KETO DIET

The Clarity of Ketogenic Diet to Reset Your Metabolism. Including: Keto Diet for Beginners, Keto Meal Preap and Keto Bread Cookbook

by

LINDA LIU

INTRODUCTION

What If I Told You That You Could Eat Your Way Skinny? You'd probably think I was crazy or assumed it had something to do with ingesting spaghetti made from tapeworms. Either way, you'd be wrong. The fact is there is a way that you could eat your way to significant and long-term fat loss results. It's called ketogenics.

Ketogenics is a term that simply refers to the process required for your body to enter a state called ketosis. Ketosis occurs when your body begins using fat as its main source of energy above all other types of energy sources including proteins and carbohydrates. Once your body enters this state it becomes much easier for your body to utilize stored fat deposits for energy thus resulting in automatic and ongoing fat loss.

So, if ketogenics is so incredible and can be your answer to fat loss and why haven't you heard of it? Well, you probably have. Ketosis is at the core of many fat loss programs and diets including the incredibly popular Atkins program. Some people fear this diet because it touts ingesting large amounts of fatty foods which some believe could be extremely harmful to your body. The fact of the matter is that when your body enters the state of ketosis it will burn most if not all of these fats for energy so very little will be stored in the body or broken down and result in fat in the bloodstream.

2

To understand why this Ketogenic Diet can be so effective at burning fat you have to look at how your body normally operates. The body's preferred source of fuel is carbohydrates and is very effective at metabolizing carbohydrates to use for fuel. Because of this fact, your body actually craves carbohydrates on a regular basis which usually leads to us overeating them. When the body eats too many carbohydrates than it can process and use, it breaks them down, converts them and stores some of them as fat for later use. If your body does not have a source of carbohydrates to use for energy, it will utilize the next available source. If you severely limit the number of carbohydrates that you eat and instead replace them with fat, your body will go through a process and adjustment that will allow it to metabolize the fat for energy as well. In addition, once the body begins to use fat as fuel it will be much easier for it to metabolize stored fat as fuel thereby helping to speed up existing fat loss.

This Book merely represents an introduction to the process of Ketogenics And Keto Recipes For Beginners. If you are interested in pursuing this type of dietary plan for use in your own fat loss program, read this book and follow every details.

Respective authors own all copyrights not held by the publisher.

The information herein is offered for informational purposes solely, and is universal as so. The presentation of the information is without contract or any type of guarantee assurance.

The trademarks that are used are without any consent and the publication of the trademark is without permission or backing by the trademark owner. All trademarks and brands within this book are for clarifying purposes only and are the owned by the owners themselves, not affiliated with this document.

TABLE OF CONTENT

CHAPTER ONE 9

INTRODUCTION TO KETOGENIC DIETS 9

What Is A Ketogenic Diet Plan? 9

The Science Behind It 10

Ketogenic Diet Mechanism.....................................15

Top 5 Keto Mistakes to Avoid..................................22

3 Types of Ketogenic Diets 27

Tips For Success on The Ketogenic Diet 29

CHAPTER TWO...32

WHAT IS KETOSIS?..32

How Do You Get Into Ketosis?.................................33

So Why Keto? 50

All About Keto 101 52

Testing for Ketosis 54

Tips for Reaching Ketosis.......................................55

Debunking The "Fat Myth 56

Calories, Macros and Net Carbs 57

What are these "macros" of which you speak? 58

CHAPTER THREE 64

KETO LIFESTYLE TACTICS 64

Historic Perspective...65

Frequently Asked Questions 75

CHAPTER FOUR...88

KETOGENIC FOOD AND SHOPPING LISTS 88

Super Keto Supplements 93

Your Brain on Keto 105

Ketosis Is a Hero for Hormones 107

Keto the Cancer Killer 112

CHAPTER FIVE 114

YOUR PERSONALIZED KETO PLAN 114

Ketogenic Diet Meal Plan 114

The Keto Basic Plan 119

Healthy Ketogenic Snack Options 122

CHAPTER SIX 141

EVERYTHING YOU NEED TO KNOW ABOUT CYCLICAL KETOGENIC DIET . 141

What Is the Cyclical Ketogenic Diet? 141

Is It the Same as Carb Cycling? 142

How to Follow It 143

Keto Diet Eating 146

Keto Diet Recipes 157

What Is Weight Loss 187

Understanding Calories For Natural Weight Loss 190

Top Weight Loss Myths 192

What You Should Know About Ketogenic Diet 195

Steps for Meal Prep Success 198

21 Days Keto Meal Plan 203

CONCLUSION 378

INTRODUCTION 382

What exactly is a ketogenic diet? 383

What is ketosis? 384

Where did the keto diet start? 384

Benefits of the keto diet..385

Keto Bread Recipes..391

CONCLUSION..679

CHAPTER ONE

INTRODUCTION TO KETOGENIC DIETS

For the best diet to rapidly burn fat using the body's natural metabolism, consider a ketogenic diet plan. Nutrition has the strongest effect on the body's production of important hormones, which regulate metabolism and allow the body to burn fat for energy and retain muscle mass, with little need for excessive exercise.

What Is A Ketogenic Diet Plan?

For many people, a ketogenic diet is a great option for weight loss. It is very different and allows the person on the diet to eat a diet that consists of foods that you may not expect.

So the ketogenic diet, or keto, is a diet that consists of very low carbs and high fat. How many diets are there where you can start your day off with bacon and eggs, loads of it, then follow it up with chicken wings for lunch and then steak and broccoli for dinner. That may sound too good to be true for many. Well on this diet this is a great day of eating and you followed the rules perfectly with that meal plan.

When you eat a very low amount of carbs your body gets put into a state of ketosis. What this means is your body burns fat for energy? How low of an amount of carbs do you need to eat in order to get into ketosis? Well, it varies from person to person, but it is a safe bet to stay under 25 net carbs. Many would suggest that when you are in the "induction phase" which is when you are actually putting your body into ketosis, you should stay under 10 net carbs.

If you aren't sure what net carbs are, let me help you. Net carbs are the amount of carbs you eat minus the amount of dietary fiber. So if on the day you eat a total of 35 grams of net carbs and 13 grams of dietary fiber, your net carbs for the day would be 22. Simple enough, right?

The Science Behind It

Its long been established in scientific circles that blood sugar was taken from food is absolutely vital for survival. Without it, a person will become sick, weak, and eventually die. However, in the past few decades, many bodybuilders have chosen to be 'guinea pigs' for their own analysis into what happens when carbohydrates - the means for bringing blood sugar into the body - are removed. The results were twofold. First, the bodybuilders achieved new levels of muscularity and conditioning. Second, they did not die, despite the scientific belief that it was impossible to maintain blood sugar levels without eating carbohydrates.

It turns out that the liver creates new blood sugar. It takes components of lactic acid and pyruvic acid which exist in the body and combines them with amino acids which enter the body through consumption of protein foods (or amino acid supplements). The liver forms new glycogen (blood sugar) at higher levels than it is consuming. Remember, the liver regularly breaks down glycogen as part of its normal routine.

In terms of effectiveness, ketogenic (low-carb) diets can be very beneficial for bodybuilders of the intermediate or advanced level, who already possess a decent amount of muscle mass. It is very hard to gain muscle while not consuming carbohydrates. Ketogenic diets are very effective because they force your body to consume fat stores for energy, instead of choosing to utilize the sugars in your blood from your daily carb consumption. There are side effects, and they are compounded greatly to negative effect when the bodybuilder doesn't consume adequate fiber through supplementation or daily no-carb vegetable ingestion.

The bottom line is that ketogenic diets are very effective for burning body fat, as long as they are done correctly. Ketogenic dieting defies scientific rationale, and there is still a great deal unknown about the long-term effects of low-carbohydrate dieting. Research it, and you might find that it's right for you when the next pre-contest diet begins!

Advantages of the Ketogenic Diet

There are a variety of advantages to the ketogenic diet. This diet was originally created as a way to manage treatment-resistant epilepsy. Today, it's been shown to help manage a variety of health problems in addition to epilepsy, including:

- Obesity
- Cardiovascular issues, including issues with cholesterol
- Neurological issues, including stroke-based damage
- Type 2 diabetes
- Alzheimer's disease
- Various types of cancer

In addition to these beneficial effects, the ketogenic diet can be used to modify hormonal and metabolic responses in the body. Altering these responses not only has clinically useful effects in disease management, but can be used to improve athletic performance and promote weight loss and muscle building in healthy individuals. These effects tend to result in increased energy levels that make ketogenic diets extremely appealing to a variety of people.

There are also cognitive benefits to ketogenic diets. Ketogenic diets have been shown to improve alertness, working memory, visual attention and the ability to switch between tasks. Positive cognitive effects have been shown in children, adolescents and adults. They occur in both healthy individuals and those with pre-existing health conditions

Benefits of a Ketogenic Diet Plan?

1. Being in Ketosis Allows the Body To Process Fat And Use It As Fuel In a Way That No Other State Allows As Easily. Carbohydrates are much easier to convert and use as fuel, so when you are providing plenty of these to your body, you need to burn and use all of those before your body will finally begin converting and using fat as fuel! *What carbs are appropriate for a diabetic –*

2. Another Benefit Of Being In A State Of Ketosis Is Those Excess Ketones Are Not Harmful To Your System In Any Way Whatsoever. Any key tones that you create which are not needed by your body are simply excreted in urine, easily and harmlessly. In fact, this excellent benefit is the reason why you

can check whether you are in a state of ketosis using urine testing strips in the morning.

(3.) When Your Body Gets Used To Being In Ketosis, It Will Actually Begin To Prefer Ketones To Glucose. This is the ideal state that you want your body to be in - no longer craving sugar whatsoever, and in fact, preferring protein as a fuel source as opposed to sugar.

4. Another Benefit Of Ketogenic Diet Weight Loss Is That Being In A Ketogenic State Is Very Useful For Controlling Insulin Levels In The Body. Insulin is one of the substances that makes you crave food, particularly for its high in sugar, and so controlling it to healthy levels is one of the key elements of weight loss.

5. Last, but certainly not least, is that the majority of people who take advantage of ketogenic diet weight loss report that being in a ketogenic state makes them feel significantly less hungry than when they are in a non-ketogenic state. It is much easier to stick to a diet - any diet - when you're not fighting cravings and hunger every step of the way. In fact, hunger pangs can often be the thing that derails a person's best

efforts! Not having to deal with them makes it easier to meet your goals, all the way around. Ketosis = less hungry

Ketogenic Diet Mechanism

The precise mechanism of action of the ketogenic diet is not known, although many possible explanations have been proposed. There are many changes that occur in the body and brain as a result of the diet, but it is unclear which of these alterations is responsible for the anticonvulsant effect. This is expected, however, as the mechanism of action of many pharmacological anticonvulsant drugs is similarly a mystery.

The key aspect of the ketogenic diet involves the restriction of carbohydrates, which are no longer able to be converted to glucose and provide for the body's metabolic and energy needs. To compensate for this, fatty acids are converted into the fuel sources through a process of oxidation in the mitochondria. *is this "good" oxidation?*

In the absence of glucose due to lack of carbohydrates in the diet, the ketone bodies β-hydroxybutyrate, acetoacetate and acetone are synthesized and are able to cross the blood-brain barrier to provide an alternative source of energy for the brain. These ketone bodies are thought to possess *brain food* anticonvulsant properties, as both acetoacetate and acetone have been shown to protect against seizures in animal models.

The stabilization of the neurons and the propagation of nervous messages may occur as a result of the efficiency of the ketone bodies as a fuel source, increasing the number of mitochondria as the body adapts to converting the fatty acids to generate ketone bodies for energy.

Neither pharmacological anticonvulsants nor the ketogenic diet is able to cure epilepsy but work due to their ability to suppress epileptic seizures. However, unlike medication options, the ketogenic diet has been shown in a study of rats to have anti-epileptogenic properties and inhibit the development of epilepsy.

There are several other theories about the mechanism of action of the ketogenic diet, including the increased acidity in the blood known as systemic acidosis, electrolyte changes and hypoglycemia. These hypotheses have not, however, been proven to be accurate and there is some evidence to indicate they are not involved in the mechanism of action.

Why Does Ketosis Have Benefits?

Ketosis occurs when there isn't enough glucose for the body to use for energy and fat is used instead. Many of the benefits of the ketogenic diet are attributed to ketosis. Because ketosis is based around elevated levels of ketones in the body, alternative methods of raising ketone levels and producing ketosis have been attempted. However, ketone supplements that supposedly induce ketosis more easily and rapidly do not result in the same benefits as adherence to the diet.

Why ketosis induces so many positive effects is not fully understood. It may act as a stressor, mimicking starvation. However, the ketogenic diet still provides the body with adequate nutrition for survival, resulting in positive metabolic and hormonal changes.

Alternatively, ketosis may simply mimic diets consumed by our ancestors, resembling dietary patterns closer to our bodies' needs from an evolutionary perspective. Ketosis could mimic a much more natural state — one that has been altered by the availability of food, nutrients and the growing popularity of the carbohydrate-rich Western diet.

Ultimately, regardless of the reason behind the benefits of ketosis, it has undisputed effects on metabolism and hormones. Many of the benefits of ketosis are based on its ability to impact cellular metabolism, essentially targeting mitochondria, the powerhouse of the cell.

Hormone levels, including corticosteroid and thyroid hormones, are also substantially impacted. These hormones influence aspects of the body like the immune system, regulating inflammation and even potentially increasing lifespans.

⭐ Ways A Ketogenic Diet Helps Squash Migraines

Foods or ingredients that allow the body to make ketones are medium-chain triglycerides like:

• MCT oil.

• Grass-fed butter

• Coconut oil

The important factor about ketones is that they help rid you of migraines. Here are the top seven ways ketones squash migraines:

1. Decreased Migraine Frequency

In recent studies, scientists have found that the ketogenic diet significantly reduced the frequency of migraines in 90% of patients. This completely dwarfs the effects of migraine drugs.

2. Glutamate Inhibition

Glutamate is found in both epilepsy and migraine patients. Medications that work in epilepsy (anti-seizure drugs) also block glutamate production. These drugs have been used to treat migraines as well. Since about 500 BC, ketones have worked to help prevent seizures, but the ketogenic diet has only been popular for the last century.

3. Processed Food

I have said many times that processed foods are bad for you, especially if you suffer from migraine. "Food-like products" are filled with preservatives, chemicals, and other triggers that could be affecting your migraine symptoms. Any diet that removes those processed foods, including the ketogenic diet, would be a good step to controlling migraine symptoms.

4. Saturated Fats

Several studies have debunked the great saturated fat myth. There are plenty of saturated fats (and other healthy fats) in a ketogenic diet, which has been found to reduce bad cholesterol and help the body produce serotonin and vitamin D, both of which help prevent migraines.

5. Hunger vs. Weight Management

Hunger is a major migraine trigger, so is weight gain/obesity. Some studies have found that weight gain and/or obesity increases the risk of migraines by 81%. Ketones help reduce hunger while controlling insulin problems, promoting weight loss, and regulating glucose levels in the blood. Weight loss and sugar control are well-known benefits to adding MCT or coconut oil to your diet. Now, as you can see, they will help control migraines by helping you feel nutritionally satisfied, more energetic, improve cognitive functioning, and lose fat.

6. Oxidative Stress

A recent study found that oxidative stress is tied to migraine triggers. In response to these findings, a new migraine medication have come out which blocks the peptide released during oxidative stress. This drug also prevents glutamate release, another migraine trigger. You don't need to depend on medication, however. A ketogenic diet will do both for you, which indicates that ketones can not only treat migraine symptoms but also determine the root cause.

7. MCT Oil

Research has found that Alzheimer's patients respond favourably to MCT (medium-chain triglyceride) oil, especially with regard to memory recall. Like Alzheimer's, migraine patients have white-matter brain lesions on their scans. Research in both diseases has found that ketones may help increase metabolism in the brain, even when oxidative stress and glucose intolerance is present.

Our minds and bodies need glucose and/or ketones to function and survive. We store about 24 hours' worth of sugar in our bodies, but we'd all die of hypoglycemia if not for the ketones. Metabolizing ketones from fat leaves our body in a healthy state of ketosis.

Migraines indicate that the brain is not metabolizing glucose into energy properly, so the logical response would be to add ketones. In addition to migraine pain symptoms, the ketogenic diet can help reduce:

• Brain fog

• Oxidative stress

• Brain Lesions

A Ketogenic Diet Can Also Help:

• Block glutamate (a major trigger)

• Eliminate processed foods (a major trigger)

• Add more saturated and healthy fats to your diet

• Control your weight

• Reduce oxidative stress

• Improve cognitive functioning

Top 5 Keto Mistakes to Avoid

For obvious reasons, we love the ketogenic diet because it helps us not stress about our health or bodies and allows us to focus on life. However, when we first got started with it we made some big-time keto mistakes.

Almost everyone makes mistakes! While mistakes usually aren't a big deal, in the keto world they can be a very bad thing mentally for you. When you get started on keto you expect to see results because you see all of the amazing results that others are achieving and you want the same thing.

When those things don't happen because of mistakes it can be very frustrating and lead you to believe that keto just isn't for you.

Here are 5 common Keto mistakes to avoid

1. Not Enough Fats

One of the hardest adjustments for people to make when starting keto is making sure they consume enough fats.

You probably ~~isn't~~ aren't used to consuming the amount of fat daily and it can be a struggle to find foods that have the fats you need.

However, on keto, if you want to lose fat, you need to consume fat so that means hitting your daily fat macros. This is why it is vital that you meal plan which is the next big mistake that people make.

2. Not Meal Planning *Chronometer app*

This is probably the biggest mistake we see from Keto dieting beginner. The ones that don't meal plan end up falling way short of their daily macros or end up slipping and eating stuff that knocks them out of ketosis because they're hungry.

Yes, meal planning takes a bit of time and preparation but nobody said this was going to be a walk in the park.

Meal planning will not only save you a bunch of headache and frustration, it's a great way to save money as well. When you meal plan, you know exactly what you're going to put into your body on any given day. That means you can make the right adjustments and understand what tweaks you might need to make to your diet.

3. Too Much Protein

Growing up all you hear is that protein is good for you and it is when it's not consumed in excess. The issue with protein on the ketogenic diet is that because your body is using fats as a fuel source, it only needs proteins to help main muscle mass.

Surprisingly enough, you need much less protein than you'd expect to make this happen. When you consume more protein than your body needs it ends up converting that protein into glucose which, in turn, can raise your blood sugar levels and knock you out of ketosis.

Most people have no problem reaching their protein macros because protein seems to be in everything. This is why it's important to meal plan so you understand how much protein you are putting into your body.

4. Looking For a Quick Fix

It's a shame it's called the ketogenic diet because the reality of the situation is that it's really a lifestyle. You don't do keto for a short period to lose weight and then go back to your old eating habits because then you'll just discover you're back at the very beginning again.

The health benefits of keto show that it's more than worth its time becoming something that you stick with for the rest of your life.

If you're looking for a quick fix then just cut out sugars from your diet. For most people, that will cause a healthy drop in weight without having to meal plan, track your macros, and other things required of you with the keto diet.

5. Not Getting Enough Sleep

Just like water, if you aren't getting the sleep you need your body can't do what it needs to do. It's important that you give your body time to reset so it can tackle another day.

Lack of sleep can also contributes to you slipping up and eating those dozen donuts as you look for quick energy sources.

How To Check Ketone Levels

Testing ketone levels in your body is the only true way to know whether or not you've entered (and remain in) ketosis. This is important to be sure you're reaping the full benefits of the ketogenic diet here.

When your body starts burning fat for fuel and enters ketosis, the ketones it creates will spill over into your urine, blood, and breath so it's possible to test for them in each area. Thankfully, there are several methods for testing your ketone levels at home:

Urine testing: You can buy urine strips that indicate your ketone level by color. These can usually be bought at your local drugstore or pharmacy for a low cost.

The downside of urine testing is that they aren't always reliable, especially if you've been in ketosis for a while. When you're more efficient at using ketones, a lower level of ketones might show up even if you're burning through them.

Other factors can affect the reading too, such as hydration and electrolyte levels.

• **Breath Testing:** Acetone is the ketone that shows up on the breath, and you can test it using a breath meter.

After purchasing the breath meter, there are no ongoing costs for testing like with urine strips. However, this method isn't the most reliable and usually shouldn't be your sole method for testing.

• **Blood Testing:** This is the most accurate way to monitor ketone levels. Using a blood glucose meter, you can check ketone levels using a blood strip. Just be warned that this method can be pricey if you test frequently.

For best results, you'll (ideally) be providing your body with optimal nutrition from rich, healthy fat sources, nutritious protein, and other foods that provide the vitamins and minerals the body needs. See our ketogenic diet food list for exactly what to eat to get keto working best for you.

3 Types of Ketogenic Diets

Ketogenic diet is a high fat low carbohydrate diet with adequate protein thrown in the meal. It is further divided into three types and depending on one's daily calorie needs, the percentage differs. Diets are often prepared on a ratio level such as 4:1 or 2:1 with the first number indicating the total fat amount in the diet compared to the protein and carbohydrate combined in each meal.

1. Standard - SKD

The first diet is the Standard or the SKD and is designed for individuals who are not active or lead a sedentary lifestyle. The meal plan limits the dieter to eat a net of 20-50 grams of carbohydrates. Fruits or vegetables that are starchy are restricted from the diet. In order for the diet to be effective, one must strictly follow the meal plan. Butter, vegetable oil and heavy creams are used heavily to replace carbohydrates in the diet.

2. Targeted - TKD

The TKD is less strict than the SKD and allows one to consume carbohydrates though only in a certain portion or amount which will not impact the ketosis that one is currently in. The TKD diet helps dieters that perform some level of exercise or workout.

3. Cyclical - CKD

The CKD is preferable for those who are into weight training or do intensive exercises and not for beginners as it requires the person undergoing the diet to stick to a SKD meal plan for the five days in a week's time and eating/loading up on carbohydrates on the next two days. It is important that dieters follow the strict regimen to ensure that their diet is successful.

Tips For Success on The Ketogenic Diet

1. Drink Tons Of Water.

While on a ketogenic diet, your body has a hard time retaining as much water as it needs, so staying properly hydrated is absolutely essential. Many experts recommend that _men intake a minimum of 3 liters of beverages each day, while the figure for women is 2.2 liters daily. A good indicator of proper hydration is the color of your urine. If your urine is clear or light yellow, you're most likely properly hydrated. Keep a bottle of water with you everywhere you go!

2. Don't Forget The Fat!

Simply put our bodies need fuel to function. When we limit our carbohydrate intake, especially to levels that induce ketosis, our bodies need an alternate fuel source. Since protein is not an efficient source of energy, our bodies turn to fat. Any fat you eat while in ketosis is used for energy, making it very difficult to store fat while in ketosis. Choose healthy, unsaturated fats as often as possible: foods like avocados, olives, nuts, and seeds are ideal.

3. Find Your Carb Limit.

All of our bodies are different. Some dieters will need to adhere to a strict low-carbohydrate diet that entails consuming less than 20 grams per day of carbs. Other dieters will find that they can comfortably stay in ketosis while consuming 50, 75, or 100 grams of carbohydrates. The only way to know for sure is trial and error. Purchase Ketostix or any brand of ketone urinalysis strips and find out your carbohydrate limit. If you find that you have a bit of wiggle room, it will make sticking to your diet that much easier.

4. Be Smart about Liquor.

One of the great aspects of the ketogenic diet is that you can drink liquor while on it without throwing your weight loss too far off course. You can drink unsweetened liquors like vodka, rum, tequila, gin, whiskey, scotch, cognac, and brandy, along with the occasional low-carb beer.

Use low-carb mixers and drink plenty of water to stay hydrated, as hangovers are notoriously bad while in ketosis. And remember, calories still count, so don't go overboard. All things in moderation.

5. Be Patient.

While the ketogenic diet is known for rapid weight loss, especially in the early stages of the diet, weight loss is always a slow, and time-consuming process. Don't freak out if the scale doesn't show weight loss, or shows slight weight increases, for a few days. Your weight varies day-to-day (and throughout the day) based upon a number of factors. Don't forget to use metrics like how your clothes fit or body measurements to see progress beyond what the scale shows.

CHAPTER TWO

WHAT IS KETOSIS?

What does "keto" stand for exactly? Keto is short for ketosis, which is the result of following the standard ketogenic diet, which is why it's also sometimes called "the ketosis diet" or "ketosis diet plan."

Following a ketogenic diet puts your body into a state of "ketosis," which is a metabolic state that occurs when most of the body's energy comes from ketone bodies in the blood, rather than from glucose from carbohydrate foods (like grains, all sources of sugar or fruit, for example). This is in contrast to a glycolytic state, where blood glucose (sugar) provides most of the body's fuel (or energy).

This state can also be achieved by multiple days of total fasting, but that isn't sustainable beyond a few days. (It's why some keto diet plans for beginners combine intermittent fasting or IMF with the keto diet for greater weight loss effects.)

Although dietary fat (especially saturated fat) often gets a bad name, provoking fear of weight gain and heart disease, it's also your body's second preferred source of energy when carbohydrates are not easily accessible.

How Do You Get Into Ketosis?

So many people ask, does the keto diet work? Yes, of course, but only if you can get your body into ketosis. Here's how you get your body into ketosis and start burning body fat for fuel in a keto diet for beginners:

Consumption of glucose from carbohydrate foods — grains, starchy vegetables, fruit, etc. — is cut way down.

This forces your body to find an alternative fuel source: fat (think avocados, coconut oil, salmon).

Meanwhile, in the absence of glucose, the body also starts to burn fat and produces ketones instead. Once ketone levels in the blood rise to a certain point, you enter into a state of ketosis.

This state of high ketone levels results in quick and consistent weight loss until you reach a healthy, stable body weight.

Wondering how many carb foods you can eat and still be "in ketosis"? The traditional ketogenic diet, created for those with epilepsy consisted of getting about 75 percent of calories from sources of fat (such as oils or fattier cuts of meat), 5 percent from carbohydrates and 20 percent from protein. For most people a less strict version (what I call a "modified keto diet") can still help promote weight loss in a safe, and often very fast, way.

In order to transition and remain in this state, aiming for about 30–50 net grams is typically the recommended amount of total carbs to start with. This is considered a more moderate or flexible approach but can be less overwhelming to begin with. Once you're more accustomed to "eating keto," you can choose to lower carbs even more if you'd like (perhaps only from time to time), down to about 20 grams of net carbs daily. This is considered the standard, "strict" amount that many keto dieters aim to adhere to for best results, but remember that everyone is a bit different.

How to Kick-Start Ketosis

Ketosis is a normal metabolic process that provides several health benefits. During ketosis, your body converts fat into compounds known as ketones and begins using them as its main source of energy.

Studies have found that diets that promote ketosis are highly beneficial for weight loss, due in part to their appetite-suppressing effects. Emerging research suggests that ketosis may also be helpful for type 2 diabetes and neurological disorders, among other conditions

That being said, achieving a state of ketosis can take some work and planning. It's not just as simple as cutting carbs.

Here are 11 effective tips to get into ketosis.

1. Minimize Your Carb Consumption

Eating a very low-carb diet is by far the most important factor in achieving ketosis. Normally, your cells use glucose, or sugar, as their main source of fuel. However, most of your cells can also use other fuel sources. This includes fatty acids, as well as ketones, which are also known as ketone bodies.

Your body stores glucose in your liver and muscles in the form of glycogen. When carb intake is very low, glycogen stores are reduced and levels of the hormone insulin decline. This allows fatty acids to be released from fat stores in your body. Your liver converts some of these fatty acids into the ketone bodies acetone, acetoacetate and beta-hydroxybutyrate. These ketones can be used as fuel by portions of the brain.

The level of carb restriction needed to induce ketosis is somewhat individualized. Some people need to limit net carbs (total carbs minus fiber) to 20 grams per day, while others can achieve ketosis while eating twice this amount or more.

For this reason, the Atkins diet specifies that carbs be restricted to 20 or fewer grams per day for two weeks to guarantee that ketosis is achieved.

After this point, small amounts of carbs can be added back to your diet very gradually, as long as ketosis is maintained.

In a one-week study, overweight people with type 2 diabetes who limited carb intake to 21 or fewer grams per day experienced daily urinary ketone excretion levels that were 27 times higher than their baseline levels.

In another study, adults with type 2 diabetes were allowed 20–50 grams of digestible carbs per day, depending on the number of grams that allowed them to maintain blood ketone levels within a target range of 0.5–3.0 mmol/L.

These carb and ketone ranges are advised for people who want to get into ketosis to promote weight loss, control blood sugar levels or reduce heart disease risk factors.

In contrast, therapeutic ketogenic diets used for epilepsy or as experimental cancer therapy often restrict carbs to fewer than 5% of calories or fewer than 15 grams per day to further drive up ketone levels. However, anyone using the diet for therapeutic purposes should only do so under the supervision of a medical professional.

BOTTOM LINE:

Limiting your carb intake to 20–50 net grams per day lowers blood sugar and insulin levels, leading to the release of stored fatty acids that your liver converts into ketones.

2. Include Coconut Oil in Your Diet

Eating coconut oil can help you get into ketosis. It contains fats called medium-chain triglycerides (MCTs). Unlike most fats, MCTs are rapidly absorbed and taken directly to the liver, where they can be used immediately for energy or converted into ketones. In fact, it's been suggested that consuming coconut oil may be one of the best ways to increase ketone levels in people with Alzheimer's disease and other nervous system disorders. Although coconut oil contains four types of MCTs, 50% of its fat comes from the kind known as lauric acid. Some research suggests that fat sources with a higher percentage of lauric acid may produce a more sustained level of ketosis. This is because it's metabolized more gradually than other MCTs.

MCTs have been used to induce ketosis in epileptic children without restricting carbs as drastically as the classic ketogenic diet.

In fact, several studies have found that a high-MCT diet containing 20% of calories from carbs produces effects similar to the classic ketogenic diet, which provides fewer than 5% of calories from carbs.

When adding coconut oil to your diet, it's a good idea to do so slowly to minimize digestive side effects like stomach cramping or diarrhea.

Start with one teaspoon per day and work up to two to three tablespoons daily over the course of a week. You can find coconut oil at your local grocery store or purchase it online

BOTTOM LINE:

Consuming coconut oil provides your body with MCTs, which are quickly absorbed and converted into ketone bodies by your liver.

3. Ramp up Your Physical Activity

A growing number of studies have found that being in ketosis may be beneficial for some types of athletic performance, including endurance exercise. In addition, being more active can help you get into ketosis. When you exercise, you deplete your body of its glycogen stores. Normally, these are replenished when you eat carbs, which are broken down into glucose and then converted to glycogen.

However, if carb intake is minimized, glycogen stores remain low. In response, your liver increases its production of ketones, which can be used as an alternate fuel source for your muscles.

One study found that at low blood ketone concentrations, exercise increases the rate at which ketones are produced. However, when blood ketones are already elevated, they do not rise with exercise and may actually decrease for a short period.In addition, working out in a fasted state has been shown to drive up ketone levels.

In a small study, nine older women exercised either before or after a meal. Their blood ketone levels were 137–314% higher when they exercised before a meal than when they exercised after a meal. Keep in mind that although exercise increases ketone production, it may take one to four weeks for your body to adapt to using ketones and fatty acids as primary fuels. During this time, physical performance may be reduced temporarily

BOTTOM LINE

Engaging in physical activity can increase ketone levels during carb restriction. This effect may be enhanced by working out in a fasted state.

4. Increase Your Healthy Fat Intake

Consuming plenty of healthy fat can boost your ketone levels and help you reach ketosis. Indeed, a very low-carb ketogenic diet not only minimizes carbs, but is also high in fat. Ketogenic diets for weight loss, metabolic health and exercise performance usually provide between 60–80% of calories from fat.

The classic ketogenic diet used for epilepsy is even higher in fat, with typically 85–90% of calories from fat. However, extremely high fat intake doesn't necessarily translate into higher ketone levels.

A three-week study of 11 healthy people compared the effects of fasting with different amounts of fat intake on breath ketone levels. Overall, ketone levels were found to be similar in people consuming 79% or 90% of calories from fat. Furthermore, because fat makes up such a large percentage of a ketogenic diet, it's important to choose high-quality sources.

Good fats include olive oil, avocado oil, coconut oil, butter, lard and tallow. In addition, there are many healthy, high-fat foods that are also very low in carbs.

However, if your goal is weight loss, it's important to make sure you're not consuming too many calories in total, as this can cause your weight loss to stall.

BOTTOM LINE:

Consuming at least 60% of calories from fat will help boost your ketone levels. Choose a variety of healthy fats from both plant and animal sources.

5. Try a Short Fast or a Fat Fast

Another way to get into ketosis is to go without eating for several hours. In fact, many people go into mild ketosis between dinner and breakfast. Children with epilepsy are sometimes fasted for 24–48 hours before they start a ketogenic diet. This is done to get into ketosis quickly so that seizures can be reduced sooner. Intermittent fasting, a dietary approach that involves regular short-term fasts, may also induce ketosis. Moreover, "fat fasting" is another ketone-boosting approach that mimics the effects of fasting.

It involves consuming about 1,000 calories per day, 85–90% of which come from fat. This combination of low calorie and very high fat intake may help you achieve ketosis quickly.

A 1965 study reported significant fat loss in overweight patients who followed a fat fast. However, other researchers have pointed out that these results appear to have been highly exaggerated. Because a fat fast is so low in protein and calories, it should be followed for a maximum of three to five days to prevent an excessive loss of muscle mass. It may also be difficult to adhere to for more than a couple of days.

BOTTOM LINE:

Fasting, intermittent fasting and a "fat fast" can all help you get into ketosis relatively quickly.

6. Maintain Adequate Protein Intake

Achieving ketosis requires a protein intake that is adequate but not excessive. The classic ketogenic diet used in epilepsy patients is restricted in both carbs and protein to maximize ketone levels. The same diet may also be beneficial for cancer patients, as it may limit tumor growth. However, for most people, cutting back on protein to increase ketone production isn't a healthy practice.

First, it's important to consume enough protein to supply the liver with amino acids that can be used for gluconeogenesis, which translates to "making new glucose."

In this process, your liver provides glucose for the few cells and organs in your body that can't use ketones as fuel, such as your red blood cells and portions of the kidneys and brain.

Second, protein intake should be high enough to maintain muscle mass when carb intake is low, especially during weight loss.

Although losing weight typically results in the loss of both muscle and fat, consuming sufficient amounts of protein on a very low-carb ketogenic diet can help preserve muscle mass. Several studies have shown that the preservation of muscle mass and physical performance is maximized when protein intake is in the range of 0.55–0.77 grams per pound (1.2–1.7 grams per kilogram) of lean mass.In weight loss studies, very low-carb diets with protein intake within this range have been found to induce and maintain ketosis.

In one study of 17 obese men, following a ketogenic diet providing 30% of calories from protein for four weeks led to blood ketone levels of 1.52 mmol/L, on average. This is well within the 0.5–3.0 mmol/L range of nutritional ketosis. To calculate your protein needs on a ketogenic diet, multiply your ideal body weight in pounds by 0.55 to 0.77 (1.2 to 1.7 in kilograms). For example, if your ideal body weight is 130 pounds (59 kg), your protein intake should be 71–100 grams.

BOTTOM LINE

Consuming too little protein can lead to muscle mass loss, whereas excessive protein intake may suppress ketone production.

7. Test Ketone Levels and Adjust Your Diet as Needed

Like many things in nutrition, achieving and maintaining a state of ketosis is highly individualized. Therefore, it can be helpful to test your ketone levels to ensure you're achieving your goals. The three types of ketones — acetone, beta-hydroxybutyrate and acetoacetate — can be measured in your breath, blood or urine. Acetone is found in your breath, and studies have confirmed testing acetone breath levels is a reliable way to monitor ketosis in people following ketogenic diets.

The Ketonix meter measures acetone in breath. After breathing into the meter, a color flashes to indicate whether you are in ketosis and how high your levels are. Ketones can also be measured with a blood ketone meter. Similar to the way a glucose meter works, a small drop of blood is placed on a strip that's inserted into the meter.

It measures the amount of beta-hydroxybutyrate in your blood, and it has also been found to be a valid indicator of ketosis levels. The disadvantage of measuring blood ketones is that the strips are very expensive.

Lastly, the ketone measured in urine is acetoacetate. Ketone urine strips are dipped into urine and turn various shades of pink or purple depending on the level of ketones present. A darker color reflects higher ketone levels.

Ketone urine strips are easy to use and fairly inexpensive. Although their accuracy in long-term use has been questioned, they should initially provide confirmation that you are in ketosis.

A recent study found that urinary ketones tend to be highest in the early morning and after dinner on a ketogenic diet. Using one or more of these methods to test ketones can help you determine whether you need to make any adjustments to get into ketosis.

8. Drink water!

It's important to also drink lots of water, the most important of all keto drinks. Getting enough water helps keep you from feeling fatigued, is important for digestion and aids in hunger suppression. It's also needed for detoxification. Aim to drink 10–12 eight-ounce glasses a day.

9. Consider using some keto supplements for greater success

A popular keto supplement are exogenous ketones (popularly called "keto diet pills") that may help you achieve results earlier as well as remain in that state. (Don't confuse exogenous ketones with raspberry ketones, as the latter don't raise ketone levels in the body or mimic endogenous ketones, so you wouldn't use raspberry ketones in your regimen.)

Also, consider supplementing with the amino acid leucine, as it can be broken down directly into acetyl-CoA, making it one of the most important ketogenic amino acids in the body. While most other amino acids are converted into glucose, the acetyl-CoA formed from leucine can be used to make ketone bodies. It's also present in keto friendly foods like eggs and cottage cheese.

10. Do not protein load?

Something that makes the keto diet different from other low-carb diets is that it does not "protein-load." Protein is not as big a part of the keto diet as fat is. Reason being: In small amounts, the body can change protein to glucose, which means if you eat too much of it, especially while in the beginning stages, it will slow down your body's transition into ketosis.

Protein intake should be between one and 1.5 grams per kilogram of your ideal body weight. To convert pounds to kilograms, divide your ideal weight by 2.2. For example, a woman who weighs 150 pounds (68 kilograms) should get about 68–102 grams of protein daily.

11. Track your macros

Your "macros" are your grams of fat, protein and net carbs (not to be confused with calorie counting!). Tracking your macros and net carbs can be tricky, so I advise you download a keto app that includes a keto diet calculator. It will help keep you on track.

9 Keto Diet Types

What is the keto diet again? And is the keto diet safe and healthy? Well, with a diet this popular, many versions and keto meal plans tend to emerge, so the answer to both questions somewhat depends on what version of the ketogenic plan you try. At present, we're at nine types of the keto diet!

Wondering how many carb foods you can eat and still be "in ketosis"? The traditional ketogenic meal plan created for those with epilepsy and is very strict with its percentages of macronutrients. But there are several other types of keto diet plans out there as well.

Here are most common keto diet types:

Standard ketogenic diet (SKD): consists of getting about 75 percent of calories from sources of fat (such as oils or fattier cuts of meat), 5 percent from carbohydrates and 20 percent from protein.

Modified ketogenic diet (MKD): this keto meal plan reduces carbohydrates to 30 percent of their total calorie intake, while increasing fat and protein to 40 percent and 30 percent respectively.

Cyclical ketogenic diet (CKD): If you find it difficult to stick to a very low-carb diet every day, especially for months on end, you might want to consider a carb-cycling diet instead. Carb cycling increases carbohydrate intake (and sometimes calories in general) only at the right time and in the right amounts, usually about 1–2 times per week (such as on weekends).

Targeted ketogenic diet (TKD): This eating plan simply tells you to follow the keto diet BUT allows you to add carbs around workouts. So on the days you exercise, you will be eating carbohydrates.

Restricted ketogenic diet (RKD): Designed to treat cancer, this ketogenic meal plan restricts calories as well as carbohydrates. Some studies indicate that calorie restriction and ketosis may help treat cancer.

High-protein ketogenic diet (HPKD): This version of the keto diet is often followed by folks who want to preserve their muscle mass like bodybuilders and older people. Rather than protein making up 20 percent of the diet, here it's 30 percent. Meanwhile, fat goes down to 65 percent of the diet and carbs stay at 5 percent. (Caution: folks with kidney issues shouldn't up their protein too much.)

Lazy keto diet: Last but not least, the Lazy keto diet often gets confused with dirty keto ... but they're different, as the "lazy" refers to simply not carefully tracking the fat and protein macros (or calories, for that matter). Meanwhile, the one aspect that remains strict? Not eating over 20 net carb grams per day. Some people find this version less intimidating to start with or end with but I will caution that your results will be less impressive.

So Why Keto?

In the absence of glucose, which is normally used by cells as a quick source of energy, the body starts to burn fat and produces ketone bodies instead (it's why the keto diet is often referred to as the ketone diet). Once ketone levels in the blood rise to a certain point, you enter into a state of ketosis — which usually results in quick and consistent weight loss until you reach a healthy, stable body weight. See this keto diet review, a before and after trying keto for 30 days.

To sum up a complex process, you reach this fat-burning state when the the liver breaks down fat into fatty acids and glycerol, through a process called beta-oxidation. There are three primary types of ketone bodies that are water-soluble molecules produced in the liver: acetoacetate, beta-hydroxybutyrate and acetone.

The body then further breaks down these fatty acids into an energy-rich substance called ketones that circulate through the bloodstream. Fatty acid molecules are broken down through the process called ketogenesis, and a specific ketone body called acetoacetate is formed and which supplies energy.

The end result of the "ketone diet" is staying fueled off of circulating high ketones (which are also sometimes called ketone bodies) — which is what's responsible for altering your metabolism in a way that some people like to say turns you into a "fat-burning machine." Both in terms of how it feels physically and mentally, along with the impact it has on the body, being in ketosis is very different than a "glycolytic state," where blood glucose (sugar) serves as the body's energy source.

So, is ketosis bad for you? Absolutely not. If anything, it's the reverse. Many consider burning ketones to be a much "cleaner" way to stay energized compared to running on carbs and sugar day in and day out. And remember, this state is not to be confused with ketoacidosis, which is a serious diabetes complication when the body produces excess ketones (or blood acids).

The goal is to keep you in this fat-burning metabolic state, in which you will lose weight until you reach your ideal set point.

Some research suggests this may be a novel approach to reverse diabetes naturally.

All About Keto 101

The ketogenic diet is super high in fat (about 80 percent of your daily calories), super low in carbohydrates (less than 5 percent of your calories), and moderate in protein (typically 15 to 20 percent of your calories). This is a pretty drastic departure from the generally recommended macronutrient distribution of 20 to 35 percent protein, 45 to 65 percent carbohydrates, and 10 to 35 percent fat.

The most important component of the keto diet is a natural and normal process called ketosis. Normally, bodies run very well on glucose. Glucose is produced when the body breaks down carbohydrates. It's a very simple process, which is why it's the body's preferred way to produce energy.

When you cut back on carbs or just haven't eaten in a while, your body looks for other sources of energy to fill the void. Fat is typically that source. When your blood sugar drops because you're not feeding your body carbs, fat is released from your cells and flood the liver. The liver turns the fat into ketone bodies, which your body uses as its second choice for energy.

What Foods Can You Eat on the Keto Diet?

A typical keto diet consists largely of:

- Meat

- Fish

- Butter

- Eggs

- Cheese

- Heavy cream

- Oils

- Nuts

- Avocados

- Seeds

- Low-carb green vegetables

This short list leaves out all of your favorite carb-heavy foods, such as grains, rice, beans, potatoes, sweets, milk, cereals, fruits and even some vegetables.

Testing for Ketosis

There are a several ways to check your ketone levels.

Ketone test strips are popular because they're simple to use. You simply swipe one through your urine stream and wait a few seconds. The tip of the strip will change color. The darker pink the strip becomes, the higher your ketone levels.

For more precise measurements, consider a blood glucose and ketone monitoring system like this one from Precision Xtra. This system takes in blood from a small finger prick and displays the most accurate blood ketone levels possible.

Finally, we have breath ketone level analyzers. Since ketones are released in your breath, you will probably notice a metallic taste in your mouth while in ketosis. At the very least, you will probably notice "keto breath," that bad bread associated with ketosis. This is caused by ketones which can be measured by a ketone breath meter. While there are many available, we haven't found one we love and recommend so we stick with ketone test strips or ketone blood monitors.

Of course, it's not necessary to do any of this to have success on a keto diet, but it can be very fulfilling to see tangible signs that you're in ketosis.

Tips for Reaching Ketosis

There are several things you can do to help your body quickly get into ketosis and we're going outline a few of them here.

Eat Plenty of Healthy Fat – In addition to limiting carbs, you'll want to make sure you're eating plenty of fat. Remember, most of your calories should come from fat. And, if you fill up on fat, you'll be less tempted to grab for a carb-heavy snack.

Watch Your Protein Intake – Also, remember that excess protein will convert into glucose (essentially doing the same thing as when you're consuming carbohydrates) so you'll want to keep your protein intake relatively low. Unless you're following the high protein ketogenic diet, shoot for no more than 25% of calories to come from protein. This means you can't load up on steak at every meal.

Add Some Light Exercise – It has been shown that exercise can increase the rate at which ketones are produced. Yep, you heard me right, being more active can help get your body into ketosis. We're not talking about heavy-duty all-out exercise, just some increased movement. Walking is a great exercise that nearly everyone can do, or you can play your favorite sport.

Increase Water Intake – Water is the perfect drink and on the keto diet you should be drinking plenty of it. Water is very important not only for hydration but also helps to fill you up, leading to less carb craving. Even more, water has been shown to speed the ketones and fat out of your body.

Try Intermittent Fasting – Since hunger decreases on a ketogenic diet, many incorporate what's known as intermittent fasting into their diet. This involves restricting the hours when you eat or skipping a meal. As an example, you can skip breakfast and just eat lunch and dinner. Many find this increases the effectiveness of low-carbing, but again it's not a necessity.

Debunking The "Fat Myth"

Dietary fat, particularly animal fat, has been demonized for a long time, so it's not surprising that many people are cautious about increasing their fat intake on keto.

Fortunately, recent research has shown that while man-made fats such as vegetable shortening and margarine contain what are known as trans fats that can do harm, natural fats like butter and olive oil produce fatty acids like omega-3 and omega-six, which can protect you from heart disease and other issues.

Another enduring myth is that you "need" carbs for energy. Remember your old coffee and pastry breakfast? Remember how after eating it you felt ready to take on the world? You should also remember the drop in energy after all the glucose was burned up, which of course gave you an excuse for another donut or a Snickers bar.

When you're running on fat, those crashes will be a thing of the past as your energy stays at steady levels.

Calories, Macros and Net Carbs

Do calories matter on a keto diet?

A question that often comes up when discussing ketogenic diets is, "do calories matter?"

If you visit certain diet forums or social media sites, you'll no doubt run into those who claim that they can eat a ton of calories and still lose weight, provided that their food matches their macro goals. They talk about adding huge amounts of butter to their steak and unlimited cheese sauce to their veggies. Unfortunately, no diet works this way. Calories still do matter.

However, since fat and protein are so satiating, while sugar and refined carbohydrates are not, calorie restriction comes naturally when following a low carb diet.

It's easy for most of us to quickly devour a pint of Ben & Jerry's ice cream, which can have well over 1200 calories, but it would be hard for that same person to eat a fatty ribeye steak with the same caloric energy.

What are these "macros" of which you speak?

Macros is the collective term for fat, protein and carbohydrate grams.

A gram of fat contains nine calories, while protein and carbohydrates each have four calories per gram.

For example, a person following a standard ketogenic diet (70% fat, 25% protein, and 5% carbs) consuming 2000 calories per day would consume roughly 1400 calories or 155 grams of fat, 500 calories or 125 grams of protein, and 100 calories or 25 grams of carbohydrates.

But, there's a little more to it than that. Keep reading...

Are all carbs the same? Net carbs and the keto diet.

Not all carbs are created equal. Not even close.

Many carbs come with a little bonus – and that bonus is FIBER!

Fiber in foods is counted as carbs, but that fiber is not digested. It's simply expelled as waste. And since we don't digest it (read: use it for energy), we can subtract the fiber grams from the total carbs to get "net carbs."

Here's a little example if you're new to this stuff.

A three-ounce bag of baby carrots has roughly 8 grams of carbs. But that same bag contains about 3 grams of fiber. When we subtract the fiber from the total carbs, we end up with 5 net carbs. This lets you enjoy a tasty snack while not blowing through your daily carb limit too quick.

Dealing with Weight-Loss Stalls Keto Health Topics FAQ

People are adopting the keto lifestyle for many reasons, but one of the most common reasons is weight loss. If you're like many keto dieters, you'll see some weight loss pretty quickly after starting your new way of eating. But after a few weeks or months, you might notice the scale isn't moving anymore. This can be frustrating and demoralizing. If your weight is not budging anymore, here are the top 5 things you can do to break a weight loss stall.

1. TRACK YOUR DAILY MACROS

You've probably read that a healthy Keto diet follows a 75:20:5 ratio. This means that 75% of your calories should come from healthy fats, 20% from protein, and 5% from carbs. These are your macros (short for macronutrients). A Keto diet doesn't just focus on the number of calories consumed, but on the sources of those calories (fat, protein, and carbs) and the ratio between them. Because sticking to the 75:20:5 macro ratio is critical to achieving and staying in ketosis, tracking your daily macros allows you to adjust your diet frequently so you can better achieve your weight loss goals.

2. TRY INTERMITTENT FASTING

Intermittent Fasting (IF) is an "eating pattern," not a "diet." With IF, you cycle between periods of eating and fasting. Rather than eating every time you feel hungry, IF limits eating to certain times throughout the day. By limiting the times you eat, you'll consume fewer calories and lose weight. However, this only works if you don't compensate for the fasting periods by eating too many calories during the eating periods. And of course, sticking to a healthy Keto diet during the eating periods is critical. Click here if you want to learn more about IF and the most popular IF methods.

3. TRACK YOUR CALORIES

Even if you're sticking to a healthy Keto diet, you'll only lose weight if you're burning more calories than you're taking in. The ideal caloric intake depends on age, metabolism, and exercise, among other things, so tracking both the calories you take in and the calories you burn allows you to adjust your diet and exercise to fit your Keto goals. There are lots of great calorie tracker websites and apps to make this process easier.

4. EXERCISE MORE OR DIFFERENTLY

You might lose weight right after starting a new exercise routine, so why do those results plateau in a matter of weeks? Our bodies adapt to exercise much faster than we think. If an exercise you used to struggle with is no longer a challenge, chances are it's not nearly as effective for weight loss as it was when you started. Try mixing up your workouts every month to keep your body guessing and burning fat. If you're running twice a week, try increasing it to every other day, or adding in short sprints to boost your heart rate. If you generally do yoga or pilates, try mixing in weight training. Give our workout programs a try to keep things fresh.

5. MEASURE INCHES, NOT POUNDS

Household scales show our weight, but they don't show our body composition (fat, muscle, bones, and organs). With a Keto diet and proper exercise, you'll lose fat and build muscle, but because muscle weighs more than fat, you might be losing body fat without seeing a change in your weight. Instead of weighing yourself, try other metrics for fat loss:

Take your measurements. Measurements can give you a more accurate picture than pounds. If you're losing inches, you're probably losing body fat.

Measure how your clothes fit. If you can fit into a pair of jeans you couldn't wear before, congrats! You're on the right track.

Set performance goals. Weight fluctuates, so instead of focusing on what you can't always control, find a more tangible goal. See how many push-ups you can do or how far you can run. If you can do more than you could last week, you're probably losing body fat and building muscle.

Measure your body fat. There are lots of different ways to do this (BMI tests, online calculators, etc.). They can often be guesstimates, but consistently measuring yourself under similar conditions can give you a more accurate picture of your body composition.

Weight loss plateaus are common and normal. Be patient with yourself and try not to let it discourage you. Our tips above will help you get back on your way to dropping pounds and reaching your health goals.

CHAPTER THREE

KETO LIFESTYLE TACTICS

All people on earth want— healthy body and mind, clear young skin, protection from chronic diseases, sound sleep, low stress, freedom from fear of obesity and in short eternal fountain of youth. The answer is so so simple.

On keto, I have experienced enormous health benefits of this lifestyle, most specifically body fat loss, increased mental focus and mental strength, increased energy, remarkably decreased hunger, freedom from having to eat every 3–4 hours, better sleep cycle, increased athletic stamina, decreased inflammation, and clear skin. Having done this for more than 9 weeks now, I feel that I am qualified to guide others about the common mistakes that can be easily avoided and the enormous potential of this diet.

Under this diet, I consume less than 30g of carbohydrates per day. I take no sugar and add enough fats to feel satisfied till the next meal. The only carbs I take is vegetables and sometimes nuts. However, there are a number of things to be taken care of while following this way of life.

Historic Perspective

For millions of years humanoid apes and then prehistoric humans ate meat filled with saturated fats and plant foods. Also fasting for long durations was very natural because it was not possible to hunt everyday or store meat in refrigerators. Fruits were not available year round. Carbohydrates were rare in nature as agriculture had not been invented yet and honey was hard to obtain. Also fruits and vegetables had not been bred for high sugar content yet. PUFA oils were rare to find and everything was organic.

These humanoids/prehistoric humans ate rarely and ate a diet full of saturated fats, proteins and vegetables. Vegetables and plant foods were full of minerals because the soil had not been exploited for farming yet. In terms of geological time, agriculture and over dependence on carbohydrates is a very new event in human history.

Cholesterol

The age old belief that cholesterol in diet gives you heart disease is a myth. There have been no studies that directly link cholesterol in food to heart disease. We need to understand that cholesterol is a healing mechanism when sugars/carbs damage the inside of the blood vessels. Without sugars/carbs damaging the blood vessels, cholesterol in the blood does not harm at all. In fact cholesterol is very important component of many hormones, brain tissue and muscle tissue. Without enough cholesterol in the body, many important functions including testosterone would not function properly. On keto life, the cholesterol might go up a little but it is not a thing to worry because you are not taking any significant amount of carbs/sugars.

Saturated vs Unsaturated fats

Saturated fats like butter, lard, palm oil and coconut oils are solids at room temperature because they have no double bonds in the carbon chain. So the molecules are long straight chains that can lay close to each other like fibers. This is the reason why saturated fats are solids. They do not have any double bonds in the carbon chain and hence they are heat stable. Unsaturated fats (PUFA) or industrially manufactured fats like canola oil, corn oil, sunflower oil, safflower oil, peanut oil, vegetable oil etc. have multiple double bonds in their carbon chains, hence the molecule itself is squiggly. These molecules are farther from each other, therefore these oils are liquids. These are not at all heat stable because of the double bonds. If you cook food in PUFA oil, then the oil molecules break down into toxic and unpredictable components like aldehydes which are carcinogenic. PUFA oils therefore cause lot of inflammation in the body. It is better to use saturated fats like coconut oil or butter for cooking because these are heat stable.

There have been no studies that have directly been able to prove that saturated fats are the cause of heart disease. Olive oil is MUFA i.e. it has a single double bond in the carbon chain. It is also not heat stable so not very suitable for cooking. However it has a great ratio of Omega 6 to Omega 3 fatty acids. Olive oil can be used raw on top of salads.

Insulin

Insulin is the hormone released to digest carbohydrates. Insulin is a fat store hormone i.e., all dietary fat will be stored for future use in presence of insulin. The basic idea is to not spike insulin through carb restriction.

Frequent meals or snacks spike insulin every time. In absence of insulin, fat will not be stored. In absence of carbs, body will try to find alternative source of energy, ergo fats will be mobilized for energy.

Apple Cider Vinegar

While ACV might have extraordinary benefits for the liver, kidneys, insulin resistance, fat burning and what not, it is highly corrosive(acidic) for the teeth. Rinse your mouth after having a apple cider vinegar drink or use a straw to drink the beverage.

Electrolytes

When you are on a low carb diet, the body is a low insulin environment. In this environment, the kidneys are losing sodium all day. There is serious chance of sodium deficiency. Throw out the old myth of sodium giving you high blood pressure. You also need 5000 mg of potassium per day. Make sure get it from vegetables (or cream of tartar if you don't eat enough veggies on a given day). Drinking huge amounts of water will also flush out the electrolytes. Drink water only when thirsty. Keto side effects can be easily avoided by eating more potassium rich vegetables (not bananas, think greens).

Magnesium

Most of the people on keto/off keto are deficient in magnesium. Without magnesium, you will feel stressed and sleep will not come easy. Magnesium soothes the entire body and is essential for muscles during exercise. Get magnesium from vegetables or Magnesium glycinate supplement, but make sure you get enough of it. I have realized that a highly sugary diet of mine (before keto) depleted my Magnesium and gave me grey hair.

Exercise

When you exercise or sweat (like say in a humid environment), you are losing valuable electrolytes especially sodium. In a low insulin body, sodium will go down very rapidly. It is imperative that you must supplement sodium otherwise you may feel excessively thirsty. I generally take Himalayan pink salt in water after a workout or a walk to feel hydrated. Do not over do salt as it may increase your thirst.

Keto flu

It is common to feel lethargic (almost sick) on your first few days of keto diet. This is because the body does not know how to use fats (ketone bodies) for energy yet. Give it some time. As you get fat adapted, you will gain energy. Ketone bodies are high intensity fuel for the body compared to carbohydrates.

Keto Rash

On a low carb diet, you might get itchy rashes on areas like arms, neck etc. I could not find a convincing reason why this happens. I learned to live with these rashes as I could easily manage these rashes with moisturizing lotion. These rashes vanished after 8 weeks on keto.

Sleep

I fixed my snoring disorder by sleeping on my sides. I would still recommend to get checked for sleep apnea. Once my weight reduced, snoring went away and I could sleep on my back again. A good night sleep helps a lot to control stress.

For me the main problem was having to wake up more than once to pee. Sodium holds on to water. If you are low on sodium, the potassium is thought to be in excess. The body tries to expel this excess potassium by feeling thirsty. Also if body is low on potassium, sodium is thought to be in excess and the body tries to rid of excess sodium by peeing. Then you drink more water and then you pee again in a vicious circle. Just get enough sodium and potassium throughout the day to avoid this.

Important: Breathing through the nose instead of the mouth while sleeping gives you the full parasympathetic restorative (healing) effects of sleep.

A major life hack, that I have learnt is to avoid lights and phone screens 2 hours before sleep. This significantly improves sleep quality. I guess, this is because brights lights suppress melatonin which is responsible for sleep.

Hunger and Intermittent Fasting

When you do not eat carbohydrates, the phenomenon of being constantly hungry vanishes. This makes intermittent fasting VERY EASY.

Keto is a powerful tool to streamline health. If you add IF to keto, the combination is seriously potent. On a diet without carbs, doing IF for 18 hours per day is not as hard as it sounds. Following a eating window really helps the overall health and regulates sleep cycle nicely.

Insulin is the opposing hormone of melatonin (the hormone responsible for sleep cycle). Therefore, digesting food is the opposite of sleeping. This is why early dinner should promote a sound sleep. Fasting, should take the sleep to the next level.

Cancer Prevention

A lot of cancers survive on sugars/carbs. When you are on intermittent fasting or extended fasting or on keto, the cancer cells are starved and die out. This might seem too simplistic but this is what I have summarized out of all the exhaustive resources online. The cancer cells are hungry for sugar. In fact, PET scan detects location of cancer/tumor by feeding radioactive sugars and tracing the path taken by the sugar (something like this). So bottom line, avoid sugar/carbs, prevent cancer.

Fat adaptation is Nirvana (believe me)

Fat adaptation should be the ultimate target. If you are on strict keto for a long period like say 2–3 months, then the body is really trained to consider fat as the primary source of fuel. The body now has cellular machinery to burn fat efficiently. The world is a different place when you have chronic high energy levels, freedom from hunger and not having constantly to think about the next meal.

Eat fats to lose fats

Dietary fats do not deposit in the body unless accompanied by sugars or carbohydrates.

Cheat days

If a person is truly fat adapted, and he cheats for a couple of meals on the keto diet, the person can still bounce right back into ketosis. I bounced back into ketosis after I indulged on an ice cream milk shake and biryani. Within a couple of days everything was normal and I was burning fat just like before. At times, I even had moderate amounts of low glycemic index foods like chickpeas, sprouted lentils and mung dal on some days (once a week) and still continued on my weight loss glory.

Kidneys

There is a slight propensity to develop kidney stones on keto diet, especially if enough vegetables are not consumed. Not that this should deter you from keto. But drinking lemon juice, enough vegetables (enough Magnesium /Potassium) everyday should prevent kidney stones. Overall, LCHF diets like keto are very good for kidneys. In fact, it has been shown to even revert kidney nephropathy (due to diabetes) in rodents.

Constipation

Some people quibble over keto not being great for bathroom schedules. My answer to this is that when you do not eat whole grains and a lot of carbs, the quantity of solid waste generated by the human body automatically reduces by more than 60%. Some people might see this as constipation. The overwhelming benefits of ketosis easily tilt the balance back in favor of keto.

Green Vegetables and Eggs

Eat a lot of green vegetables (collard greens, broccoli, asparagus, lettuce, spinach, kale, lemons, avocado) every day to avoid most common side effects of LCHF. I try to stuff myself with as much vegetables as I can. Eggs are super food because they have all the good fats and vitamins. Also eggs satisfy you for a very long time. The human body can feel that you are eating nutrition dense food and hence it stops being hungry very soon. If you are always hungry, it means that you are nutrition deficient.

Organic foods

Omega 3 and Omega 6 are in equal amounts in nature and both are important for the human body. However, in industrial societies like ours, most oils are Omega 6 (canola, peanut oils). Only in organic naturally grown foods, the ratio is still maintained.

Cravings

When you eat nutritionally dense foods and cut out all carbs, cravings for junk food die out. Fatty foods fill you up very soon and it is difficult to overeat fats. Going long hours without food becomes easy. Life becomes easy when you do not have to worry about eating healthy every 3 to 4 hours.

As you can see, there are a lot of side effects and common pitfalls of this way of eating. However, the benefits of ketogenic diet are overwhelming. Fats/ketone bodies are like rocket fuel for the brain and the muscles. I used to be lethargic, low on mental energy and chronically tired on carb diet, but not anymore.

If this is done without fully understanding the basics, it is likely to be dangerous. Fortunately, the internet is filled with supportive online communities, online resources and a lot of relevant information.

Frequently Asked Questions

How Long Does It Take To Get Into Ketosis?

A ketogenic diet is not a diet that you can whimfully choose to go on and off of at any point. It takes time for your body to adjust and go into a state known as ketosis. This process? Anywhere from 2 – 7 days, depending on your body type, activity levels, and what you're eating. The fastest way to get into ketosis is to exercise on an empty stomach, restrict your carbohydrate intake to 20g or less per day, and be vigilant with your water intake.

Where Can I Find Low Carb Recipes?

Everywhere on the internet! There's recipes on almost every health website nowadays, and a quick Google of what you want will definitely help you out. You can even convert high carb recipes that use sugar or fruits in them to low carb recipes with artificial sweeteners or by getting rid of the fruit.

How Should I Track My Carb Intake?

The most common ways to track your carbs is through MyFitnessPal and their mobile app. You cannot track net carbs on the app, although you CAN track your total carb intake and your total fiber intake. To get your net carbs, simply subtract your total fiber intake from your total carb intake.

Do I Need To Count Calories?

At the end of the day, calories matter. Calories in/calories out is such a simple equation that it will never stand true to any one person. Metabolic disorders, endocrine disorders, and food sensitivities will also play a part in all of this. Your job? Well, to eat properly. Never go too far into a deficit, and never snack on foods that are considered "bad".

With a ketogenic diet you rarely have to worry about calories because the fats and proteins will fill you up and keep you full for a long period of time. But, if you exercise, you sometimes have to be vigilant. With exercise comes a greater calorie deficit, and you must eat to make up for it.

Can I Eat Too Much Fat?

In short, yes, you can eat too much fat. In the above question, I talked about calories and how they're still important for us. In the end, we still need to be at a caloric deficit for us to lose weight. Eating too much fat will push you over that calorie deficit, and turn it into a calorie surplus. While most people will find it hard to actually overeat on a low carb high fat diet, it is still possible.

You can use the keto calculator to calculate your macros and see how much fats, proteins, and carbs you should be eating a day. Keep in mind when you fill this out, you can edit the values of your protein and carbs (and should, depending on your activity levels).

How Much Weight Will I Lose?

The amount of weight you lose is totally dependent on you. Obviously adding exercise to your regimen will speed up your weight loss. Cutting out things that are common "stall" causers is also a good thing. Artificial sweeteners, dairy, wheat products and by products (wheat gluten, wheat flours, and anything with an identifiable wheat product in it).

Water weight loss is common when you first start a low carb diet. Ketosis has a diuretic effect to it that can cause many pounds of weight loss in only a few days. While I hate being the bearer of bad news, this isn't fat. But on a side (and more positive) note, that shows that your body is starting to adjust itself into a fat burning machine!

How Can I Tell if I Am In Ketosis?

The most common way is to use Ketostix. They can be picked up at your local pharmacy usually. Keep in mind, though, that they're incredibly inaccurate. Normally, they will give you an idea as to if you're in ketosis or not. Any pink or purple on the stick shows that ketones are being produced in your body. Darker colors usually mean that you're dehydrated and the ketone levels are more concentrated in your urine.

Ketostix measure the amount of acetone in your urine, which are mostly unused ketones. The ketone that is used by your body and brain for energy is called Beta-hydroxybutyrate (BHB), and is not measured by Ketostix.

For a more reliable and accurate way to measure your ketone levels, you must use a blood ketone meter. These will show you the proper amount of ketones in your blood, and aren't as easily changed through hydration (or lack thereof).

If you have a blood ketone meter, this is what the readings mean:

- Light Ketosis: 0.5 mmol/L – 0.8 mmol/L
- Medium Ketosis: 0.9 mmol/L – 1.4 mmol/L
- Deep Ketosis (best for weight loss): 1.5 mmol/L – 3.0 mmol/L

How Does Ketosis Work?

In a nutshell, ketosis is a state that our body enters when we don't eat carbohydrates. It's a way for our body to use fats (body fats included) as the primary energy we need. It's not only healthy for us, it's actually more efficient for our brains to use.

How do we get that energy from the fats? Well that "ketosis" state we are in allows our liver to break fats down into molecules called ketones. Those ketones provide the energy we need.

How does that all fall into weight loss? Through calorie deficit, we aren't actually eating enough energy for our body to live, so we have to dig into our own fat stores to get the energy we need.

What About Heart Attacks From All This Fat?

The main three fat groups we eat are saturated fats, polyunsaturated fats, and monounsaturated fats. The general consensus used to be that saturated fats were terrible for us and there was a clear link between saturated fats and heart disease. In recent years, though, saturated fats have shown to not only NOT cause heart attacks, but improve cholesterol levels. You can eat them without worry.

Polyunsaturated fats are a bit more tricky. There are 2 sides of the story here. Processed polyunsaturated fats (like margarine spreads and vegetable oils) are terrible for us, and usually include trans fats. They DO have a causation effect with heart disease and should be avoided. However, there are naturally occurring polyunsaturated fats in foods like fish, which are great for us and will improve cholesterol. It's your job to seek out the healthy fats and eliminate the unhealthy fats.

Last but not least, there's monounsaturated fats. These are pretty known to be "healthy" and are generally accepted as so. Olive oil is a pirmary example of something that is more proportionately a monounsaturated fat – being healthy for us and lowering our cholesterol.

What Are Macros and Should I Count Them?

Macros is a condensed term for the word macronutrients. The "big 3" macronutrients are fats, proteins, and carbohydrates. As mentioned before, calories still matter – and it's best you track all of them at the beginning. This not only gets you in a good habit, but also allows you to see how you are doing. You'd be surprised at how much we lie to ourselves, and how many unknown carbs can creep into our diet.

Tracking your macros also helps you if you come to a stall in your weight loss. You can pinpoint and nitpick at things in your diet that could well be causing this. When you track your macros, make sure you think in terms of GRAMS. Don't think in terms of percentages. I see tons of new people thinking "well I did 5% carbs, 20% protein, and 75% fat – perfect" but that isn't the case. Grams give a much more accurate description of what you're eating, so use those!

Keep in mind that if you're off on your macros by a bit, it's not a huge deal. You have wiggle room to go up or down by 10-15g of fats and proteins, in most cases. If some days you go over, and some days you're under, don't freak out. As long as you're keeping your calories in check and they're not too far in a deficit, you're fine!

What Foods Can I Eat?

It's a very common question to ask what you can eat. The main thing is to stay away from carbs. In a nutshell, that's sugars, breads, pastas, and rice. It might sound so simple when you look at it that way, but it's not all that simple. Potato chips, tomato sauce, and even salad dressings can have carbs in them.

Even vegetables have carbs in them, but they are a necessary part of our diet, and that's why we are allowed up to 30g of carbs a day – wiggle room, if you will, for some small amounts of residual carbohydrates from foods we need

I Just Started and Feel Like Crap. What Should I Do?

A very common happening when people start a ketogenic diet is getting headaches and "brain fogginess". Since ketosis has a diuretic effect on our bodies, we end up peeing a lot more than usual. Factor that in with our bodies burning up the lasting glycogen stores, and you have yourself a big disaster on your hands. You're peeing out electrolytes and you need to replace them.

Stay hydrated and eat salt. Broth, salty foods like bacon and deli meat, or salted nuts. These are good things to eat and drink while you're transitioning into ketosis, and are good things to help keep you sane and functional.

Constipation, What To Do?

It's fairly common for people starting out on keto to have irregular bowel movements. Below is a list of common advice given to people for constipation or bowel movement problems.

- Take a Magnesium Supplement
- Drink Plenty of Water
- Eat One Tbsp. of Coconut Oil
- Stop Eating Nuts (if you do)
- Eat More Fibrous Vegetables
- Try Eating Chia Seeds or Flax Seeds
- Try Coffee or Tea
- Can I Drink Alcohol On This Diet?

Alcohol can be consumed while on keto, but you must be wary. Those hidden carbs can creep in again.

The main takeaway point is to go after liquor. Wine, beer, and cocktails all have carbohydrates in them. Clear liquor is your best bet, but make sure you are steering clear of flavored liquors, as they can hold carbs in them.

I Stopped Losing Weight. What Can I Do?

Weight loss plateaus happen to everyone at least once. There's a number of things that could be the problem but I will keep this one short. You can try a different number of methods that may help you out – ranging from cutting certain foods out of your diet to changing your eating patterns through intermittent fasting or fat fasting.

Here's a list of common suggestions that are normally advised to people that aren't losing weight:

- Cut Out Dairy
- Up Your Fat Intake
- Decrease Your Carb Intake
- Stop Eating Nuts
- Stop Eating Gluten
- Cut Out Artificial Sweeteners
- Look for Hidden Carbs
- Begin Cutting Processed Food from Diet
- Switch to Measuring Instead of Weighing

I Work Out, Should I Be Worried?

There's 2 types of people that work out. People who run and people who lift weights. If you're someone who does a lot of cardio – running, biking, marathons, or the like, then you don't need to worry. Studies show that aerobic training (endurance training) isn't effected by low carbohydrate diets.

Now, the story changes if you lift weights. You have to know your end goal here. As a short answer, carbohydrates do help your performance and also help with recovery of muscles.

That means faster gains, and better strength performance in your training sessions. There's two routes you can take here – TKD and CKD.

TKD is a targeted ketogenic diet, where you're intaking just enough carbs before your workout to knock you out of ketosis for the duration of your workout. How it works is that you supply a glycogen source to your muscle to use, and then once it is used up after you finish your workout you will resume a ketotic state.

CKD is a cyclical ketogenic diet, and is also known as a more advanced technique. This shouldn't be used if you're new to keto, or new to training. It's more for bodybuilding and competitors that are wanting to stay on a ketogenic diet while still building muscle in their intense workouts. In this method, you stay on a regular ketogenic diet for a period of time (usually 5 days) and then do what is known as a carb-up for a period of time (usually 2 days, or the weekend). In a CKD, you are essentially replenishing all of your glycogen stores for all the training you'll do for the rest of the week, and your goal is to deplete that glycogen.

What Supplements Should I Take?

Sometimes it's common for people to get cramps or just not feel "right" after starting a ketogenic diet. Some supplements that are commonly suggested for people include:

- Multivitamin for Women
- Multivitamin for Men
- Magnesium Supplement
- Vitamin B Complex
- Vitamin D Supplement
- Potassium Supplement

Always check with your doctor before introducing vitamins into your diet.

CHAPTER FOUR

KETOGENIC FOOD AND SHOPPING LISTS

The Keto Diet does limit the foods you can eat, but "limit" doesn't mean you are left with few options. Here are all of the foods that you can safely consume while on the Keto Diet.

SEAFOOD

Anchovies

Fresh Fish

Bass

~~Carp~~

Flounder

Haddock

Halibut

Mackerel

Salmon

Sardines

Sole

~~Tilapia~~

Trout

Tuna

CHEESE

American

Bleu Cheese

Cheddar

Cottage Cheese

Cream Cheese

Feta

Gouda

Mozzarella

Parmesan

Provolone

Ricotta Cheese

Swiss

Clams

Crab Meat

Lobster

Mussels

Oysters

Shrimp

Squid

DRESSINGS

Red Wine Vinegar

Bleu Cheese

Creamy Caesar

Ranch

Olive Oil

FATS & OILS

Almond Butter

Avocado Oil

Butter

Cocoa Butter

Coconut Oil

Fish Oil

Flax Seed Oil

Grape Seed Oil

Hemp Seed Oil

Macadamia Oil

MCT Oil

Full Fat Mayonnaise

Olive Oil

Walnut Oil

NUTS & LEGUMES

Almonds

Brazil Nuts

Coconut

Hazelnuts

Macadamias

Pecans

Pistachios

Walnuts

FLOURS, MEALS, & POWDERS

Acorn Flour

Almond Flour

Almond Meal

SEEDS

Chia

Flax

Hemp

Pumpkin

Safflower

Sesame

Cocoa Powder

Coconut Flour

Flax Seed Meal

Protein Powder

Psyllium Husk

Sesame Seed Flour

Splenda

EGGS, POULTRY & FOWL

Eggs

Chicken

Duck

Goose

Quail

Turkey

DAIRY & DAIRY SUBSTITUTES

Almond Milk (unsweetened)

Coconut Cream

Coconut Milk (unsweetened)

Greek Yogurt

Heavy Cream

Sour Cream (full fat)

Soy Milk (unsweetened)

Whipped Cream

Grass Fed Butter

FRUITS & BERRIES

Avocado

Blackberry

Blueberry

Cranberry

Lemon

Lime

Green Olive

Raspberry

Strawberry

Rhubarb

Tomato

MEAT	VEGETABLES
Beef	Arugula
Tongue	Asparagus
Ribs	Bok Choy
Roast	Broccoli
Pastrami	Broccoli Rabe
Sausage	Cabbage
Corned	Cauliflower
Ground 70%-90% Lean	Celery
Hot Dog / Frankfurter	Chard
Steak	Chicory Greens
Bologna	Cucumber
Lamb	Eggplant
Pepperoni	Endive
Pork	Fennel
Bacon	Garlic
Chops	Green Bean
Ham	Jalapeño
~~Liverwurst~~	Lettuce (Green Leaf,
Loin	Romaine)
Proscuitto	Parsley
Sausage	Radish
Veal	Spinach
Venison	Soy Bean

Zucchini

Super Keto Supplements

As the popularity of the ketogenic diet continues to grow so does interest in how to optimize health while following this high-fat, low-carb eating plan. Because the keto diet cuts out a number of food options, it's a good idea to supplement with specific nutrients.

Not to mention, some supplements can help dieters reduce adverse effects of the keto flu and even enhance athletic performance when training on a low-carb diet.

Here are the best supplements to take on a keto diet.

1. Magnesium

Magnesium is a mineral that boosts energy, regulates blood sugar levels and supports your immune system. Research suggests that due to magnesium-depleting medications, reliance on processed foods and other factors, a good portion of the population has or is at risk of developing a magnesium deficience.

On a ketogenic diet, it may be even more difficult to meet your magnesium needs, as many magnesium-rich foods like beans and fruits are also high in carbs.

For these reasons, taking 200–400 mg of magnesium per day may be beneficial if you're on a keto diet.

Supplementing with magnesium can help reduce muscle cramps, difficulty sleeping and irritability — all symptoms commonly experienced by those transitioning to a ketogenic diet

Some of the most absorbable forms of magnesium include magnesium glycinate, magnesium gluconate and magnesium citrate. If you wish to increase your magnesium intake through keto-friendly foods, focus on incorporating these low-carb, magnesium-rich options:

- Spinach
- Avocado
- Swiss chard
- Pumpkin seeds
- Mackerel

N.B: Those following a ketogenic diet may be at a higher risk of developing a magnesium deficiency. Taking a magnesium supplement or eating more low-carb, magnesium-rich foods can help you meet your daily requirements.

2. MCT Oil

Medium-chain triglycerides, or MCTs, are a popular supplement among keto dieters.

They're metabolized differently than long-chain triglycerides, the most common type of fat found in food.

MCTs are broken down by your liver and quickly enter your bloodstream where they can be used as a fuel source for your brain and muscles.

Coconut oil is one of the richest natural sources of MCTs, with about 17% of its fatty acids being in the form of MCTs with potential metabolic benefits. However, taking MCT oil (made by isolating MCTs from coconut or palm oil) provides an even more concentrated dose of MCTs and can be helpful for those following a ketogenic diet.

Supplementing with MCT oil can help keto dieters since it can quickly up your fat intake, which increases ketone levels and helps you stay in ketosis. It has also been shown to promote weight loss and increase feelings of fullness, which can be helpful for those using the ketogenic diet as a weight loss tool.

MCT oil can be easily added to shakes and smoothies or simply taken by the spoonful for a quick fat boost.

It's a good idea to start with a small dose (1 teaspoon or 5 ml) of MCT oil to see how your body reacts before increasing to the suggested dosage listed on the supplement bottle. MCT oil can cause symptoms like diarrhea and nausea in some people.

N.B: MCT oil is a type of rapidly digested fat that can be used to help ketogenic dieters boost fat intake and stay in ketosis.

3. Omega-3 Fatty Acids

Omega-3 fatty acid supplements, such as fish or krill oil, are rich in the omega-3 fatty acids eicosapentaenoic acid (EPA) and docosahexaenoic acid (DHA), which benefit health in many ways.

EPA and DHA have been found to reduce inflammation, lower heart disease risk and prevent mental decline. Western diets tend to be higher in omega-6 fatty acids (found in foods like vegetable oils and processed foods) and lower in omega-3s (found in fatty fish).

This imbalance can promote inflammation in the body and has been linked to an increase in many inflammatory diseases. Omega-3 supplements can be particularly beneficial for people on ketogenic diets, as they can help maintain a healthy omega-3 to omega-6 ratio when following a high-fat diet.

What's more, omega-3 supplements can maximize the ketogenic diet's impact on overall health.

One study showed that people following a ketogenic diet who supplemented with omega-3 fatty acids from krill oil experienced greater decreases in triglycerides, insulin and inflammatory markers than those who did not. When shopping for omega-3 supplements, choose a reputable brand that provides at least a combined 500 mg of EPA and DHA per 1,000 mg serving.

Those on blood-thinning medications should consult a doctor before taking omega-3 supplements, as they can increase your risk of bleeding by further thinning your blood. To boost your intake of omega-3 fatty acids through keto-friendly foods, eat more salmon, sardines and anchovies.

N.B: Omega-3 fatty acid supplements can reduce inflammation, lower heart disease risk factors and help ensure a healthy balance of omega-3s to omega-6s.

4. Vitamin D

Having optimal levels of vitamin D is important for everyone's health, including people following ketogenic diets.

The keto diet doesn't necessarily put you at a higher risk of developing a vitamin D deficiency, but since vitamin D deficiency is common in general, supplementing with this vitamin is a good idea. Vitamin D is important for many bodily functions, including facilitating the absorption of calcium, a nutrient that could be lacking on a ketogenic diet, especially in those who are lactose intolerant. Vitamin D is also responsible for supporting your immune system, regulating cellular growth, promoting bone health and lowering inflammation in your body. Since few foods are good sources of this important vitamin, many health professionals recommend vitamin D supplements to ensure proper intake.

Your doctor can run a blood test to determine if you're deficient in vitamin D and help prescribe a proper dosage based on your needs.

N.B: Since vitamin D deficiency is common, it may be a good idea for people following the ketogenic diet to get their vitamin D levels checked and supplement accordingly.

5. Digestive Enzymes

One of the main complaints of those new to the ketogenic diet is that the high fat content of this eating pattern is tough on their digestive system.

Since the keto diet may consist of up to 75% fat, those used to consuming diets lower in fat can experience unpleasant gastrointestinal symptoms like nausea and diarrhea. In addition, though the ketogenic diet is only moderate in protein, it may still be a higher amount than some people are used to, which can also cause digestive side effects.

If you're experiencing digestive issues like nausea, diarrhea and bloating when transitioning to a ketogenic diet, a digestive enzyme blend that contains enzymes that break down fats (lipases) and proteins (proteases) may help optimize digestion.

What's more, proteolytic enzymes, which are enzymes that help break down and digest protein, have been shown to reduce post-workout soreness, which can be a bonus for workout enthusiasts on a keto diet.

N.B: Taking a digestive supplement that contains both protease and lipase enzymes, which break down protein and fat respectively, may help relieve digestive symptoms related to transitioning to a keto diet.

6. Exogenous Ketones

Exogenous ketones are ketones supplied through an external source, while endogenous ketones are the type produced naturally by your body through a process called ketogenesis.

Exogenous ketone supplements are commonly used by those following a ketogenic diet to increase blood ketone levels.

Aside from potentially helping you reach ketosis quicker, exogenous ketone supplements have been linked to other benefits as well.

For example, they have been shown to boost athletic performance, speed muscle recovery and decrease appetite.

However, research on exogenous ketones is limited, and many experts argue that these supplements aren't necessary for keto dieters. Additionally, most of the studies on exogenous ketones used a more powerful type of exogenous ketones called ketone esters, not ketone salts, which is the most common form found in supplements available to consumers.

While some people may find these supplements helpful, more research is needed to establish their potential benefits and risks.

N.B: Exogenous ketones may help raise ketone levels, decrease appetite and increase athletic performance.

However, more research is needed to establish the effectiveness of these supplements.

7. Greens Powder

Increasing vegetable intake is something that everyone should focus on. Vegetables contain a wide variety of vitamins, minerals and powerful plant compounds that can fight inflammation, lower disease risk and help your body function at optimal levels.

Though not everyone following a keto diet is necessarily lacking in their vegetable intake, this eating plan does make it more difficult to consume enough plant foods. A quick and easy way to boost your vegetable intake is by adding a greens powder to your supplement regimen.

Most greens powders contain a mixture of powdered plants like spinach, spirulina, chlorella, kale, broccoli, wheatgrass and more.

Greens powders can be added to drinks, shakes and smoothies, making them a convenient way to increase your intake of healthy produce. Those following ketogenic diets can also focus on adding more whole-food, low-carb vegetables to their meals and snacks. While it shouldn't be used as a replacement for fresh produce, a well-balanced greens powder is an excellent and easy way for keto dieters to add a nutrient boost to their meal plan.

N.B: Greens powders contain powdered forms of healthy plants like spinach, spirulina and kale. They can provide a convenient source of nutrients to those following ketogenic diets.

8. Electrolyte Supplements or Mineral-Rich Foods

Focusing on adding minerals through diet is important for people following a ketogenic diet, especially when first switching to this way of eating. The first weeks can be challenging as the body adapts to the very low number of carbs consumed.

Transitioning to a ketogenic diet results in increased water loss from the body.

Levels of sodium, potassium and magnesium can drop as well, leading to symptoms of the keto flu, such as headaches, muscle cramps and fatigue. Additionally, athletes following a keto diet may experience even greater fluid and electrolyte losses through sweating

Adding sodium through diet is the best strategy. Simply salting foods or sipping on a broth made with bouillon cubes should cover most people's increased sodium needs. Increasing your intake of potassium- and magnesium-rich foods can counteract losses of these important minerals, too.

Dark leafy greens, nuts, avocados and seeds are all keto-friendly foods that are high in both magnesium and potassium. Electrolyte supplements containing sodium, potassium and magnesium are available as well.

N.B: People following a ketogenic diet should focus on increasing their consumption of sodium, potassium and magnesium to prevent unpleasant symptoms like headache, muscle cramps and fatigue.

9. Supplements to Boost Athletic Performance

Athletes looking to boost performance while on a ketogenic diet may benefit from taking the following supplements:

Creatine monohydrate: Creatine monohydrate is an extensively researched dietary supplement that has been shown to promote muscle gain, improve exercise performance and increase strength

Caffeine: An extra cup of coffee or green tea can benefit athletic performance and boost energy levels, especially in athletes transitioning to a keto diet

Branched-chain amino acids (BCAAs): Branched-chain amino acid supplements have been found to reduce exercise-related muscle damage, muscle soreness and fatigue during exercise

HMB (beta-hydroxy beta-methylbutyrate): HMB may help decrease muscle loss and increase muscle mass, especially in those who are just beginning an exercise program or increasing the intensity of their workouts

Beta-alanine: Supplementing with the amino acid beta-alanine may help prevent fatigue and muscle burnout when following a ketogenic diet

N.B: Athletes following a ketogenic diet may benefit from certain supplements that preserve muscle mass, boost performance and prevent fatigue.

The high-fat, low-carb ketogenic diet is followed for various reasons, from promoting weight loss to boosting athletic performance.Some supplements can make the transition to this way of eating easier and help reduce symptoms of the keto flu.

What's more, many supplements can improve the nutritional value of a ketogenic diet plan and even enhance athletic performance. Taking these supplements can help optimize nutrition and allow you to thrive while on a keto diet.

Your Brain on Keto

Ketones are burned using different pathways and enzymes than sugar, causing a cascade of effects that improve brain health. Let's go over some of the ways that ketone bodies benefit the brain:

Ketones are a neuroprotective antioxidant. They have been found in many animal models to act as an antioxidant, preventing harmful reactive oxygen species from damaging brain cells.

Ketones are a more efficient energy source than sugar. Ketone bodies, beta-hydroxybutyrate in particular, are a more efficient source of energy per unit oxygen than glucose. Burning ketones may be an essential part of maintaining the health of aging brain cells because brain cells tend to lose their ability to use glucose efficiently as fuel over time.

Ketones increase mitochondrial efficiency and production. The ketogenic diet causes a coordinated upregulation of mitochondrial genes and genes involved in energy metabolism while stimulating the biogenesis of mitochondria. Altogether, this enhances the capacity of brain cells, protecting them from strokes and neurodegenerative diseases like Alzheimer's disease and Parkinson's disease.

Ketones increase GABAergic tone and decrease glutamatergic tone. Glutamate, the brain's main excitatory neurotransmitter, is the precursor for GABA, the brain's main inhibitory neurotransmitter. Glutamate is essential for neural communication, memory formation, learning, and regulation, but in certain conditions, glutamate can become excitotoxic. In other words, nerve cells can become damaged or killed by excessive stimulation of glutamate, which sets the stage for a variety of issues like multiple sclerosis, Alzheimer's disease, amyotrophic lateral sclerosis (ALS), and Parkinson's disease. Although the mechanisms are unclear, ketones have been found to decrease glutamatergic tone and increase GABAergic tone, which helps prevent brain cell damage and improve function.

Ketones trigger the expression BDNF. BDNF or Brain-derived neurotrophic factor is a protein that acts on specific neurons in throughout the nervous system. It helps to support the survival of existing neurons while encouraging the growth and differentiation of new neurons and neuronal connections. Ketones have been found to trigger the expression of BDNF in ways that can improve the function of the hippocampus, cortex, and basal forebrain—areas of the brain, which are vital in learning, memory, and higher thinking.

Whether you want to boost brain function, prevent neurodegenerative disease, or reduce the severity of a brain-related issue, the ketogenic diet one of the best ways to do it. By using the ketogenic diet to enter ketosis, you provide your body and brain with a more efficient fuel source that decreases inflammation and neuronal damage, improves brain cell growth and function, and regulates your brain's neurotransmitters.

As an added bonus, you will be eating highly-satiating, healthy foods that will help you eat fewer calories, improve health, and lose fat rapidly. This is what makes the ketogenic diet a win-win for many people, especially those with neurological conditions.

Ketosis Is a Hero for Hormones

Ketosis is the ultimate goal of the ketogenic diet. It's defined as a metabolic state of greater ketone production and enhanced fat burning. But it also comes with a plethora of health benefits. For women, however, ketosis apparently triggers a range of unpleasant side effects.

A properly executed ketogenic diet can help restore balance to out-of-whack female sex hormones. In my practice, I've also seen it mitigate weight gain, hot flashes, near-zero energy, low sex drive, bone loss, mood swings, and other troublesome symptoms associated with perimenopause, menopause, PMS, and post-menopause. Women who are going through major homone changes or dealing with symptoms related to homone flunctuation, I employ ketogenic nutrition to help them fix their hormones and keep them feeling healthy, especially as they get older. Here's how and why the ketogenic diet can come to your rescue:

1. It focuses on fat for better hormone support.

Fat is your best friend on a ketogenic diet. On a true keto diet, roughly 75 percent of your calories should come from healthy fat sources such as avocados, nuts and seeds, coconut oil, butter, olives and olive oil, and other high-fat foods. These "good" fats support hormone production and maintain hormone balance because they are the building blocks for estrogen, progesterone, and testosterone. For too long, we've been told to be wary of fat, and thus we slashed fat in favor of carbs. This was a mistake, and personally, I believe that this low-fat movement contributed to the hormonal challenges many women face today.

2. It boosts insulin sensitivity by reducing carb intake.

A keto diet restricts carbohydrates to 20 to 50 grams a day. This helps balance insulin levels. Insulin is a master hormone that controls blood sugar, and when it's too high and out of balance, your sex hormone levels can drop.

Luckily, following a ketogenic diet makes your body more "insulin sensitive." This means insulin is well-regulated, in balance, and used properly by your cells. When you're insulin sensitive, all sorts of metabolic miracles happen. You stay slim and get fit more easily; you lower your risk of cardiovascular disease, Alzheimer's disease, and dementia; you tend to not have hot flashes or night sweats; and you rebuild your bone health so that you're less at risk for frailty and osteoporosis. Cravings become a distant memory, and you feel and look healthy and energized.

3. It eases premenstrual syndrome (PMS) by detoxing the body.

PMS produces a lot of really uncomfortable symptoms, including cramps, cravings, moodiness, irritability, depression, acne, and fatigue. The underlying cause is often estrogen dominance, or having too much estrogen and not enough progesterone. One of the causes of estrogen dominance is a diet comprised of too much sugar and refined carbohydrates—a problem easily eliminated by going on a ketogenic diet.

Another cause of estrogen dominance is exposure to estrogens in the environment. These are toxic forms of estrogen that not only worsen PMS symptoms, but they are through to increase the risk of breast cancer, endometriosis, infertility, and autoimmune diseases. In my version of a keto diet, you're encouraged to eat foods that detoxify these nasty estrogens like veggies such as broccoli, cauliflower, Brussels sprouts, cabbage, and greens and delicious herbs and spices like oregano, thyme, rosemary, sage, and turmeric.

4. It boosts reproductive health by combating PCOS.

One of the main causes of infertility in women is polycystic ovary syndrome, or PCOS. This condition develops from poorly balanced sex hormones, and more than half of the women diagnosed with PCOS are obese or overweight, have poor blood sugar regulation, and have insulin resistance. There's no cure for PCOS, but because insulin problems are associated with PCOS, a ketogenic diet is a viable solution. Duke University researchers found that women with PCOS who followed a keto diet were able to balance their levels of insulin and testosterone and experience improvements in weight, infertility, and menstruation among other factors. Two women in the study got pregnant despite previous infertility problems, and everyone lost weight.

5. It zaps stress to protect the adrenals.

In response to life's many stressors, the adrenal glands release the hormone cortisol to galvanize energy so we can react quickly to whatever challenge we're facing. If our stress goes unresolved, the adrenals keep pumping out cortisol, resulting in too much cortisol floating around. The ongoing secretion of high amounts of cortisol robs your body of progesterone, estrogen, and testosterone, and if this keeps happening, you're more likely to experience imbalanced sex hormones, high blood sugar, loss of muscle, low sex drive, and burnout.

To combat this, enjoy all those low-carbohydrate vegetables you typically eat on a ketogenic diet (plenty of green leafy vegetables, parsley, kale, beet greens, broccoli, cauliflower, and so forth). They may help normalize cortisol, support your adrenal glands, and improve your natural progesterone levels.

The keto diet isn't for everyone, but for a lot of women in my practice it's been a game-changer for hormonal imbalance and hormone-related symptoms. If you're suffering or just not feeling your best, the keto diet is definitely worth a try!

Keto the Cancer Killer

The keto diet limits carbs, which are known to increase glucose and insulin. It forces the body to burn fat as fuel. Some of the fat is converted to ketones, which are used by the brain and many other tissues as another type of fuel.

"Because cancer cells prefer to use glucose, diets that limit glucose may be beneficial," ketogenic diets will limit the ability of cancer to grow, which gives the patient's immune system time to respond. With ketogenic diets, lowering carbohydrates will reduce your levels of glucose, the fuel that feeds cancer cells. This will put your body into ketosis and will assist in depleting cancer cells of their energy supply.

Cancer cells are unlike normal cells in many ways, but one of their traits that is most unique regards insulin receptors. They have ten times more insulin receptors on their cellular surface. This enables cancer cells to gorge themselves in glucose and nutrients coming from the bloodstream at a very high rate. As you continue to consume glucose as your primary diet source, cancer cells will continue to thrive and spread. It is no surprise that the lowest survival rate in cancer patients is among those with the highest blood sugar levels.

Cancer cells have damaged mitochondria and lack the ability to create energy from aerobic respiration. They cannot metabolize fatty acids for energy. For this reason, cancer cells thrive in oxygen-depleted environments. Instead, cancer cells metabolize glucose and amino acids. Restricting glucose or the amino acid glutamine is essential to starve off cancer.

CHAPTER FIVE

YOUR PERSONALIZED KETO PLAN

If you find yourself in a conversation about dieting or weight loss, chances are you'll hear of the ketogenic, or keto, diet. That's because the keto diet has become one of the most popular methods worldwide to shed excess weight and improve health.

Research has demonstrated that adopting this low-carb, high-fat diet can promote fat loss and even improve certain conditions such as type 2 diabetes and cognitive decline. This page explains what to eat and avoid while following a keto diet and provides a one-week keto meal plan to get you started.

Ketogenic Diet Meal Plan

Switching over to a ketogenic diet can seem overwhelming, but it doesn't have to be difficult.

Your focus should be on reducing carbs while increasing the fat and protein content of meals and snacks. In order to reach and remain in a state of ketosis, carbs must be restricted.

While certain people might only achieve ketosis by eating less than 20 grams of carbs per day, others may be successful with a much higher carb intake.

Generally, the lower your carbohydrate intake, the easier it is to reach and stay in ketosis. This is why sticking to keto-friendly foods and avoiding items rich in carbs is the best way to successfully lose weight on a ketogenic diet.

Keto-Friendly Foods to Eat

When following a ketogenic diet, meals and snacks should center around the following foods:

Eggs: Pastured, organic whole eggs make the best choice.

Poultry: Chicken and turkey.

Fatty fish: Wild-caught salmon, herring and mackerel.

Meat: Grass-fed beef, venison, pork, organ meats and bison.

Full-fat dairy: Yogurt, butter and cream.

Full- fat cheese: Cheddar, mozzarella, brie, goat cheese and cream cheese.

Nuts and seeds: Macadamia nuts, almonds, walnuts, pumpkin seeds, peanuts and flaxseeds.

Nut butter: Natural peanut, almond and cashew butters.

Healthy fats: Coconut oil, olive oil, avocado oil, coconut butter and sesame oil.

Avocados: Whole avocados can be added to almost any meal or snack.

Non-starchy vegetables: Greens, broccoli, tomatoes, mushrooms and peppers.

Condiments: Salt, pepper, vinegar, lemon juice, fresh herbs and spices.

Foods to Avoid

Avoid foods rich in carbs while following a keto diet.

The following foods should be restricted:

Bread and baked goods: White bread, whole-wheat bread, crackers, cookies, doughnuts and rolls.

Sweets and sugary foods: Sugar, ice cream, candy, maple syrup, agave syrup and coconut sugar.

Sweetened beverages: Soda, juice, sweetened teas and sports drinks.

Pasta: Spaghetti and noodles.

Grains and grain products: Wheat, rice, oats, breakfast cereals and tortillas.

Starchy vegetables: Potatoes, sweet potatoes, butternut squash, corn, peas and pumpkin.

Beans and legumes: Black beans, chickpeas, lentils and kidney beans.

Fruit: Citrus, grapes, bananas and pineapple.

High-carb sauces: Barbecue sauce, sugary salad dressings and dipping sauces.

Certain alcoholic beverages: Beer and sugary mixed drinks.

Though carbs should be restricted, low-glycemic fruits such as berries can be enjoyed in limited amounts as long as you're maintaining a keto-friendly macronutrient range.

Be sure to choose healthy food sources and steer clear of processed foods and unhealthy fats.

The following items should be avoided:

Unhealthy fats: Margarine, shortening and vegetable oils such as canola and corn oil.

Processed foods: Fast food, packaged foods and processed meats such as hot dogs and lunch meats.

Diet foods: Foods that contain artificial colors, preservatives and sweeteners such as sugar alcohols and aspartame.

Keto-Friendly Beverages

Sugar can be found in a wide variety of beverages including juice, soda, iced tea and coffee drinks.While on a ketogenic diet, high-carb drinks must be avoided just like high-carb foods.

It's no small matter that sugary beverages have also been linked to various health issues — from obesity to an increased risk of diabetes.

Thankfully, there are many tasty, sugar-free options for those on the keto diet.

Keto-friendly beverage choices include:

Water: Water is the best choice for hydration and should be consumed throughout the day.

Sparkling water: Sparkling water can make an excellent soda replacement.

Unsweetened coffee: Try heavy cream to add flavor to your cup of joe.

Unsweetened green tea: Green tea is delicious and provides many health benefits.

If you want to add some extra flavor to your water, try experimenting with different keto-friendly flavor combinations.

For example, tossing some fresh mint and lemon peel into your water bottle can make hydration a breeze.

Though alcohol should be restricted, enjoying a low-carb drink like vodka or tequila mixed with soda water is perfectly fine on occasion.

The Keto Basic Plan

A Sample Keto Menu for One Week

The following menu provides less than 50 grams of total carbs per day.

As mentioned above, some people may have to reduce carbohydrates even further in order to reach ketosis.

This is a general one-week ketogenic menu that can be altered depending on individual dietary needs.

MONDAY

Breakfast: Two eggs fried in pastured butter served with sauteed greens.

Lunch: A bunless grass-fed burger topped with cheese, mushrooms and avocado atop a bed of greens.

Dinner: Pork chops with green beans sauteed in coconut oil.

TUESDAY

Breakfast: Mushroom omelet.

Lunch: Tuna salad with celery and tomato atop a bed of greens.

Dinner: Roast chicken with cream sauce and sauteed broccoli.

WEDNESDAY

Breakfast: Bell pepper stuffed with cheese and eggs.

Lunch: Arugula salad with hard-boiled eggs, turkey, avocado and blue cheese.

Dinner: Grilled salmon with spinach sauteed in coconut oil.

THURSDAY

Breakfast: Full-fat yogurt topped with Keto granola.

Lunch: Steak bowl with cauliflower rice, cheese, herbs, avocado and salsa.

Dinner: Bison steak with cheesy broccoli.

FRIDAY

Breakfast: Baked avocado egg boats.

Lunch: Caesar salad with chicken.

Dinner: Pork chops with vegetables.

SATURDAY

Breakfast: Cauliflower toast topped with cheese and avocado.

Lunch: Bunless salmon burgers topped with pesto.

Dinner: Meatballs served with zucchini noodles and parmesan cheese.

SUNDAY

Breakfast: Coconut milk chia pudding topped with coconut and walnuts.

Lunch: Cobb salad made with greens, hard-boiled eggs, avocado, cheese and turkey.

Dinner: Coconut chicken curry.

As you can see, ketogenic meals can be diverse and flavorful.

Although many ketogenic meals are based around animal products, there is a wide variety of vegetarian options to choose from as well.

Healthy Ketogenic Snack Options

Snacking between meals can help moderate hunger and keep you on track while following a ketogenic diet. Because the ketogenic diet is so filling, you may only need one or two snacks per day, depending on your activity level.

Here are some excellent, keto-friendly snack options:

- Almonds and cheddar cheese
- Half an avocado stuffed with chicken salad
- Guacamole with low-carb veggies
- Trail mix made with unsweetened coconut, nuts and seeds
- Hard-boiled eggs
- Coconut chips
- Kale chips
- Olives and sliced salami
- Celery and peppers with herbed cream cheese dip
- Berries with heavy whipping cream
- Jerky
- Cheese roll-ups
- Parmesan crisps
- Macadamia nuts
- Greens with high-fat dressing and avocado
- Keto smoothie made with coconut milk, cocoa and avocado
- Avocado cocoa mousse

Though these keto snacks can maintain fullness between meals, they can also contribute to weight gain if you're snacking too much throughout the day.

It's important to eat the appropriate number of calories based on your activity level, weight loss goal, age and gender. If you're unsure how many calories you should be eating, check out this article to learn how to calculate energy needs.

The Keto Fasting Plan

There are a few approaches when it comes to intermittent fasting.

Skipped meals. This is when you skip over a meal to induce extra time of fasting. Usually people choose breakfast, but others prefer to skip lunch.

Eating windows. Usually this condenses your entire macronutrient intake between a 4 and 7 hour window. The rest of the time you are in a fasting state.

24-48 hour cleanse. This is where you go into extended fasting periods, and do not eat for 1-2 days.

I don't recommend that you go straight for a 1-2 day fast, but begin by restricting yourself to certain eating windows. Typically people restrict themselves to the hours of 5pm – 11pm. People often refer to their fasting windows by numbers: 19/5 or 21/3, for example, means 19 hours of fasting and 5 hours eating or 21 hours fasting and 3 hours eating, respectively.

Once you have the hang of eating on a schedule, you can try short periods of 18-24 hour fasting. Then you can judge if intermittent fasting is for you.

Whether you decide to do it every day, once a week, or twice a week is up to you – do what makes you feel best and listen to your body.

How Does Intermittent Fasting Work?

The whole point of intermittent fasting is to allow ourselves to increase the amount of food we can intake at one time. Our bodies naturally can only take in a certain amount of food at once, so we are creating a sort of limit on our calorie intake.

This is also a great method for people that overeat. I tend to see people that forget to count the snacks that they have throughout the day, and wonder why they are putting weight on.

Your body will adjust itself to fasting, and you will find yourself not as hungry as you used to be. This allows you to properly record and maintain the nutrient values of what you intake.

In this fasting state, our bodies can break down extra fat that's stored for the energy it needs. When we're in ketosis, our body already mimics a fasting state, being that we have little to no glucose in our bloodstream, so we use the fats in our bodies as energy.

Intermittent fasting is using the same reasoning – instead of using the fats we are eating to gain energy, we are using our stored fat. That being said, you might think it's great – you can just fast and lose more weight. You have to take into account that later on, you will need to eat extra fat in order to hit your daily macros (the most important thing). If you're overeating on fats here, you will store the excess.

While there are some weight loss advantages to fasting, it's more for the convenience of timing. Do not fast solely for the weight loss if you do not enjoy doing it. There are other benefits, though, and we'll discuss these too.

Intermittent Fasting – Meal Timing Matters

Intermittent fasting is a term that we use to describe the dietary practice of restricting your food consumption to a specific window of time. A popular intermittent fasting strategy, for example, is fasting during an 18 hour window of time and eating during the 6 hour window of time that is left in the day.

Let's say your last meal was at 6 pm last night and you ate nothing else after that. To implement an intermittent fast, simply restrict eating until 12 pm the next afternoon (yes, sleeping time counts as fasting time). To do this every day, only eat between 12 pm and 6 pm and fast for the remainder of the day.

There are many different variations of intermittent fasting as well. Dr. Dom D'Agostino, the well-known ketogenic diet researcher, suggests doing a longer intermittent fast for 3 days, 3 times a year. This means not eating for 3 days, and eating normally until the next fast. Daily intermittent fasts are recommended as well. He says that it is ideal to have one to two meals after fasting for most of the day to reap the benefits of intermittent fasting every day.

You are probably wondering how there could possibly be a benefit to eating less frequently that goes beyond what you are already getting with a ketogenic diet. Restricting carbs and eating enough fat and protein does come with a plethora of health benefits, but when you add intermittent fasting to your lifestyle you can increase energy and reverse aging by harnessing the power of a nobel prize winning process.

The Keto Vegan Plan

Overview of the vegan ketogenic diet

You might have noticed a lot of animal-based proteins in the "what to eat on a ketogenic diet" list. Many of vegans' go-to sources of protein like beans and legumes are off-limits because they put you over the recommended range of carbohydrates per day. That said, soy-based proteins and high-protein veggies like spinach, kale, broccoli, sprouts, mushrooms and brussels sprouts are still allowed. Reaching to a state of ketosis on a vegan diet requires careful macronutrient calculation, so it's often best to consult a doctor, nutritionist or dietician.

Vegan ketogenic diet food list: What foods to eat and avoid

The vegan ketogenic diet food list looks quite similar to the standard ketogenic diet food list — minus the beef, poultry, eggs and fish. Here are foods to avoid:

High-carb fruits: Bananas, clementines, apples, kiwis and blueberries

All grains: Whole wheat breads, quinoa, oats and corn

Processed, natural and artificial sugars: White sugar, cane sugar, agave, honey, maple syrup, Equal and Splenda

Tubers: Potatoes, taro and yams

Legumes: Lentils, black beans, peas and chickpeas

Here is a list of vegan keto-friendly foods to eat:

Fat: Coconut oil, coconut cream/milk, avocado, plant-based oils, nuts and seeds

Healthy protein: nut-based yogurts, soy proteins and high-protein veggies

Carbohydrates: Tomatoes, broccoli, onion, kale, spinach, brussels sprouts and raspberries

Vegan keto diet grocery list

Ready to go shopping? Here is a vegan keto diet grocery list to take along. The list is broken up by macronutrient, but there is some overlap when it comes to foods like nuts and seeds as they contain fat and protein. When buying packaged foods like tofu, tempeh and seitan, read ingredient labels to make sure there are no added sugars.

Vegan keto proteins

Tofu

Tempeh

Seitan

Dairy-free yogurt (high-fat)

Vegan keto fats

Nuts like pistachios and almonds

Seeds like hemp seeds, sunflower seeds and pumpkin seeds

Avocado

Plant-based oil like coconut oil, olive oil or hemp oil

Vegan keto carbohydrates

Leafy greens like kale and spinach

Mushrooms like shiitake, lion's mane and oyster

Berries like blackberries and raspberries

Vegetables like broccoli, cauliflower and zucchini

Raw vegan ketogenic diet

Turning your vegan ketogenic meal plan into a raw vegan ketogenic one isn't too tricky. Instead of cooking or roasting veggies, nuts and seeds, consume them raw. To make leafy greens more appealing and digestible, massage them with a plant-based oil before serving. Finally, if you're struggling to get the correct ratio of protein in your daily diet, consider a raw vegan protein supplement (Garden of Life and Sunwarrior brands offer these powders).

7 day vegan keto diet plan

By eating foods from the "Do Eat" list, you can follow a vegan Keto diet and meet most of your nutritional bases. They provide all macronutrients (carbs, fats, and proteins) without packing up carbs.

Also, most of your foods while on a vegan Ketogenic diet come from this list, so have this list handy. I admit. Making every Keto recipe without animal products vegan takes some efforts.

But with some easy food swaps and some careful planning, you can veganize most keto recipe out there!

Day 1:

Breakfast: Chocolate-Covered Macadamia Smoothie

Lunch: Low-carb avocados salad with almond

Dinner: Tofu stir-fry served over cauliflower rice

Day 2:

Breakfast: Baked Tofu, avocado, and vegan pesto

Lunch: Zucchini noodles with pesto and vegan cheese.

Dinner: Grilled Zucchini avocado salads with walnuts and a drizzle of MCT oil.

Day 3:

Breakfast: Chia almond pudding made with full-fat coconut milk.

Lunch: Broccoli creamy coconut soup.

Dinner: Baked asparagus with tofu drizzled with avocado oil

Day 4:

Breakfast: Coconut yogurt topped with crushed nuts, seeds, and unsweetened shredded coconut.

Lunch: Crispy Tofu & Cauliflower Rice Stir-Fry

Dinner: Seitan Negimaki

Day 5:

Breakfast: Tofu scramble with vegan cheese, mushrooms, and spinach.

Lunch: Vegetable and tofu salad with avocado dressing.

Dinner: Eggplant lasagna made with vegan cheese.

Day 6:

Breakfast: Peanut Butter avocado smoothie

Lunch: Green curry kale & crispy coconut tempeh

Dinner: Cauliflower tofu fried rice.

Day 7:

Breakfast: Coconut almond chia pudding.

Lunch: Green salad with tempeh avocado, vegan cheese, and pumpkin seeds.

Dinner: Vegan cauliflower mac and cheese.

The Keto Collagen-Boosting Plan

You may have heard of collagen, but keto collagen...? Do a quick google search and you might not find too much out there. Ketogenic nutrition is just coming into the mainstream. The good news is, keto is quickly becoming one of the best-researched diets on the planet. The science and anecdotal experience from keto dieters is promising. From fat loss to higher brain function, to soaring energy, the list of keto diet benefits are long — and growing!

Here, we'll talk about the importance of adding a high-quality collagen supplement to your diet, plus when to use collagen.

What is Keto Collagen?

Keto Collagen is a blend of MCTs and grass-fed collagen powder. These are some of the healthiest fats and proteins on the planet.

The purpose of keto collagen is to give you great energy and recovery in one convenient scoop. A ketogenic diet can be difficult to get used to. Keto collagen will help you set yourself up for success, especially in those first few weeks when the keto flu can hit.

The Purpose of MCTs in Keto Collagen

When you're in a ketogenic state, your body switches from using glucose and glycogen (stored glucose) as fuel and starts to burn fat as fuel.

But even when you're not in ketosis, you need fat to:

- Make hormones
- Make neurotransmitters
- For cell function
- For brain function
- For energy

First, What Are MCTs?

Like most foods, there are healthy and unhealthy types and sources. MCTs are one of the most efficient and highest quality fats on the planet.

Short for medium-chain triglycerides, MCTs are a type of fatty acid that bypass normal digestion and rarely get stored as body fat. Instead, they're processed through your liver and turned into ketones, which your brain and body use as a super efficient energy source.

Bottom line: MCTs are a quick, clean energy source you will burn, not store as body fat.

The benefits of MCTs include:

Better Weight Loss – MCTs are easily digested and have a thermogenic (energy-creating) effect, aka, they're known for "boosting your metabolism."

Better Energy – MCTs are fast-acting source of energy. They break down into ketones which can then be used as fuel for your body.

Better Digestion – MCTs support your gut microbiome by combating harmful bacteria and parasites.

Better Overall Health – MCTs contain antioxidant properties which reduce internal inflammation. This is great news for your heart, brain, and nervous system.

The Purpose of Collagen in Keto Collagen

Collagen provides the best protein for your skin, hair, joints, and other soft tissue. That's why it's quickly becoming one of the most popular supplements on the planet.

The word collagen comes from Greek roots that literally mean "glue-producing." Collagen makes up 25% of your body's protein content and is helpful in soft-tissue repair.

Collagen Aids In:

- Energy production
- Building healthy DNA
- Detoxification and digestion
- Rebuilding joints, tendons, cartilage, skin, nails, hair, and your gut lining

Collagen Is:

A type of protein – 1 of over 10,000 in your body.

In water, collagen breaks into gelatin. They are the same amino acids with a different chemical structure. Think of them as the same tool, but different packaging.

Collagen protein from grass-fed beef is made in the same way that bone broth is made, low and slow heating to preserve the nutrition.

How To Use Keto Collagen

Keto Collagen was made to aid in energy and recovery. So, anytime you're asking yourself how you can use Keto Collagen, think, "When could I use some good, convenient energy and recovery?" Here are some popular ways we see people using Keto Collagen.

WHEN TO USE KETO COLLAGEN

In The Morning or Afternoon During Work

MCTs metabolize quickly in your body, which means they turn from fatty acid into ketones for your body to burn as energy. Since your brain uses about 20% of your total daily energy expenditure, some Keto Collagen before or during work isn't a bad idea.

This is not a stimulant for the perception of alertness. Keto Collagen is real energy.

Before/During/After Exercise

MCTs are fuel for your body and mind, especially on a low-carb diet. When we talk about "fat-burning" we are literally describing fatty acids like MCTs being metabolized into ketones and shuttling energy to your cells.

Collagen protein plays a huge role in the regeneration of muscles, joints, connective tissues, and ligaments, so many people like to take collagen supplements before or after a workout.

Anytime Ketogenic Protein/Fat Snack

Get the best quality protein and fats, anytime, without carbohydrates or fake ingredients.

HOW MUCH KETO COLLAGEN TO USE

This depends on you and your goals. Many people start with half a scoop and increase from there. You can experiment with 0.5-3 scoops per day, depending on how much you're exercising, your weight-loss or weight-gain goals, or if you're traveling and don't have easy access to healthy options.

Keto Collagen is a completely clean product. It doesn't contain any soy, dairy, gluten, artificial sweeteners, or anything that doesn't directly improve your health. It also tastes phenomenal. Perfect Keto comes in a delicious chocolate flavor that goes great in almost any beverage, coffee or smoothie you can dream up. It's also great in just plain water!

CHAPTER SIX

EVERYTHING YOU NEED TO KNOW ABOUT CYCLICAL KETOGENIC DIET

Though often considered inflexible, the ketogenic diet has many different variations. The standard keto diet is by far the most popular form, but there are several other ways to follow this low-carb, high-fat regime — including the cyclical ketogenic diet.

The cyclical keto diet involves rotating between a strict high-fat, low-carb ketogenic meal plan and higher carb intake.

What Is the Cyclical Ketogenic Diet?

The ketogenic diet is a high-fat, very low-carb diet. When following a ketogenic diet, you normally restrict carbs to under 50 grams per day. When carb intake is drastically reduced, your body must burn fat for energy instead of glucose, or blood sugar, in a process known as ketosis.

While in ketosis, your body uses ketones — byproducts of fat breakdown produced by your liver — as an alternate energy source. Though the cyclical ketogenic diet is a variation of the standard ketogenic diet, there are major differences between the two.

Cyclical ketogenic dieting involves adhering to a standard ketogenic diet protocol 5–6 days per week, followed by 1–2 days of higher carb consumption.

These higher-carb days are often referred to as "refeeding days," as they're meant to replenish your body's depleted glucose reserves. If you undertake a cyclical ketogenic diet, you switch out of ketosis during refeeding days in order to reap the benefits of carb consumption for a temporary period.

The cyclical ketogenic diet is popular among those seeking muscle growth and improved exercise performance. Though research to support this claim is lacking, some people speculate that the cyclical diet is superior to the standard version for boosting strength and muscle.

Is It the Same as Carb Cycling?

The cyclical ketogenic diet is often compared to carb cycling — but it's not the same thing.

Carb cycling involves cutting carbs on certain days of the week while upping your intake on others. Typically, each week is divided between 4–6 days of lower carb intake and 1–3 days of higher intake.

While the method is the same, carb cycling doesn't reduce overall carb intake drastically enough to reach ketosis.

Carb cycling is often used to promote weight loss, boost athletic performance and encourage muscle growth.

How to Follow It

There is no standard set of rules for a cyclical ketogenic diet. However, anyone wanting to start it should follow a standard ketogenic diet 5–6 days per week, adding 1–2 days of higher carb intake.

Stick to a Standard Keto Diet 5–6 Days per Week

During standard ketogenic days, it's important to consume fewer than 50 grams of carbs per day. During this phase of the cyclical keto diet, healthy fats should deliver approximately 75% of your total calorie intake.

Healthy fat options include:

- Eggs
- Coconut oil and unsweetened coconut
- Avocado
- Full-fat dairy products
- Low-carb nuts and seeds
- Nut butters
- Fatty meats
- MCT oil

Proteins should make up around 15–20% of your total calories, while carb intake is typically restricted to under 10%. Be sure to follow the standard keto diet 5–6 days per week.

Increase Carb Consumption 1–2 Days per Week

The second phase of the cyclical keto diet involves choosing 1–2 days per week to "refeed" your glycogen stores.

During refeeding days, you should consume more carbs in order to break ketosis.

On refeeding days:

Carbs should comprise 60–70% of your total calories.

Protein should account for 15–20% of your total calories.

Fats should deliver just 5–10% of your total calories.

Though the goal of the refeeding phase is to increase the number of carbs, carb quality also matters.

Instead of relying on unhealthy sources like white bread and baked goods, you should get the majority of your carbs from healthy sources.

Some examples of nutritious, complex carbs include:

- Sweet potatoes
- Butternut squash
- Brown rice
- Oats
- Quinoa
- Whole-wheat or brown-rice pasta
- Beans and lentils

These carbs are high in vitamins, minerals and fiber, which fuel your body and keep blood sugar levels stabilized.

Avoid foods and beverages high in sugar — like candy, juice, soda and cake — as they're devoid of nutrients and lead to blood sugar irregularity, which can cause increased hunger and irritability

Keto Diet Eating

Studies have found that this very low-carb, high-fat diet is effective for weight loss, diabetes and epilepsy. There's also early evidence to show that it may be beneficial for certain cancers, Alzheimer's disease and other diseases, too. A ketogenic diet typically limits carbs to 20–50 grams per day. While this may seem challenging, many nutritious foods can easily fit into this way of eating.

Here are 13 healthy foods to eat on a ketogenic diet.

1. Seafood

Fish and shellfish are very keto-friendly foods. Salmon and other fish are rich in B vitamins, potassium and selenium, yet virtually carb-free.However, the carbs in different types of shellfish vary. For instance, while shrimp and most crabs contain no carbs, other types of shellfish do. While these shellfish can still be included on a ketogenic diet, it's important to account for these carbs when you're trying to stay within a narrow range.

Here are the carb counts for 3.5-ounce (100-gram) servings of some popular types of shellfish.

- Clams: 5 grams
- Mussels: 7 grams
- Octopus: 4 grams
- Oysters: 4 grams
- Squid: 3 grams

Salmon, sardines, mackerel and other fatty fish are very high in omega-3 fats, which have been found to lower insulin levels and increase insulin sensitivity in overweight and obese people.In addition, frequent fish intake has been linked to a decreased risk of disease and improved mental health

2. Low-Carb Vegetables

Non-starchy vegetables are low in calories and carbs, but high in many nutrients, including vitamin C and several minerals. Vegetables and other plants contain fiber, which your body doesn't digest and absorb like other carbs.

Therefore, look at their digestible (or net) carb count, which is total carbs minus fiber.

Most vegetables contain very few net carbs. However, consuming one serving of "starchy" vegetables like potatoes, yams or beets could put you over your entire carb limit for the day. The net carb count for non-starchy vegetables ranges from less than 1 gram for 1 cup of raw spinach to 8 grams for 1 cup of cooked Brussels sprouts. Vegetables also contain antioxidants that help protect against free radicals, which are unstable molecules that can cause cell damage. What's more, cruciferous vegetables like kale, broccoli and cauliflower have been linked to decreased cancer and heart disease risk.

Low-carb veggies make great substitutes for higher-carb foods. For instance, cauliflower can be used to mimic rice or mashed potatoes, "zoodles" can be created from zucchini and spaghetti squash is a natural substitute for spaghetti.

3. Cheese

Cheese is both nutritious and delicious.

There are hundreds of types of cheese. Fortunately, all of them are very low in carbs and high in fat, which makes them a great fit for a ketogenic diet. One ounce (28 grams) of cheddar cheese provides 1 gram of carbs, 7 grams of protein and 20%

of the RDI for calcium. Cheese is high in saturated fat, but it hasn't been shown to increase the risk of heart disease. In fact, some studies suggest that cheese may help protect against heart disease.

Cheese also contains conjugated linoleic acid, which is a fat that has been linked to fat loss and improvements in body composition. In addition, eating cheese regularly may help reduce the loss of muscle mass and strength that occurs with aging.

A 12-week study in older adults found that those who consumed 7 ounces (210 grams) of ricotta cheese per day experienced increases in muscle mass and muscle strength over the course of the study.

4. Avocados

Avocados are incredibly healthy. 3.5 ounces (100 grams), or about one-half of a medium avocado, contain 9 grams of carbs.

However, 7 of these are fiber, so its net carb count is only 2 grams. Avocados are high in several vitamins and minerals, including potassium, an important mineral many people may not get enough of. What's more, a higher potassium intake may help make the transition to a ketogenic diet easier. In addition, avocados may help improve cholesterol and triglyceride levels.

In one study, when people consumed a diet high in avocados, they experienced a 22% decrease in "bad" LDL cholesterol and triglycerides and an 11% increase in "good" HDL cholesterol.

5. Meat and Poultry

Meat and poultry are considered staple foods on a ketogenic diet. Fresh meat and poultry contain no carbs and are rich in B vitamins and several minerals, including potassium, selenium and zinc.

They're also a great source of high-quality protein, which has been shown to help preserve muscle mass during a very low-carb diet. One study in older women found that consuming a diet high in fatty meat led to HDL cholesterol levels that were 8% higher than on a low-fat, high-carb diet. It's best to choose grass-fed meat, if possible. That's because animals that eat grass produce meat with higher amounts of omega-3 fats, conjugated linoleic acid and antioxidants than meat from grain-fed animals.

6. Eggs

Eggs are one of the healthiest and most versatile foods on the planet. One large egg contains less than 1 gram of carbs and fewer than 6 grams of protein, making eggs an ideal food for a ketogenic lifestyle. In addition, eggs have been shown to trigger hormones that increase feelings of fullness and keep blood sugar levels stable, leading to lower calorie intakes for up to 24 hours.It's important to eat the entire egg, as most of an egg's nutrients are found in the yolk. This includes the antioxidants lutein and zeaxanthin, which help protect eye health.

Although egg yolks are high in cholesterol, consuming them doesn't raise blood cholesterol levels in most people. In fact, eggs appear to modify the shape of LDL in a way that reduces the risk of heart disease.

7. Coconut Oil

Coconut oil has unique properties that make it well suited for a ketogenic diet.

To begin with, it contains medium-chain triglycerides (MCTs). Unlike long-chain fats, MCTs are taken up directly by the liver and converted into ketones or used as a rapid source of energy.

In fact, coconut oil has been used to increase ketone levels in people with Alzheimer's disease and other disorders of the brain and nervous system, The main fatty acid in coconut oil is lauric acid, a slightly longer-chain fat. It has been suggested that coconut oil's mix of MCTs and lauric acid may promote a sustained level of ketosis, What's more, coconut oil may help obese adults lose weight and belly fat. In one study, men who ate 2 tablespoons (30 ml) of coconut oil per day lost 1 inch (2.5 cm), on average, from their waistlines without making any other dietary changes

8. Plain Greek Yogurt and Cottage Cheese

Plain Greek yogurt and cottage cheese are healthy, high-protein foods. While they contain some carbs, they can still be included in a ketogenic lifestyle.

5 ounces (150 grams) of plain Greek yogurt provides 5 grams of carbs and 11 grams of protein. That amount of cottage cheese provides 5 grams of carbs and 18 grams of protein. Both yogurt and cottage cheese have been shown to help decrease appetite and promote feelings of fullness. Either one makes a tasty snack on its own.

However, both can also be combined with chopped nuts, cinnamon and optional sugar-free sweetener for a quick and easy keto treat.

9. Olive Oil

Olive oil provides impressive benefits for your heart.It's high in oleic acid, a monounsaturated fat that has been found to decrease heart disease risk factors in many studies. In addition, extra-virgin olive oil is high in antioxidants known as phenols. These compounds further protect heart health by decreasing inflammation and improving artery function, As a pure fat source, olive oil contains no carbs. It's an ideal base for salad dressings and healthy mayonnaise.

Because it isn't as stable as saturated fats at high temperatures, it's best to use olive oil for low-heat cooking or add it to foods after they have been cooked.

10. Nuts and Seeds

Nuts and seeds are healthy, high-fat and low-carb foods.

Frequent nut consumption has been linked to a reduced risk of heart disease, certain cancers, depression and other chronic diseases, furthermore, nuts and seeds are high in fiber, which can help you feel full and absorb fewer calories overall. Although all nuts and seeds are low in net carbs, the amount varies quite a bit among the different types.

Here are the carb counts for 1 ounce (28 grams) of some popular nuts and seed.

- Almonds: 3 grams net carbs (6 grams total carbs)
- Brazil nuts: 1 gram net carbs (3 grams total carbs)
- Cashews: 8 grams net carbs (9 grams total carbs)
- Macadamia nuts: 2 grams net carbs (4 grams total carbs)
- Pecans: 1 gram net carbs (4 grams total carbs)
- Pistachios: 5 grams net carbs (8 grams total carbs)
- Walnuts: 2 grams net carbs (4 grams total carbs)
- Chia seeds: 1 gram net carbs (12 grams total carbs)
- Flaxseeds: 0 grams net carbs (8 grams total carbs)
- Pumpkin seeds: 4 grams net carbs (5 grams total carbs)
- Sesame seeds: 3 grams net carbs (7 grams total carbs)

11. Berries

Most fruits are too high in carbs to include on a ketogenic diet, but berries are an exception.

Berries are low in carbs and high in fiber. In fact, raspberries and blackberries contain as much fiber as digestible carbs.

These tiny fruits are loaded with antioxidants that have been credited with reducing inflammation and protecting against disease. Here are the carb counts for 3.5 ounces (100 grams) of some berries.

- Blackberries: 5 grams net carbs (10 grams total carbs)
- Blueberries: 12 grams net carbs (14 grams total carbs)
- Raspberries: 6 grams net carbs (12 grams total carbs)
- Strawberries: 6 grams net carbs (8 grams total carbs)

12. Butter and Cream

Butter and cream are good fats to include on a ketogenic diet. Each contains only trace amounts of carbs per serving.

For many years, butter and cream were believed to cause or contribute to heart disease due to their high saturated fat contents. However, several large studies have shown that, for most people, saturated fat isn't linked to heart disease.

In fact, some studies suggest that a moderate consumption of high-fat dairy may possibly reduce the risk of heart attack and stroke. Like other fatty dairy products, butter and cream are rich in conjugated linoleic acid, the fatty acid that may promote fat loss

13. Shirataki Noodles

Shirataki noodles are a fantastic addition to a ketogenic diet. You can find them online.

They contain less than 1 gram of carbs and 5 calories per serving because they are mainly water. In fact, these noodles are made from a viscous fiber called glucomannan, which can absorb up to 50 times its weight in water,Viscous fiber forms a gel that slows down food's movement through your digestive tract. This can help decrease hunger and blood sugar spikes, making it beneficial for weight loss and diabetes managemen. Shirataki noodles come in a variety of shapes, including rice, fettuccine and linguine. They can be substituted for regular noodles in all types of recipes.

Keto Diet Recipes

Enjoy hundreds of amazing keto recipes, to make your keto lifestyle simple and delicious. What is everyone else eating? The following ten are our most popular keto options that thousands of readers come back to, time after time.

Keto pizza

Pizza, meet keto... A simple take on how to get your pizza fix without the carbs. It's everything you want — pepperoni, cheese and tomato-sauce deliciousness.

INGREDIENTS

Topping

3 tbsp unsweetened tomato sauce

1 tsp dried oregano

5 oz. Shredded cheese

1½ oz. Pepperoni

Olives (optional)

Crust

4 eggs

6 oz. shredded cheese, preferably mozzarella or provolone

For serving

2 oz. leafy greens

4 tbsp olive oil

Sea salt and ground black pepper

INSTRUCTIONS

Preheat the oven to 400°F (200°C).

Start by making the crust. Crack eggs into a medium-sized bowl and add shredded cheese. Give it a good stir to combine.

Use a spatula to spread the cheese and egg batter on a baking sheet lined with parchment paper. You can form two round circles or just make one large rectangular pizza. Bake in the oven for 15 minutes until the pizza crust turns golden. Remove and let cool for a minute or two.

Increase the oven temperature to 450°F (225°C).

Spread tomato sauce on the crust and sprinkle oregano on top. Top with cheese and place the pepperoni and olives on top.

Bake for another 5-10 minutes or until the pizza has turned a golden brown color.

Serve with a fresh salad on the side.

Keto Mushroom omelet

Looking for a quick and easy way to start your day? This hearty omelet is super healthy, and just takes a few minutes to make! Fresh mushrooms make a delicious filling. Enjoy this keto meal anytime — breakfast, lunch or dinner!

INGREDIENTS

3 eggs

1 oz. Butter, for frying

1 oz. shredded cheese

1/5 yellow onion

3 mushrooms

Salt and pepper

INSTRUCTIONS

Crack the eggs into a mixing bowl with a pinch of salt and pepper. Whisk the eggs with a fork until smooth and frothy.

Add salt and spices to taste.

Melt butter in a frying pan. Once the butter has melted, pour in the egg mixture.

When the omelet begins to cook and get firm, but still has a little raw egg on top, sprinkle cheese, mushrooms and onion on top (optional).

Using a spatula, carefully ease around the edges of the omelet, and then fold it over in half. When it starts to turn golden brown underneath, remove the pan from the heat and slide the omelet on to a plate.

Keto Browned Butter Asparagus with Creamy Eggs

Three of our much-loved keto foods take center stage in this tasty medley. Creamy eggs... sautéed asparagus... browned butter. Mmmmm— c'est magnifique! What a simple way to enjoy a sophisticated appetizer or breakfast!

INGREDIENTS

2 oz. Butter

4 eggs

3 oz. grated parmesan cheese

½ cup sour cream

Salt

Cayenne pepper

25 oz. Green asparagus

1 tbsp olive oil

1½ tbsp lemon juice

3 oz. butter

INSTRUCTIONS

Melt the butter over medium heat and add the eggs. Stir until scrambled. Cook through, but do not overcook the eggs.

Spoon the hot eggs into a blender. Add the cheese and sour cream and blend until smooth and creamy. Add salt and cayenne pepper to taste.

Roast the asparagus in olive oil over medium heat in a large frying pan. Add salt and pepper, remove from frying pan for now, and set aside.

Sauté the butter in the frying pan until it is golden brown and has a nutty smell. Remove from heat, let cool, and add the lemon juice.

Put the asparagus back into the frying pan and stir together with the butter until it gets hot.

Serve the asparagus with the sautéed butter and the creamy eggs.

Chorizo with creamed green cabbage

Spicy chorizo paired with creamy cabbage? Yes, please! This tasty and low-carb combination of the two is topped off with a lemony gremolata for a kiss of citrus flavor.

INGREDIENTS

Creamed green cabbage

25 oz. green cabbage

2 oz. Butter

1¼ cups heavy whipping cream

Salt and pepper

½ cup fresh parsley, finely chopped

½ lemon, the zest

Fried chorizo

25 oz. chorizo or other high-quality sausage

2 tbsp butter, for frying

INSTRUCTIONS

Fry the chorizo in butter in a skillet over medium heat. Keep warm until serving.

Shred the cabbage using a food processor, mandolin or sharp knife.

Sauté cabbage with remaining butter in the same skillet over medium heat. Stir occasionally for a few minutes, until cabbage is golden brown.

Add heavy whipping cream, and bring to a light boil. Reduce heat, and let simmer until the cream is reduced. Season with salt and pepper.

Add parsley and lemon zest before serving with the fried chorizo.

Keto pancakes with berries and whipped cream

Try these incredible keto cottage cheese pancakes and you'll never go back to regular flapjacks! Our berry topping gives them just the right amount of sweetness and the kids will love them too!

INGREDIENTS

Toppings

½ cup fresh raspberries or fresh blueberries or fresh strawberries

1 cup heavy whipping cream

4 eggs

7 oz. Cottage cheese

1 tbsp ground psyllium husk powder

2 oz. butter or coconut oil

INSTRUCTIONS

Add eggs, cottage cheese and psyllium husk to a medium size bowl and mix together. Let sit for 5-10 minutes to thicken up a bit.

Heat up butter or oil in a non-stick skillet. Fry the pancakes on medium-low heat for 3–4 minutes on each side. Don't make them too big or they will be hard to flip.

Add cream to a separate bowl and whip until soft peaks form.

Serve the pancakes with the whipped cream and berries of your choice.

Keto blue-cheese dressing

Wonderfully creamy. So versatile. Enjoy this tangy keto sauce on salads, meat, or chicken. And it works as a super tasty dip for veggies. Can you say winning?

INGREDIENTS

5 oz. Blue cheese

¾ cup Greek yogurt

½ cup mayonnaise

2 tbsp fresh parsley, finely chopped

Salt and pepper

Heavy whipping cream or water (optional)

INSTRUCTIONS

Place the cheese into a small bowl and use a fork to break it up into coarse chunks.

Add yoghurt and mayonnaise and mix well.

Let sit for a few minutes to allow the flavors to develop.

Salt and pepper to taste. Dilute with water or heavy cream if needed.

Keto BLT with cloud bread

Just the mere mention of "BLT" and the clouds start to part! We paired this mouthwatering, keto version with fluffy cloud bread, also known as oopsie bread. Oops, it's bread! Gluten-free and grain free, you just need to dive in and indulge.

INGREDIENTS

Cloud bread

3 eggs

4¼ oz. Cream cheese

1 pinch salt

½ tbsp ground psyllium husk powder

½ tsp baking powder

¼ tsp cream of tartar (optional)

Toppings

8 tbsp mayonnaise

5 oz. Bacon

2 oz. Lettuce

1 tomato, thinly sliced

Fresh basil (optional)

INSTRUCTIONS

Cloud bread

Preheat oven to 300°F (150°C).

Separate the eggs. Put the egg whites in one bowl and the yolks in another.

Whip egg whites together with salt (and cream of tartar, if you are using any) until very stiff. Preferably using a hand held electric mixer. You should be able to turn the bowl over without the egg whites moving.

Add cream cheese to the egg yolks and mix well. To make the oopsie more bread-like, add in the optional psyllium seed husk and baking powder.

Gently fold the egg whites into the egg yolk mixture — try to keep the air in the egg whites.

Put 8 cloud bread pieces on a paper-lined baking tray.

Bake in the middle of the oven for about 25 minutes, until they turn golden.

Keto meat pie

Keep everyone happy with this satisfying, cheese-topped keto masterpiece. Meat pie may be a little old-school, but it's time to rediscover its deliciousness. Any cook can get rave reviews from this easy-to-follow recipe. Serve lukewarm for peak flavor. Great for packed lunches, too.

INGREDIENTS

Pie crust

¾ cup almond flour

4 tbsp sesame seeds

4 tbsp coconut flour

1 tbsp ground psyllium husk powder

1 tsp baking powder

1 pinch salt

3 tbsp olive oil or coconut oil, melted

1 egg

4 tbsp water

Topping

8 oz. cottage cheese

7 oz. Shredded cheese

Filling

½ yellow onion, finely chopped

1 garlic clove, finely chopped

2 tbsp butter or olive oil

20 oz. ground beef or ground lamb

1 tbsp dried oregano or dried basil

Salt and pepper

4 tbsp tomato paste or ajvar relish

½ cup water

INSTRUCTIONS

Preheat the oven to 350°F (175°C).

Fry onion and garlic in butter or olive oil over medium heat for a few minutes, until onion is soft. Add ground beef and keep frying. Add oregano or basil. Salt and pepper to taste.

Add tomato paste or ajvar relish. Add water. Lower the heat and let simmer for at least 20 minutes. While the meat simmers, make the dough for the crust.

Mix all the crust ingredients in a food processor for a few minutes until the dough turns into a ball. If you don't have a food processor, you can mix by hand with a fork.

Place a round piece of parchment paper in a well-greased springform pan or deep-dish pie pan — 9-10 inches (23-25 cm) in diameter — to make it easier to remove the pie when it's done. Spread the dough in the pan and up along the sides. Use a spatula or well-greased fingers. Once the crust is shaped to the pan, prick the bottom of the crust with a fork.

Pre-bake the crust for 10-15 minutes. Remove from the oven and place the meat in the crust. Mix cottage cheese and shredded cheese together, and layer on top of the pie.

Bake on lower rack for 30-40 minutes or until the pie has turned a golden color.

Keto Mexican scrambled eggs

Spice up your breakfast with this flavorful keto egg dish. Jalapenos, tomatoes, and scallions enhance the scrambled eggs with just the right amount of zing. Guaranteed to liven up your day!

INGREDIENTS

6 eggs

1 scallion

2 pickled jalapeños, finely chopped

1 tomato, finely chopped

3 oz. Shredded cheese

2 tbsp butter, for frying

Salt and pepper

INSTRUCTIONS

Finely chop the scallions, jalapeños and tomatoes. Fry in butter for 3 minutes on medium heat.

Beat the eggs and pour into the pan. Scramble for 2 minutes. Add cheese and seasonings.

Keto coconut porridge

Feel like hot cereal this morning? For satisfying, warm-in-the-belly comfort food, check out this keto delight. Pure happiness in a bowl!

INGREDIENTS

1 oz. Butter or coconut oil

1 egg

1 tbsp coconut flour

1 pinch ground psyllium husk powder

4 tbsp coconut cream

1 pinch salt

INSTRUCTIONS

Add all ingredients to a non-stick saucepan. Mix well and place over low heat. Stir constantly until you achieve your desired texture.

Serve with coconut milk or cream. Top your porridge with a few fresh or frozen berries and enjoy!

In **conclusion,** we have provided you some of the most crucial aspects regarding keto diet. We hope that you not only were able to learn something, but that you also will be able to successfully apply it. Follow our advice and you will be one step closer to being an expert in this subject.

INTRODUCTION

There are many diets in the world, and often people would engage in radical behaviors or follow some extreme diets without becoming aware of the biological and physiological consequences of their actions. Fasting was one such diet that was at first practiced for theoretical beliefs in purity, abstinence and such, and only after were the biological processes at played understood, researched, and practice refinely. What was discovered is that fasting produces the same results as a carbohydrate free diet, and that by restricting the carbs in your diet you can achieve rapid weight loss.

This approach is called the ketogenic diet, and it is also named because the form of abstinence from carbs causes bodies called ketones to be produced by the liver, which then helps your body process fat as a primary source of energy instead of glucose. Why is that?

Traditionally our bodies burn glucose as our primary form of fuel. Glucose is derived from carbohydrates, with excess glucose getting stored in the muscles and liver as glycogen. The excess glucose which remains after that process is then turned into fat. When we cut all carbs from our diet, we no longer have access to glucose, which forces our bodies to burn through the glycogen reserves and then start oxidizing fat. This would be fine but for the fact that certain tissues such as parts of our brain can only be sustained by glucose, then it'd be where ketone production comes in.

The production of ketones allows those tissues to substitute ketones for glucose and allow us to survive without any carbs at all. If you eat less than 100 grams per day you will trigger this process, resulting in a diet that is based solely on fat and protein and which burns fat and protein as a source of fuel. Unless it's managed correctly, such a diet can cause your body to cannibalize your lean body mass as well as your fat, resulting in a dramatic drop in weight that cannot be wholly attributed to fat loss.

Where do ketones come from? They are produced by the liver as a byproduct of free fatty acid breakdown. Ketones are thus derived from fat, and their production also has consequences on the hormone levels in your body which are normally used to regulate glucose movement in your bloodstream such as insulin. That is why many people report feeling sluggish or exhausted when on the ketogenic diet.

What Is Weight Loss

Weight loss is a basic issue in today's general public with obesity on the increase and individuals at long last acknowledging what being overweight is doing to their bodies, their well being and in the end their ways of life.

Weight loss is useful for some conditions. It is of genuine advantage in diabetes, hypertension, shortness of breath, joint issues and raised cholesterol.

Weight loss is conceivable with exercise and sound dinners alone, yet including great quality protein and building incline bulk will help you lose all the more rapidly, helping you to keep the weight off and stay solid.

Weight loss is essentially ensured on the off chance that one adheres to the controls of the eating regimen.

Weight loss essentials: eat a larger number of calories than you utilize, then you'll put on weight; utilize more than you eat, then you'll lose it. Weight loss is presently an objective which can be truly effective in the event that we adhere to a preparation of administration, abstaining from food arrangement. Be that as it may, just for a few, surgery might also be the main trust.

Surgical procedures have advanced in the course of recent decades. And most of them are compelling, as they do normally have significant weight reduction in such a short time.

In any case, all specialists do concur that the most ideal approach to keep up weight loss is to take after a healthy way of lifestyle. Whichever approach you lean toward, the way to long haul achievement is a moderate consistency of weight loss. It is demonstrated that it is essential to prepare yourself up mentally for your weight loss journey and the way of lifestyle changes you are going to experience.

For people who are morbidly obese, surgery which sidesteps parts of the stomach and small digestive system may now and then be the main successful method for creating maintained and noteworthy weight loss.

The essential factor in accomplishing and keeping up weight loss is a long lasting responsibility to general exercise and sensible dietary patterns. You will find that all levels of your life are enhanced with weight loss which brings you so much individual fulfillment.

Understanding Calories For Natural Weight Loss

The word "calorie" is often thrown left and right by anyone discussing weight loss. Yet very seldom do people understand the meaning of calories, and their purpose in natural weight loss. Read on to learn some common myths about calories, and how you can use calories to naturally lose weight.

The first common myth of the calorie is that all calories are created equal. In fact, some weight loss "experts" would even recommend eating anything you want, and as long as your calorie intake is less than your calories used, you'll lose weight. Neither of these are the case, and trying to lose weight in this manner is a guaranteed recipe for failure.

A calorie is only as good as its source. An un-enriched slice of white bread and an organic mango may have the same calorie value, but the body's ability to break it down into useable energy, not to mention its nutritional value, is nowhere close.

By eating high-caloric and low-nutritional foods, it's entirely possible to be over-eating and being under-nourished. This is a sure formula for obesity. Instead, by eating high-nutritional foods and avoiding toxic foods (which includes limiting your meat intake, particularly non-lean-meats,) you can still eat a whole lot and successfully lose weight.

Keeping track of your calories may be a good idea for understanding your own body. Keep a notebook of what foods you ate and your daily activities, plus their corresponding calorie values. By recording and going over your food choices, you can learn from the results of your habits and change them to whatever suits you best.

Understanding calories is much more than simply counting how much you're eating and how much you're exercising. Understanding the quality of the calories you're taking in is just as important, if not more. Natural weight loss involves nurturing your body to its natural form - Not starving an already under-nourished body even further to achieve a certain look.

Top Weight Loss Myths

Weight loss myths have been around from many years, whether they are listed on the internet or any popular magazine, they have been a hot topic among both figure-conscious and obese people. This book will detail some top weight loss myths that people think could help them in losing weight. These myths are really common and are often followed by the people planning to lose weight. Believing these myths may cause more harm than good to you. Find out the answers behind most common weight loss myths.

Getting rid of your favorite food

By treating yourself with your favorite food every now and then would help you control calorie intake and will prevent you from binging. Moderation is the right way to find success in your weight loss mission.

I should not eat between the meals

Well, many of us might be following this weight loss myth. On the contrary, a light snack in between the meals would help in controlling your blood sugar level, enhancing your metabolism, and burning more calories. This will also help you manage your calorie intake while taking big meals.

Drastically cutting down the calories will result in faster weight loss

When you lower down your calorie intake drastically, you actually send your body into "The Starvation Mode". In this mode your body starts saving calories and uses less energy to save them for the future use. Your metabolism is reduced and you tend to gain weight instead of losing it.

Fat is not good

Most of the people struggling to lose weight often follow this weight loss myth. Fat is also an essential part of our diet. Fats help in enhancing the taste and aroma of the food. Some of the good fatty acids that will help you in achieving your weight loss plan are Omega3 Fatty acids that are prominently found in shellfish and fish.

Following a diet strictly, leaving no room for cheating

When you eliminate certain food groups completely or concentrate on just one of them, you are bound to get less effective results. You will soon feel tired of eating the allowed food group and may feel really deprived, this will increase your chances to quit the strict diet and binge onto fatty and banned food group thus leading to weight gain.

Eating late night may increase my weight

This is one of the most popular myths usually followed by body builders and figure conscious people. It doesn't matter if you are eating in the day or midnight, your body turns all the extra calories into fat within a period of time. In fact, eating some light snack before getting into bed would rather help you get a better sleep.

What You Should Know About Ketogenic Diet

A ketogenic diet may help you lose more weight in the first 3 to 6 months than some other diets. This may be because it takes more calories to change fat into energy than it does to change carbs into energy. It's also possible that a high-fat, high-protein diet satisfies you more, so you eat less, but that hasn't been proved yet.

What's a Ketogenic Diet?

"Ketogenic" is a term for a low-carb diet (like the Atkins diet). The idea is for you to get more calories from protein and fat and less from carbohydrates. You cut back most on the carbs that are easy to digest, like sugar, soda, pastries, and white bread.

Is a ketogenic diet healthy?

We have solid evidence showing that a ketogenic diet reduces seizures in children, sometimes as effectively as medication. Because of these neuroprotective effects, questions have been raised about the possible benefits for other brain disorders such as Parkinson's, Alzheimer's, multiple sclerosis, sleep disorders, autism, and even brain cancer. However, there are no human studies to support recommending ketosis to treat these conditions.

Weight loss is the primary reason my patients use the ketogenic diet. Previous research shows good evidence of a faster weight loss when patients go on a ketogenic or very low carbohydrate diet compared to participants on a more traditional low-fat diet, or even a mediterranean diet. However, that difference in weight loss seems to disappear over time.

A ketogenic diet also has been shown to improve blood sugar control for patients with type 2 diabetes, at least in the short term. There is even more controversy when we consider the effect on cholesterol levels. A few studies show some patients have increase in cholesterol levels in the beginning, only to see cholesterol fall a few months later. However, there is no long-term research analyzing its effects over time on diabetes and high cholesterol.

How It Works

When you eat less than 50 grams of carbs a day, your body eventually runs out of fuel (blood sugar) it can use quickly. This typically takes 3 to 4 days. Then you'll start to break down protein and fat for energy, which can make you lose weight. This is called ketosis. It's important to note that the ketogenic diet is a short term diet that's focussed on weight loss rather than the pursuit of health benefits.

Who Uses It?

People use a ketogenic diet most often to lose weight, but it can help manage certain medical conditions, like epilepsy, too. It also may help people with heart disease, certain brain diseases, and even acne, but there needs to be more research in those areas. Talk with your doctor first to find out if it's safe for you to try a ketogenic diet, especially if you have type 1 diabetes.

Steps for Meal Prep Success

These steps to food prep are perfect for a beginner who likes the idea of meal prep but isn't sure where to start. With a little work, you'll head into your food prep session with a plan of attack to help you make the most of your time.

Here is what a sample meal prep day looks like, but what you do depends on the dishes being made. As always, adjust the following to make it your own:

Step 1: Meal planning

Select the meals you will prep for and find the recipes you want to use.

Step 2: Go shopping

Create a shopping list. Review the ingredients needed for each recipe and compare them to what you already have in your pantry or refrigerator. Make sure to write out measurements of expensive ingredients, like beef or chicken. It's sometimes cheaper to order the exact amount from the butcher counter as opposed to picking it up prepackaged. If you do purchase your meat in bulk, you can divide it as needed for each recipe, which is also more cost efficient.

Step 3: Store ingredients

If you go shopping on a day or two before your meal prep day, make sure to immediately store your food in the refrigerator or freezer. Meat, fish, or chicken that will be used within the next 48 hours should be portioned and stored in the refrigerator. The remaining raw proteins should be properly labelled and stored in the freezer. If you're shopping the same day you're prepping food, place cold items in the refrigerator to maintain their temperature until you start your meal prep.

Step 4: Prep ingredients

The trick is to have all the ingredients prepped and measured, so when the recipe calls for it, there isn't much to do except adding it in. That's exactly what you're trying to accomplish here—to make cooking go as smoothly as possible. Take out all the ingredients you'll need based on the recipe's ingredient list. Read each recipe thoroughly, including the instructions, so you understand each step you need to take. Wash, chop, dice, mince, zest, or juice any vegetable, fruit, herb, seed, or nut if needed. Marinate any meat, fish, or poultry. Prepare any other ingredients you'll need for each recipe so they're ready to be used.

Step 5: Slow cook

The first recipe to prepare is one in the slow cooker. This is because the slow cooker takes between 4 and 6 hours (or more) to cook the dish. There isn't much to do except prepping and tossing the ingredients inside (okay, and press the "cook" button), and after that you can move onto another task.

Step 6: Prep sauces, dips, and dressings

Hopefully you have a salad or two on your meal prep list for the week. Salads typically have dressings that are quick and easy (5 minutes, tops) to whisk together. Salad dressings can last 2 weeks, so make them as 1-cup portion so they could last for a while. The same goes for salsa, hummus, chimichurri, and other sauces and dips. These are easy-to-make recipes that are ready within 10 to 15 minutes and require no or minimal cooking.

Step 7: Cook ingredients

Another step in meal prep is cooking the separate ingredients needed for a recipe. This could be roasting or steaming vegetables, cooking starches like brown rice or quinoa, or toasting nuts or seeds. You want all parts of the dish to be ready before the dish is put together.

Step 8: Put it together

Once you have all the components of the dish prepped and cooked, it's time to put it all together. Toss them together to make the dish, or put the meal together by cooking the components together to make it, like a stir-fry. What you combine depends on the recipe you're making.

Step 9: Box it up

Once the dish is complete, divide it into portions for the refrigerator or freezer. For a dish like meatballs, you may decide to divide it into two large containers, one for the refrigerator and one for the freezer. If you're planning on bringing a 4-ounce serving of Lemony Chicken Breasts with a side of quinoa to work, then pack those two items together in a single container. If you made muffins or quiches, wrap them individually so you can grab and go. Portion out spiced nuts or popcorn for easy-to-grab snack packs for work. Sometimes you won't be cooking the dish until right before you eat it, like an egg scramble or smoothie, but you can still package the ingredients together so they're ready to go.

21 Days Keto Meal Plan

Day: 1

Breakfast

Dairy Free Coconut Yogurt

Prep Time: 5 mins

Cook Time: 24 hrs

Total Time: 24 hrs 5 mins

Servings: 6 servings

Ingredients

- 2 15 oz. cans organic coconut cream, chilled in the refrigerator 4 hours
- 2 dairy-free probiotic pills with bacterial strains L. bulgaricus, S. thermophilus and L. casei
- 1 tablespoon honey

Instructions

- Open coconut cream and separate the liquid from the cream.
- In a food processor or high-speed blender, add the cream with the probiotic pills and honey. Process on high for 3 minutes until pills are broken down.
- Check the consistency of the yogurt. If it's too thick, add a little of the coconut water and blend.
- Transfer the yogurt to a glass jar and seal with lid.
- Preheat the oven to 100°F. Place the glass jar in the oven for 24 hours to ferment.

- Once fermented, remove from the oven, cool and stir the yogurt. Chill in the refrigerator for at least 2 hours.

Lunch

Creamy Mushroom Chicken

Prep Time: 5 minutes

Cook Time: 20 minutes

Total Time: 25 minutes

Servings: 2 servings

Ingredients

- 2 pastured chicken cutlets
- 1 small onion
- 5 cremini mushrooms
- 1/2 teaspoon pink Himalayan salt, more to taste
- 1/2 teaspoon dried thyme
- 3 tablespoons of Kerry gold butter, unsalted
- 1/3 cup full fat canned coconut milk

Instructions

- Heat a cast iron skillet on medium heat. While it comes to temperature slice your mushroom and onions.
- Once your skillet is hot, add in two tablespoons of butter. When melted add in the sliced mushrooms, sprinkle with ¼ teaspoon salt. Sauté until browned, then add in the onions. Keep stirring until softened, about 6 more minutes. Remove the mushroom and onion mix from the skillet.
- Add in the last tbsp. of butter. Sprinkle your chicken cutlets with the remaining salt and thyme. Place in the skillet side by side. Cook for five minutes on one side. Then flip over. Cook another 5 minutes.
- Then add the mushroom and onion mix back in. Pour the coconut milk right over it. Make sure you shake your can so you get a good mix of coconut milk with fat.

- Let simmer for one minute, remove from heat and serve! Perfect saucy protein to go with a big green salad!

Nutrition Info

Calories: 334 kcal

Fat: 27.3g

Carbohydrates: 3.2g

Protein: 24.3g

Dinner

Creamed Spinach with Parmesan Recipe

Prep Time: 5 minutes

Cook Time: 10 minutes

Servings: 4 servings

Ingredients

- 2 tablespoons butter
- 3 cloves minced garlic
- 10 ounces fresh chopped spinach
- 1/2 cup heavy cream
- 3 ounces cream cheese (softened)
- 1/4 teaspoon dried basil
- 1/4 teaspoon dried oregano
- 1/4 cup grated parmesan
- salt and pepper

Instructions

- Melt the butter in a large saucepan over medium heat.
- Add the garlic and sauté for 1 to 2 minutes until fragrant then stir in the spinach.
- Cook for 3 to 4 minutes until it is just wilted.
- Stir in the heavy cream, cream cheese, basil, oregano, salt, and pepper.

- Cook for 4 to 5 minutes, stirring constantly, until the cream cheese melts.
- Sprinkle with parmesan cheese and serve hot.

Nutrition Info

220 Calories

20.5g of Fat

6.5g of Protein

3g of Net Carbs

Day: 2

Breakfast

Kale & Mushroom Sausage Patties

Total time: 20 mins

Cook Time: 10 mins

Prep Time: 10 mins

Serves: 5 servings

Ingredients

- 1 lb ground pork
- 6 oz fresh mushrooms, chopped

- 1 bunch of kale, thinly sliced
- 2 tablesppons coconut oil
- 2 garlic cloves, minced
- ½ teaspoon salt
- ½ teaspoon garlic powder
- ½ teaspoon onion powder
- ¼ teaspoon fennel seed
- Pinch of ground ginger
- Pinch of nutmeg

Instructions

- In a large skillet, melt one tablespoon of coconut oil.
- Add the kale, mushrooms, and garlic and sauté until the veggies are cooked.
- Place the ground pork in a mixing bowl and add the veggies and spices. Mix well and form into 10 patties.
- Melt another tablespoon of coconut oil over medium heat and add half the sausage patties; cook until golden brown on each side and cooked in the middle. Repeat with the other half.

Nutrition Info

14 grams of protein

2 grams of carbohydrates

18 grams of fat

Lunch

Low Carb Keto Chili

Prep Time: 5 minutes

Cook Time: 30 minutes

Total Time: 35 minutes

Servings: 6 servings

Ingredients

- 1/2 tablespoon avocado oil
- 2 ribs celery, chopped
- 2 lbs. 85/15 ground beef
- 1 teaspoon ground chipotle chili powder
- 1 tablespoon chili powder
- 2 teaspoons garlic powder
- 1 tablespoon cumin
- 1 teaspoon salt
- 1 teaspoon black pepper
- 1 15 oz. can no-salt-added tomato sauce
- 1 16.2 oz. container Kettle & Fire Beef Bone Broth

Instructions

- In a large pot, heat avocado oil over medium heat. Add chopped celery and cook until softened, about 3-4 minutes. Transfer celery to separate bowl and set aside.
- In same pot, add beef and spices and brown beef until cooked throughout.
- Lower heat to medium-low, add tomato sauce and beef bone broth to cooked beef, and simmer covered for 10 minutes, stirring occasionally.

- Add celery back to pot and stir until well-incorporated.
- Garnish, serve, and enjoy!

Nutrition Info

Calories: 359 kcal

Fat: 22.8g

Carbohydrates: 6.7g (Net: 5.2g)

Protein: 34.4g

Dinner

Quick and Easy Sloppy Joes Recipe

Prep Time: 15 minutes

Cook Time: 20 minutes

Servings: 4 servings

Ingredients

- 1 pound ground beef (80% lean)
- 1 pound medium stalk celery (diced)
- 1 small yellow onion (diced)

- 2 cloves minced garlic
- 3/4 cup beef broth
- 1/4 cup tomato paste
- 2 tablespoons So-Nourished powdered erythritol
- 2 teaspoons Worcestershire sauce
- 1 teaspoon dijon mustard
- salt and pepper

Instructions

- Cook the beef in a large skillet over medium-high heat until browned, breaking it up with a spoon.
- Stir in the celery, onion, and garlic and cook for 5 to 6 minutes until tender.
- Add the remaining ingredients and stir well to combine.
- Reduce heat and simmer on low for 20 minutes until it starts to thicken.
- Serve the sloppy joes on keto bread or in lettuce cups.

Nutrition Info

240 Calories

7.5g of Fat

36g of Protein

4.5g of Net Carbs

Day: 3

Breakfast

Zucchini Egg Cups

Prep Time: 10 mins

Total Time: 40 mins

Servings: 12 servings

Ingredients

- Cooking spray, for pan
- 2 zucchini, peeled into strips
- 1/4 lb. ham, chopped
- 1/2 cup cherry tomatoes, quartered
- 8 eggs
- 1/2 cup heavy cream
- Kosher salt
- Freshly ground black pepper
- 1/2 teaspoon dried oregano
- 1 cup Pinch red pepper flakes
- 1 cup shredded cheddar

Instructions

- Preheat oven to 400° and grease a muffin tin with cooking spray. Line the inside and bottom of the muffin tin with zucchini strips, to form a crust. Sprinkle ham and cherry tomatoes inside each crust.
- In a medium bowl whisk together eggs, heavy, cream, oregano, and red pepper flakes then season with salt and pepper. Pour egg mixture over ham and tomatoes then top with cheese.

- Bake until eggs are set, 30 minutes.

Lunch

Low Carb Keto Lasagna

Prep Time: 10 minutes

Cook Time: 45 minutes

Total Time: 55 minutes

Servings: 6 servings

Ingredients

- 1 tablespoon butter, ghee, coconut oil, or lard
- 1/2lb spicy Italian sausage or sweet Italian sausage
- 15oz ricotta cheese
- 2 tablespoons coconut flour
- medium-high large whole egg
- 1 1/2 teaspoons salt
- 1/2 teaspoon pepper
- 1 teaspoon garlic powder
- a large clove garlic (finely chopped)
- 1 1/2 cups mozzarella cheese
- 1/3 cup parmesan cheese
- 4 large zucchinis (sliced long ways to 1/4" pieces)
- 16oz Rao's marinara sauce
- 1 tablespoon mixed Italian herb seasoning
- 1/4 to 1/2 teaspoon red pepper flake (depending on how spicy you want this dish)
- 1/4 cup basil

Instructions

- Slice the zucchini then sprinkle generously with sea salt. Place your salted zucchini on a paper towel for 30 minutes. Once 30 minutes is up, wring the zucchini noodles with a paper towel one last time to extract any moisture.

- Heat 1 tablespoon of butter or fat of choice in a large skillet over medium-high heat. Crumble and brown Italian sausage. Remove from heat and let cool.

- Preheat oven to 375 degrees and coat a 9×9 baking dish with cooking spray or butter.

- Add ricotta cheese, 1 cup of mozzarella cheese, 2 tablespoons of parmesan cheese, 1 egg, coconut flour, salt, garlic, garlic powder, and pepper to a small bowl and mix until smooth. Set aside. Add Italian seasoning and red pepper flakes to a jar of marinara, stir well. Set aside.

- Add a layer of sliced zucchini to the bottom of greased dish. Spread 1/4 cup of cheese mixture over zucchini, sprinkle with 1/4 of the Italian sausage and then add a layer of sauce. Repeat process 3-4 times until ingredients are all gone, ending with a layer of sauce. Add remaining mozzarella cheese and sprinkle with remaining parmesan cheese.

- Cover with foil and bake for 30 minutes. Remove foil and bake for an additional 15 minutes until golden brown. Remove from oven and let sit for 5-10 minutes before serving. Sprinkle with fresh basil if desired.

Nutrition Info

Calories: 364 kcal

Fat: 21g

Carbohydrates: 12g

Protein: 32g

Dinner

Cheesy Pizza Chicken in a Skillet Recipe

Prep Time: 10 minutes

Cook Time: 30 minutes

Servings: 6 servings

Ingredients

- 1 tablespoon olive oil
- 6 bone-in chicken thighs
- 1 cup low carb tomato sauce
- 3 ounces sliced pepperoni
- 1 1/2 cups shredded mozzarella cheese
- salt and pepper

Instructions

- Preheat the oven to 350°F.
- Heat the oil in a 12-inch cast-iron skillet over medium heat.
- Season the chicken with salt and pepper then add to the skillet.
- Cook for 3 to 4 minutes on each side until browned.
- Pour the low-carb tomato sauce over the chicken and spread it evenly.
- Top the chicken with pepperoni slices and sprinkle with mozzarella.
- Bake for 25 minutes until the cheese is melted then place under a broiler to brown the cheese.
- Remove from heat and let rest for 5 minutes before serving.

Nutrition Info

360 Calories

28g of Fat

25.5g of Protein

1g of Net Carbs

Day: 4

Breakfast

Chocolate-Raspberry Chia Pudding Shots

Prep Time: 1 hour

Servings: 2 servings

Ingredients:

- ¼ cup chia seeds
- 1/2 cup coconut milk
- 1/4 cup almond milk
- 1 tablespoon cacao powder
- 1 tablespoon Stevia
- 1/2 cup raspberries

Instructions

- In a container, bring together all the ingredients (with the exception of the raspberries) and shake vivaciously. Let sit for 2 minutes and after that fill four shot glasses.

- Refrigerate for no less than 60 minutes (ideally across the night) until the point that blend thickens into pudding. Top with raspberries.

Nutrition Info

Calories: 241 kcal
Protein: 4g
Fats: 20g
Net Carbs: 4g

Lunch

Beberé Enchilada Style Stuffed Peppers

Prep Time: 10 minutes

Cook Time: 50 minutes

Total Time: 1 hour

Servings: 5 servings

Ingredients

- 2lb 85% lean pastured ground beef
- 1 cup organic frozen cauliflower rice
- 3 tablespoons Kerry Gold butter
- 1/2 maui onion
- 1 large carrot
- 2 cloves garlic
- 2 teaspoons smoked sea salt

- 2 teaspoons beberé
- 5 large bell peppers
- 5 dollops organic, lactose free sour cream

Instructions

- Heat a large skillet on medium heat. In the meantime dice your carrot, onion and garlic.
- Add the butter to the skillet; once it's melted add in the diced veggies.
- Sauté, stirring occasionally until tender, about 8 minutes.
- Add in the beef, salt and bebere, stir well, breaking up the beef until crumbly and browned. Mix in the cauliflower rice. Stir until well incorporated. Remove the skillet from the heat.
- Pre-heat the oven to 400F. While the oven heats cut the tops off of your peppers, remove the core and seeds. Then spoon the beef mixture into them. Arrange the peppers in a casserole dish.
- Top each one with a dollop of sour cream. Sprinkle a little extra spice mix on top.
- Bake for 40 minutes! Serve hot!

Nutrition Info

Calories: 516 kcal

Fat: 38.8g

Carbohydrates: 8.4g

Protein: 35g

Dinner

Lemon Butter Sauce for Fish

Prep: 5 mins

Cook: 10 mins

Total: 15 mins

Servings: 2 servings

Ingredients

Lemon Butter Sauce:

- 60 g / 4 tablespoons unsalted butter , cut into pieces
- 1 tablespoon fresh lemon juice
- Salt and finely ground pepper

Crispy Pan Fried Fish:

- 2 thin white fish fillets (120-150g / 4-5oz each), skinless boneless (I used Bream, Note 1)
- Salt and pepper
- 2 tablespoons white flour
- 2 tablespoons oil (I use canola)

Serving:

- Lemon wedges
- Finely chopped parsley, optional

Instructions

- Place the butter in a light coloured saucepan or small skillet over medium heat.

- Melt butter then leave on the stove, whisking / stirring very now and then. When the butter turns golden brown and it smells nutty - about 3 minutes, remove from stove immediately and pour into small bowl. (Note 2)

- Add lemon juice and a pinch of salt and pepper. Stir then taste when it has cooled slightly. Adjust lemon/salt to taste.

- Set aside - it will stay pourable for 20 - 30 minutes. See Note 3 for storing.

Crispy Pan Fried Fish:

- Pat fish dry using paper towels. Sprinkle with salt & pepper, then flour. Use fingers to spread flour. Turn and repeat. Shake excess flour off well, slapping between hands if necessary.

- Heat oil in a non stick skillet over high heat. When the oil is shimmering and there are faint wisps of smoke, add fish. Cook for 1 1/2 minutes until golden and crispy on the edges, then turn and cook the other side for 1 1/2 minutes (cook longer if you have thicker fillets).

- Remove immediately onto serving plates. Drizzle each with about 1 tbsp of Sauce (avoid dark specks settled at the bottom of the bowl), garnish with parsley and serve with lemon on the side.

Nutrition Info

Calories: 393 kcal

Day: 5

Breakfast

Keto Chicken Parmesan

Prep Time: 20 mins

Cook Time: 8 mins

Total Time: 28 mins

Servings: 2 servings

Ingredients

- 1 (8 ounce) skinless, boneless chicken breast
- 1 egg
- 1 tablespoon heavy whipping cream
- 1 1/2 ounces pork rinds, crushed
- 1 ounce grated Parmesan cheese
- 1/2 teaspoon salt
- 1/2 teaspoon garlic powder
- 1/2 teaspoon red pepper flakes (optional)
- 1/2 teaspoon ground black pepper
- 1/2 teaspoon Italian seasoning
- 1/2 cup jarred tomato sauce (such as Rao's®)
- 1/4 cup shredded mozzarella cheese
- 1 tablespoon ghee (clarified butter)

Instructions

- Set oven rack about 6 inches from the heat source and preheat the oven's broiler.
- Slice chicken breast through the middle horizontally from one side to within 1/2 inch of the other side. Open

the two sides and spread them out like an open book. Pound chicken flat until about 1/2-inch thick.

- Beat egg and cream together in a bowl.
- Combine crushed pork rinds, Parmesan cheese, salt, garlic powder, red pepper flakes, ground black pepper, and Italian seasoning in bowl; transfer breading to a plate.
- Dip chicken into egg mixture; coat completely. Press chicken into breading; thickly coat both sides.
- Heat a skillet over medium-high heat; add ghee. Place chicken in the pan; cook until no longer pink in the center and the juices run clear, about 3 minutes per side. An instant-read thermometer inserted into the center should read at least 165 degrees F (74 degrees C). Be careful to keep breading in place.
- Transfer chicken to a baking sheet. Cover with tomato sauce; top with mozzarella cheese.
- Broil until cheese is bubbling and barely browned, about 2 minutes.

Nutrition Info

Calories: 442 cals

Lunch

Almond Coconut Curry on Veggies

Total Time: 15 minutes

Servings: 4 servings

Ingredients

For the curry mixture

For the veges

- 1 teaspoon coconut oil
- 400 ml coconut milk
- 2 cups mushrooms
- 125 g almond butter (100% ground almonds)
- 4 cups spinach
- 1 tablespoon tomato paste
- 2 cups brocolli (chopped into florets)
- 1 tablespoon curry powder

Instructions

For the curry mixture

- Put the coconut drain, almond spread, tomato glue and curry powder in a blender. Mix for around 20 seconds or until smooth.
- Add the curry blend to a pan on low-medium warmth and warmth for 10-15 minutes or until warmed through. Blend habitually to abstain from staying.

For the veges

- Heat the coconut oil in a container on medium-high warmth and include the broccoli and mushrooms. Sear for around 3 minutes. Include the spinach and warmth for one more moment.
- Serve the veges in a bowl with the curry blend poured over the best.

Recipe Notes:

You can make the almond margarine by granulating almonds in a sustenance processor.

The curry blend isolates whenever left to sit in the refrigerator for some time, so make certain to mix it completely before utilizing on the off chance that you have put away it in the ice chest.

Nutrition Info

Calories: 438 kcal

Fats: 41g

Protein: 11g

Net Carbs: 9g

Dinner

Crab Stuffed Mushrooms With Cream Cheese

An easy recipe for crab stuffed mushrooms with cream cheese. Low carb, keto, and gluten free.

Prep Time: 15 minutes

Cook Time: 30 minutes

Servings: 4 servings

Ingredients

- 20 ounces cremini (baby bella) mushrooms (20-25 individual mushrooms)
- 2 tablespoons finely grated parmesan cheese
- 1 tablespoon chopped fresh parsley
- salt

Filling:

- 4 ounces cream cheese softened to room temperature
- 4 ounces crab meat finely chopped
- 5 cloves garlic minced
- 1 teaspoon dried oregano
- 1/2 teaspoon paprika
- 1/2 teaspoon black pepper
- 1/4 teaspoon salt

Instructions

- Preheat the oven to 400 F. Prepare a baking sheet lined with parchment paper.
- Snap stems from mushrooms, discarding the stems and placing the mushroom caps on the baking sheet 1 inch apart from each other. Season the mushroom caps with salt.

- In a large mixing bowl, combine all filling ingredients and stir until well-mixed without any lumps of cream cheese. Stuff the mushroom caps with the mixture. Evenly sprinkle parmesan cheese on top of the stuffed mushrooms.
- Bake at 400 F until the mushrooms are very tender and the stuffing is nicely browned on top, about 30 minutes. Top with parsley and serve while hot.

Nutrition Info

Calories: 160 kcal

Total Carb: 5.5g

Sugars: 0g

Protein: 9g

Day: 6

Breakfast

Keto Banana Nut Muffins

Tired of eggs for keto breakfast? These Keto Banana Nut Muffins are so simple and delicious, your kids will love helping you make them on the weekends just as much as they'll love helping you eat them!

Prep Time: 10 Minutes

Cook Time: 20 Minutes

Total Time: 30 minutes

Servings: 10 Muffins

Ingredients

Muffin Battter

- 1 1/4 Cup almond flour (I use this)
- 1/2 Cup powdered erythritol (I use this)
- 2 tablespoons ground flax (feel free to omit if you don't have it...it just adds a bit more depth to the flavors)
- 2 teaspoons baking powder
- 1/2 teaspoons ground cinnamon
- 5 tablespoon butter, melted
- 2 1/2 teaspoons banana extract
- 1 teaspoon vanilla extract
- 1/4 cup unsweetened almond milk
- 1/4 cup sour cream
- 2 eggs

Walnut Crumble

- 3/4 cup chopped walnuts

- 1 tablespoon butter, cold and cut in 4 pieces
- 1 tablespoon almond flour
- 1 tablespoon powdered erythritol

Instructions

- Preheat oven to 350

- Prepare muffin tin with 10 paper liners, and set aside

- In a large bowl, mix almond flour, erythritol (or preferred sweetener) flax, baking powder and cinnamon

- Stir in butter, banana extract, vanilla extract, almond milk, and sour cream.

- Add eggs to mixture and gently stir until fully combined.

- Fill muffin tins about 1/2-3/4 full with mixture.

Crumble Topping

- Add walnuts, butter, and almond flour to food processor.

- Pulse a few times until nuts are chopped into small pieces. If mixture seems too dry (sometimes some walnuts are softer than others) feel free to add another tablespoon of butter.

- Sprinkle bits of the mixture evenly over batter and gently press down.

- Sprinkle erythritol on top of crumble mixture.

- Bake for 20 minutes or until golden and toothpick comes out clean. Let cool for at least 30 minutes, an hour or more if possible. This lets them firm up.

- If they seem to be cooking faster, take them out sooner to avoid burning. Alternatively, if they are still wet looking, return them to the oven for a few minutes keeping a close eye on them.

Lunch

Loaded Chicken Salad

A delicious salad filled with plenty of vegetables and delicious grilled meat!

Prep Time: 10 minutes
Cook Time: 8 minutes
Total Time: 18 minutes

Ingredients

- 1 boneless chicken breast (about 300g, with or without skin)
- 1 tablespoon extra virgin olive oil
- 1/4 teaspoon Himalayan salt

- 1/4 teaspoon black pepper
- 1 avocado
- 100 g mozzarella balls
- 1 large tomato (any colour)
- 1 jar of artichoke hearts (my jar was 170g)
- 1/2 red onion
- 5 asparagus
- 20 leaves basil
- 4 cups baby spinach (200g used)

Dressing

- 2 tablespoons extra virgin olive oil
- 1 1/2 tbsp balsamic vinegar
- 1 teaspoon dijon mustard
- 1 clove garlic
- pinch Himalayan salt
- pinch black pepper

Instructions

- Peel and dice the avocado. Slice the red onion. Dice the tomato. Pile the basil leaves together, roll them up and slice. Cut the stems off the asparagus and slice in half. Mince the garlic.

- Slice the chicken breast in half lengthwise. Sprinkle the 1/4 teaspoon of salt and pepper on each sides. Heat the 1 tablespoon of olive oil in a cast iron skillet and place the chicken breasts in. Fry on each side, about 3 minutes each side, until they have a nice golden brown colour and cooked through. Add the asparagus beside the chicken breasts and cook a few minutes until soft and grilled. Take out the chicken and slice.

- In a small bowl, combine the minced garlic, olive oil, balsamic vinegar, dijon, and salt & pepper.

- Add the baby spinach to a large bowl or plate. Cover with the grilled chicken, avocado, mozzarella, tomatoes, artichoke, red onions, asparagus and basil leaves. Pour the dressing over and enjoy!

Nutrition Info

Calorics: 430 kcal
Calories from Fat: 264 kcal
Total Fat: 29.36g
Sugars: 3.16g
Protein: 31.73g

Dinner

Keto Instant Pot Crack Chicken Recipe

Prep time: 5 mins

Cook time: 20 mins

Total time: 25 mins

Serves: 8 servings

Ingredients

- 2 slices bacon, chopped
- 2 lbs (910 g) boneless, skinless chicken breasts
- 2 (8 oz/227 g) blocks cream cheese
- ½ cup (120 ml) water
- 2 tablespoons apple cider vinegar
- 1 tablespoon dried chives
- 1½ teaspoons garlic powder
- 1½ teaspoons onion powder
- 1 teaspoon crushed red pepper flakes
- 1 teaspoon dried dill
- ¼ teaspoon salt
- ¼ teaspoon black pepper
- ½ cup (2 oz/57 g) shredded cheddar
- 1 scallion, green and white parts, thinly sliced

Instructions

- Turn pressure cooker on, press "Sauté", and wait 2 minutes for the pot to heat up. Add the chopped bacon and cook until crispy. Transfer to a plate and set aside. Press "Cancel" to stop sautéing.
- Add the chicken, cream cheese, water, vinegar, chives, garlic powder, onion powder, crushed red pepper

flakes, dill, salt, and black pepper to the pot. Turn the pot on Manual, High Pressure for 15 minutes and then do a quick release.

- Use tongs to transfer the chicken to a large plate, shred it with 2 forks, and return it back to the pot.
- Stir in the cheddar cheese.
- Top with the crispy bacon and scallion, and serve.

Nutrition Info

Calories: 437 kcal

Fat: 27.6g

Net Carbs: 4.3g

Carbohydrates: 4.5g

Protein: 41.2g

Day: 7

Breakfast

Brussels Sprouts Hash

Prep Time: 10 mins

Total Time: 40 mins

Servingss: 4 servings

Ingredients

- 6 slices bacon, cut into 1" pieces
- 1/2 onion, chopped

- 1 lb. brussels sprouts, trimmed and quartered
- kosher salt
- Freshly ground black pepper
- 1/4 teaspoon red pepper flakes
- 3 tablespoons water
- 2 garlic cloves, minced
- 4 large eggs

Instructions

- In a large skillet over medium heat, fry bacon until crispy. Turn off heat and transfer bacon to a paper towel-lined plate. Keep most of bacon fat in skillet, removing any black pieces from the bacon.
- Turn heat back to medium and add onion and brussels sprouts to the skillet. Cook, stirring occasionally, until the vegetables begin to soften and turn golden. Season with salt, pepper, and red pepper flakes.
- Add 2 tablespoons of water and cover the skillet. Cook until the Brussels sprouts are tender and the water has evaporated, about 5 minutes. (If all the water evaporates before the Brussels sprouts are tender, add more water to the skillet and cover for a couple minutes more.) Add garlic to skillet and cook until fragrant, 1 minute.

- Using a wooden spoon, make four holes in the hash to reveal bottom of skillet. Crack an egg into each hole and season each egg with salt and pepper. Replace lid and cook until eggs are cooked to your liking, about 5 minutes for a just runny egg. Sprinkle cooked bacon bits over the entire skillet. Serve warm.

Lunch

Cinnamon Pork Chops & Mock Apples

Prep Time: 5 minutes

Cook Time: 40 minutes

Total Time: 45 minutes

Ingredients

- 2 tablespoons of ghee
- 1/2 teaspoon sea salt
- 4 pork chops boneless
- 2 chayote chopped to 1/2-inch chunks
- 2 tablespoons monkfruit sweetener or low carb sweetener of choice
- 1 teaspoon cinnamon
- 1/8 teaspoon nutmeg
- 1 tablespoon apple cider vinegar

Instructions

- Melt ghee in a large skillet over medium heat, add pork chops and cook for 5 minutes.

- Flip the pork chops and add chayote and sprinkle sweetener, cinnamon, nutmeg, and apple cider vinegar over the top. Cook for an additional 4-5 minutes, or until the pork chops reach the appropriate temperature (145 F for medium rare, 160 for medium).

- Remove the pork chops and place in a meal prep container if preparing meals for the week, otherwise keep pork chops warm until ready to serve.

- Bring the chayote mixture to a boil for several minutes. Reduce heat to low medium and simmer with cover, stirring occasionally, for 30 to 40 minutes. When done, the chayote will be fork tender and similar in texture to baked apple.

- Divide the chayote mock apples between four meal prep containers or serve immediately alongside the warm pork chops.

Recipe Notes

2g net carbohydrates per serving - which gives you room for a couple more things if you'd like to add that to your meal prep container or tailor things to your personal macros.

Nutrition Info

Net Carbs: 4.85g
Protein: 35.43g
Fat: 30.22g

Calories: 455kcal

Dinner

Italian Wedding Soup Recipe

Prep Time 15 minutes

Cook Time 30 minutes

Servings: 6 servings

Ingredients

- 1 pound ground beef (80% lean)
- 1/2 cup almond flour
- 1/2 cup grated parmesan
- 1 teaspoon dried Italian seasoning
- 1 large egg
- 2 tablespoons olive oil
- 2 medium stalks celery (diced)
- 1/2 small yellow onion (diced)
- 3 cloves minced garlic
- 6 cups chicken broth
- 1 teaspoon fresh chopped oregano
- 1 teaspoon fresh chopped thyme
- 2 cups cauliflower rice
- 2 cups fresh baby spinach
- salt and pepper

Instructions

- Combine the ground beef, almond flour, parmesan cheese, Italian seasoning, and egg in a mixing bowl.
- Season with salt and pepper them mix well by hand and shape into ½-inch balls.
- Place the meatballs on a plate and refrigerate until ready to use.
- Heat the oil in a large saucepan over medium heat.
- Add the celery and onion then season with salt and pepper – cook for 6 to 7 minutes until tender, stirring often.
- Stir in the garlic and cook for 1 minute more.
- Add the broth, oregano, and thyme then bring to a boil.
- Reduce heat and simmer for 10 minutes then stir in the cauliflower rice and meatballs.
- Cook for 5 minutes or until the meatballs are cooked through.
- Stir in the spinach and cook for 1 to 2 minutes until wilted then adjust seasoning to taste and serve hot.

Nutrition Info

420 Calories

26g of Fat

6.5g of Protein

4g of Net Carbs

Day: 8

Breakfast

3-Ingredient Bacon and Egg Cups

Total time: 40 mins

Cook Time: 30 mins

Prep Time: 10 mins

Serves: 6 servings

Ingredients

- 18 slices of regular-cut bacon
- 6 eggs

- 2 tablespoons chopped fresh parsley
- Salt and pepper to taste (optional)

Instructions

- Preheat the oven to 350°F and spray a six-cavity, large muffin pan with coconut oil.
- Create a lattice for each egg cup by weaving three bacon slices together. Press down into each muffin cavity so there are as little holes as possible.
- Crack an egg into each cavity.
- Bake for 25 to 30 minutes until the eggs are fully cooked.
- Use a spoon to remove the bacon and egg cups from the muffin pan. Garnish with freshly chopped parsley and serve.

Lunch

Superfood Meatballs

Prep Time: 10 minutes

Cook Time: 40 minutes

Total Time: 50 minutes

Servings: 10 servings

Ingredients

- 3lbs 85% lean grass fed ground beef
- 1lb pastured chicken livers
- 1 large shallot
- 4 medium carrots
- 3 garlic cloves
- 2 tablespoons grass fed butter
- 1 teaspoon dried oregano

- 2 tablespoons coconut aminos (separated)
- 3 teaspoon salt (separated)
- 2 teaspoon black pepper
- 1 tablespoon dried thyme (dried)
- 1 tablespoon garlic powder
- Olive oil

Instructions

- Heat a large cast iron skillet on medium heat. While it heats, mince the shallots, carrots and garlic until fine. When the skillet comes to temperature add in the vegetables and sauté until aromatic and tender, about 8 minutes, stir often.
- Add in the chicken livers along with 1 teaspoon salt and dried oregano. Cook, stirring often, until the livers are browned all over. Add in the 1 tablespoon coconut aminos and 1 tablespoon apple cider vinegar and cook until reduced and livers are cooked.
- Remove from heat, and let cool a few minutes. Transfer to a food processor and pulse until it looks like ground beef. Then transfer to a large bowl, to cool to room temp.

- Pre-heat oven to 425F. Add the ground beef to the bowl with the remaining salt and the rest of the seasoning. Mix well. Shape 1 ½ inch balls, will make aprx 30.
- Drizzle olive oil all over the sheet pan. With oiled hands, coat each meatball in a little olive oil and you handle it to place it on the sheet pan. Then lightly drizzle them with the remaining coconut aminos.
- Place in the oven, roast at 425F for 5 minutes. Then turn the temperature down to 350F and roast another 20 minutes before removing from the oven.
- These meatballs are perfect for meal prep or feeding a crowd. Dunk them in ranch, pile on some guac or drizzle with lemon tahini sauce for some extra fats!

Nutrition Info

Calories: 323 kcal
Fat: 21g
Carbohydrates: 4.3g
Protein: 31.8g

Dinner

2 Ingredient Keto Pasta

Prep Time: 10 minutes

Cook Time: 1 minute

Servings: 1 serving

Ingredients:

- 1 cup shredded part skim low moisture mozzarella cheese
- 1 large egg

Instructions

- Add the mozzarella to a large microwave-safe bowl and microwave for about 1 minute. Stir until cheese is completely melted. If needed, heat for an additional 30 seconds or until cheese is completely melted.

- Allow the mozzarella to cool for 1 minute, so that it will not cook the egg. You don't want to cool the cheese too long though because it needs to stay melted.

- Add in egg and stir and mix into the cheese, until you have a uniform yellow dough.

- Place your dough on a flat surface lined with parchment paper. Place another parchment paper on top of the dough.

- Use a rolling pin over the top piece of parchment paper, and roll dough until it is 1/8 inch thick.

- Remove the top piece of parchment and cut the dough into ½ inch wide strips. Refrigerate the pasta for at least 6 hours or overnight.

- When ready to cook, bring a pot of water to boil. Do not add salt to the water. Add in pasta. Cook for about 40 seconds to 1 minute. Be careful not to cook too long, otherwise the pasta will lose its form, break down and become a melted cheese mess.

- Remove pasta from pot and run under cold water to cool it down. Gently separate strands sticking together. Allow pasta to cool until it is only slightly warm to the touch. When the pasta cools, it will firm back up, so that it is no longer just melty cheese and it will taste more like pasta rather than just cheese sticks. Serve with your favorite pasta sauce.

Nutrition Info

Calories: 358 kcal
Calories from Fat: 198 kcal
Total Fat: 22g
Saturated Fat: 12g
Sugars: 1g
Protein: 33g

Day: 9

Breakfast

Bacon-Wrapped Avocado Fries

Prep Time: 10 mins

Total time: 40 mins

Cook Time: 30 mins

Serves: 20 servings

Ingredients

- 2 avocados
- 20 strips of pasture-raised bacon

Instructions

- Preheat the oven to 425°F and line a baking sheet with parchment paper. Remove the pits from the avocados and slice the avocado into thin strips lengthwise (5 per half).
- Wrap each avocado slice with one strip of bacon, and place on the baking sheet. Bake for 25-30 minutes or until the bacon is crisp. Allow to cool for 5 minutes before serving.

Lunch

BBQ Pulled Beef Sando

Prep Time: 8 minutes

Cook Time: 8 hours-12 hours

Servings: 4 servings

Ingredients

- 3lbs Boneless Chuck Roast
- 2 teaspoons Pink Himalayan Salt
- 2 teaspoon garlic powder
- 1 teaspoon onion powder
- 1 teaspoon black pepper
- 1 tablespoon smoked paprika
- 2 tablespoons tomato paste
- 1/4 cup apple cider vinegar

- 2 tablespoons coconut aminos
- 1/2 cup bone broth
- 1/4 cup melted Kerrygold Butter

Instructions

- Trim the fat off of the beef and cut in to two large pieces.
- In a small bowl mix together the salt, garlic, onion, paprika and black pepper. Then rub it all over the beef. Place the beef in your slow cooker.
- In another bowl melt the butter, whisk in the tomato paste, vinegar and coconut aminos. Pour it all over the beef. Then add the bone broth to the slow cooker, pouring it around the beef.
- Set on low and cook for 10-12 hours. When done, remove the beef, set the slow cooker to high and let the sauce thicken. Shred the beef then add it back in to the slow cooker and toss with sauce. Serve!

Nutrition Info

Calories: 184 kcal
Fat: 15.1g
Carbohydrates: 3.6g

Protein: 5.1g

Dinner

Pigs in a Blanket Recipe

Prep Time: 15 minutes

Cook Time: 20 minutes

Servings: 6 servings

Ingredients

- 2 cups shredded mozzarella
- 2 ounces cream cheese (softened)
- 1/2 cup coconut flour

- 1 teaspoon dried oregano
- 3/4 teaspoon onion powder
- 1/2 teaspoon garlic powder
- 1/2 teaspoon baking powder
- 2 large eggs (whisked)
- 12 all-beef hotdogs
- 1 teaspoon sesame seeds

Instructions

- Preheat the oven to 400°F and line a baking sheet with parchment.
- Combine the mozzarella and cream cheese in a microwave-safe bowl and heat until melted then stir smooth and set aside.
- Combine the coconut flour, oregano, onion powder, garlic powder, baking powder, and eggs in a mixing bowl then stir in the melted cheese until a dough forms – wet your hands because it will be sticky.
- Divide the dough into 12 pieces and roll into balls.
- Roll out each dough ball between two pieces of parchment into 8-inch circles.
- Wrap each dough circle around a hotdog and place on the baking sheet.

- Sprinkle with sesame seeds then bake for 15 to 20 minutes until browned.

Nutrition Info

370 Calories

23.5g of Fat

24.5g of Protein

7.5g of Net Carbs

Day: 10

Breakfast

Keto Pancakes

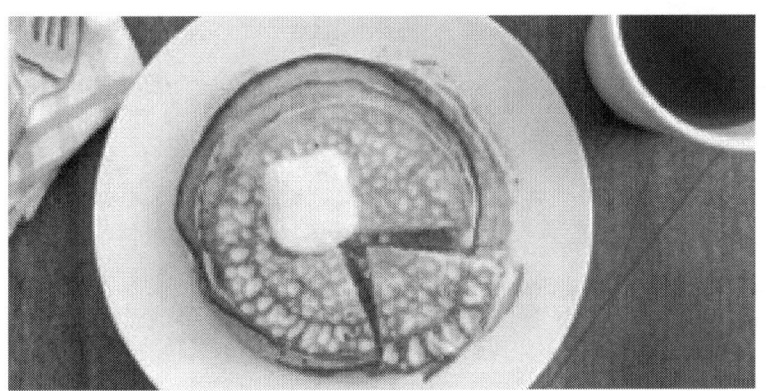

Prep Time: 5 mins

Total Time: 15 mins

Servingss: 4 servings

Ingredients

- 1/2 cup almond flour
- 4 oz. cream cheese, softened
- 4 large eggs
- 1 teaspoon lemon zest
- Butter, for frying and serving

Instructions

- In a medium bowl, whisk together almond flour, cream cheese, eggs, and lemon zest until smooth.
- In a nonstick skillet over medium heat, melt 1 tablespoon butter. Pour in about 3 tablespoons batter and cook until golden, 2 minutes. Flip and cook 2 minutes more. Transfer to a plate and continue with the rest of the batter.
- Serve topped with butter.

Lunch

Salmon & Avocado Nori Rolls (Paleo Sushi)

Prep time: 10 mins

Total time: 10 mins

Serves: 1 serving

Ingredients

- 3 square nori sheets (seaweed wrappers)

- 150-180 g / 5-6 oz cooked salmon or tinned salmon
- ½ red pepper, sliced into thin strips
- ½ avocado, sliced into strips
- ½ small cucumber, sliced into strips
- 1 spring onion/scallion, cut into 2-3" pieces
- 2 tablespoons mayonnaise
- 1 tablespoon hot sauce or Sriracha sauce
- 1 teaspoon black or white sesame seeds
- Coconut aminos for dipping, optional

Instructions

- Place the nori sheet on a flat surface, such as a cutting board, shiny side down. Look at the fibres of the wrapper to see which way it needs to be rolled.
- Add a third of the salmon to the right or left third of the nori sheet and top with two strips of pepper, cucumber and avocado. Add some green onion and a drizzle of mayonnaise and hot sauce. You can sprinkle with sesame seeds now or at a later stage, once the rolls are cut.
- Lightly wet the top part of the nori sheet (the side you are rolling towards), just 1-2 cm of the wrapper. Pick up the opposite outer edge of the roll and start wrapping it over the ingredients, using your fingers to keep it nice

and tight. This can take a bit of practice, but don't worry if your roll doesn't look perfect. Roll it until the top edge of the wrapper overlaps the roll and press it tightly to stick. Place the roll on the cutting board with the seam facing down and then cut into bite-size pieces.

- Serve right away with some coconut aminos or extra mayo for dipping, or pack in a container to take for lunch or keep as a snack in the fridge.

Dinner

Cheesy Meatball Casserole Recipe

Prep Time: 15 minutes

Cook Time: 45 minutes

Servings: 8 servings

Ingredients

- 1 pound ground beef (80% lean)

- 1 pound ground sausage
- 1 cup shredded mozzarella
- 1/2 cup grated parmesan
- 1 cup shredded zucchini (pressed to remove moisture)
- 1 large egg
- 1 tablespoon minced garlic
- 2 teaspoons dried basil
- 1 teaspoon dried oregano
- salt and pepper
- 1 cup sugar-free tomato sauce
- 2 cups shredded provolone cheese

Instructions

- Preheat the oven to 400°F and grease a large casserole dish with cooking spray.
- Combine the ground beef, ground sausage, mozzarella, parmesan, zucchini, egg, and seasonings in a large bowl and mix well by hand.
- Shape the mixture into 24 meatballs and arrange them in the casserole dish.
- Pour the sauce over the meatballs and top with the shredded provolone cheese.
- Bake for 30 minutes then drain the cooking liquid.

- Let the casserole bake for another 10 to 15 minutes until the cheese is melted and browned.

Nutrition Info

515 Calories

38g of Fat

39g of Protein

2.5g of Net Carbs

Day: 11

Breakfast

Keto Cannoli Stuffed Crepes – Low Carb

Prep Time: 15 minutes

Cook Time: 20 minutes

Total Time: 35 minutes

Servings: 4 servings

Ingredients

For the crepes:

- 8 ounces cream cheese, softened
- 8 eggs
- 1/2 teaspoon ground cinnamon
- 1 tablespoon granulated erythritol sweetener
- 2 tablespoons butter, for the pan

For the cannoli filling:

- 6 ounces mascarpone cheese, softened
- 1 cup whole milk ricotta cheese
- 1/2 teaspoon lemon zest
- 1/2 teaspoon ground cinnamon
- 1/4 teaspoon unsweetened vanilla extract
- 1/4 cup powdered erythritol sweetener

Instructions

For the crepes:

- Combine all of the crepes ingredients in a blender and blend until smooth.
- Let the batter rest for 5 minutes and then give it a stir to break up any additional air bubbles.
- Heat 1 teaspoon of butter in a 10 inch or larger nonstick saute pan over medium heat.
- When the butter is melted and bubbling, pour in about 1/4 cup of batter (you can eyeball it) and if necessary, gently tilt the pan in a circular motion to create a 6-inch (-ish) round crepe.
- Cook for two minutes, or until the top is no longer glossy and bubbles have formed almost to the middle of the crepe.
- Carefully flip and cook for another 30 seconds. Remove and place on a plate.
- Repeat until you have 8 usable crepes.

Nutrition Info

Serving Size: 2 stuffed crepes

Calories: 478 kcal

Fat: 42g

Carbohydrates: 4g

Fiber: 0g

Protein: 16g

Lunch

Delicious Lemon Herb Low Carb Keto Meatloaf

Prep Time: 10 minutes

Cook Time: 50 minutes

Total Time: 1 hour

Servings: 6 servings

Ingredients

- 2 pounds 85% lean grass fed ground beef

- 1/2 tablespoon fine Himalayan salt
- 1 teaspoon black pepper
- 1/4 cup Nutritional Yeast
- 2 large eggs
- 2 tablespoons avocado oil
- 1 tablespoon lemon zest
- 1/4 cup chopped parsley
- 1/4 cup chopped fresh oregano
- 4 cloves garlic

Instructions

- Pre-heat oven to 400F.
- In a large bowl mix the ground beef, salt, black pepper and nutritional yeast.
- In a blender or food processor mix the eggs, oil, herbs and garlic. Blend until the eggs are froth and the herbs, lemon and garlic are minced and mixed.
- Add the egg blend to the beef and mix to combine.
- Add the beef to a small, 8×4 loaf pan. Smooth and flatten out.
- Set in the oven, middle rack for 50-60 minutes.

- Carefully remove from the oven and tilt the loaf pan over the sink to drain the fluid. Let it cool for 5-10 minutes before slicing into.
- Garnish with fresh lemon and enjoy!

Nutrition Info

Calories: 344 kcal

Fat: 29g

Carbohydrates: 4g

Fiber: 2g

Protein: 33g

Dinner

Cheesy Taco Pie Recipe

Prep Time: 15 minute
Cook Time: 30 minutes

Servings: 4 servings

Ingredients

- 1 pound ground beef (80% lean)
- 1 tablespoon chili powder
- 1 tablespoon ground cumin
- 1 tablespoon garlic powder
- 1 cup heavy cream
- 6 large eggs
- 1 cup shredded cheddar cheese
- salt and pepper
- sour cream (to serve)
- Diced Avocado (to serve)

Instructions

- Preheat the oven to 350°F and grease a 9-inch glass pie plate with cooking spray.
- Cook the beef in a large skillet over medium heat until browned, breaking it up into chunks with a wooden spoon.
- Stir in the chili powder, cumin, garlic powder, salt, and pepper then reduce heat and cook on medium-low for 5 minutes to thicken.

- Spoon the beef mixture into the pie plate and set aside.
- Whisk together the heavy cream and eggs then pour over the beef.
- Sprinkle with cheese and bake for 30 minutes until the cheese is melted and browned.
- Remove from the oven and let rest for 5 minutes.
- Cut into wedges then serve with sour cream and diced avocado, if desired.

Nutrition Info

430 Calories

32g of Fat

32g of Protein

2.5g of Net Carbs

Day: 12

Breakfast

Bacon Spinach Frittata

Total time: 25 mins

Cook Time: 20 mins

Prep Time: 5 mins

Ingredients

- 8 large eggs
- 4 large egg whites
- 1 cup almond milk (or other nut milk)
- ¼ onion, diced

- 1 grape tomatoes, quartered
- 2 cups spinach
- 6 strips nitrate-free bacon, cooked & crumbled, and grease reserved to cook the eggs

Instructions

- Preheat oven to 400 degrees.
- Cook the bacon in a cast iron skillet over medium-high heat until cooked through, remove the bacon from the pan and reserve the bacon grease, setting the pan off to the side for now. Crumble the bacon, once cooled, and set aside.
- In a medium to large bowl, whisk together eggs, egg whites, and milk. Set aside.
- In the bacon grease, sauté the onions and for 2-3 minutes until tender. Add tomato and spinach and cook for 1-2 more minutes. Spinach should just begin to wilt.
- Pour your egg mixture in the skillet and add bacon pieces. Let cook for 4-6 minutes. The eggs should just begin to set.
- Bake for 8-12 minutes, until eggs are completely cooked through.

Lunch

Lemon Balsamic Chicken

No, not all Italian food is a mountain of carbs. Today's lemon balsamic chicken recipe draws inspiration from the South of Italy with its fresh flavor and good fats.

Prep Time: 5 minutes
Cook Time: 30 minutes
Total Time: 35 minutes
Servings: 6 servings

Ingredients

- 8 boneless skinless chicken thighs (about 2 lbs)

- 3 tablespoons pastured butter
- 1 cup sliced onion
- 1 cup shredded purple cabbage
- 2 tablespoons minced lemon rind
- 2 bay leaves
- 2 teaspoons pink Himalayan salt
- 1 teaspoon dried Italian herb blend
- 1 teaspoon coarse black pepper
- 1.5 tablespoons balsamic vinegar
- 5 tablespoons olive oil

Instructions

- Heat your electric pressure cooker on sauté mode. Add in 2 tablespoons of butter.
- While it melts, peel and slice your onion. Go ahead and prep your lemon rind and your cabbage, too!
- Add the onion, cabbage and lemon to the pressure. Sauté, stirring often until tender.
- Add in the chicken thighs, seasonings and bay leaves. Stir well and cook, browning the chicken for a 2-3 minutes.

- Pour in the vinegar. Cancel the sauté function. Close the lid, select pressure cook. Set it to poultry or high for 20 minutes.
- Once it has finished, let the pressure releases naturally. Open the lid, stir the chicken to shred. Mix in the last tablespoon of butter.
- Spoon this delicious saucy chicken all over your zoodles, drizzle with olive oil or avocado oil! Enjoy!

Nutrition Info

Calories: 325 kcal

Fat: 17.8g

Carbohydrates: 6.9g

Fiber: 4g

Protein: 29g

Dinner

Miracle Noodle Broccoli Alfredo Recipe

Prep Time 10 minutes

Cook Time 10 minutes

Servings: 4 servings

Ingredients

- 2 ounces cream cheese (softened)
- 1 ounce butter
- 1/4 cup heavy cream
- 1/4 cup grated parmesan cheese
- 1/4 teaspoon garlic powder
- 1 teaspoon olive oil
- 1 1/2 cups broccoli florets
- 2 packages Miracle Noodles (fettuccini style)
- salt and pepper

Instructions

- Combine the cream cheese and butter in a small saucepan over low heat.
- When the butter and cream cheese are melted, whisk in the heavy cream and parmesan cheese until smooth and well combined.
- Add the garlic powder, salt, and pepper then remove from heat.
- Heat the oil in a large skillet over medium heat and add the broccoli.
- Season the broccoli with salt and pepper and stir-fry for about 3 to 4 minutes until bright green.
- Rinse the Miracle Noodles in cool water then pat dry.

- Add the noodles to the skillet with the broccoli and cook for about 5 minutes, stirring often.
- Pour the sauce over the noodles and broccoli then cook until heated through. Serve hot.

Nutrition Info

175 Calories

16g of Fat

4.5g of Protein

2.5g of Net Carbs

Day: 13

Breakfast

Curry Tofu Scramble with Avocado

Prep Time: 5 minutes

Total Time: 20 minutes

Cook Time: 13 minutes

Servings: 3 servings

Ingredients:

- 1 tablespoon coconut oil
- 2 tablespoons olive oil
- 300 g tofu (extra firm)
- 1 teaspoon turmeric
- 1 tablespoon nutritional yeast
- 1 tablespoon curry powder
- 1/2 cup zucchini (chopped)
- 1 cup mushrooms (chopped)
- 1 tomato (chopped)
- cilantro (optional)(to garnish)
- 300-gram avocado

Instructions:

- The initial step is to dry the tofu so it ingests the flavor.
- Cut the tofu into 1 inch long strips, spread out the strips on a paper towel,
- Put another paper towel to finish everything and after that a slashing board.
- Place something substantial over this, for example, a few books.
- Abandon it to sit for around 15 minutes.

- Add the coconut oil to the dish and disintegrate the tofu into the skillet with your hands.
- Cook for around 5 minutes, mixing every now and again.
- Include the turmeric, nourishing yeast and curry powder and 1 tablespoon of the olive oil,
- Blend and cook for a further 4 minutes.
- Add whatever remains of the olive oil, zucchini, mushroom and tomato and sear for a further 4 minutes blending much of the time.
- Serve with 1 little medium size avocado (roughly 100g) cut.

Nutrition Info

Calories: 381 kcal

Fats: 32g

Protein: 11g

Net Carbs: 8g

Lunch

Easy White Turkey Chili

Prep Time: 5 minutes

Cook Time: 15 minutes

Total Time: 20 minutes

Servings: 5 servings

Ingredients

- 1 lb Organic ground turkey (or ground beef, lamb or pork)
- 2 cups riced cauliflower
- 2 tablespoons coconut oil
- 1/2 Vidalia onion
- 2 garlic cloves
- 2 cups full fat coconut milk (or heavy cream)
- 1 tablespoon mustard
- 1 teaspoon of: salt, black pepper, thyme, celery salt, garlic powder

Instructions

- In a large pot, heat the coconut oil.
- In the meantime mince the onion and garlic. Add it to the hot oil.
- Stir for 2-3 minutes then add in the ground turkey.
- Break up with the spatula and stir constantly until crumbled.
- Add in the seasoning mix and riced cauliflower and stir well.

- Once the meat is browned add in the coconut milk, bring to a simmer and reduce for 5-8 minutes, stirring often.
- At this point it's ready to serve. Or you can let it reduce by half until thick and serve as a dip.
- Mix in shredded cheese for an extra thick sauce.

Topping Suggestions:

- Avocado
- Jalapenos
- Bacon
- Shredded aged cheddar cheese
- Cherry Tomatoes
- Hot Sauce

Nutrition Info

Calories: 388 kcal
Fat: 30.5g
Carbohydrates: 5.5g
Protein: 28.8g

Dinner

Bacon Cheddar Chicken Calzones Recipe

Prep Time: 10 minutes

Cook Time: 50 minutes

Servings: 6 servings

Ingredients

- 2 cups shredded chicken

- 1 cup shredded cheddar cheese
- 4 slices bacon (cooked and crumbled)
- 2 tablespoons sour cream
- 2 tablespoons mayonnaise
- 8 ounces shredded mozzarella cheese
- 2 ounces cream cheese (softned)
- 1 large egg (whisked)
- 6 tablespoons almond flour
- 6 tablespoons coconut flour
- 6 tablespoons ground flaxseed
- 1 egg white (whisked)

Instructions

- Preheat the oven to 350°F and line a baking sheet with parchment paper.
- Stir together the shredded chicken, cheddar cheese, bacon, sour cream, and mayonnaise in a mixing bowl until well combined then set aside.
- Combine the mozzarella and cream cheese in a microwave-safe bowl and heat on high heat for 60 seconds.
- Stir the mixture and heat at 30-second intervals, stirring between each, until melted.

- Add the egg, almond flour, coconut flour, and ground flaxseed and stir until fully incorporated – you can also use a stand mixer with the dough hook attachment.
- Turn out the dough onto a piece of parchment and roll into a large rectangle then cut into three pieces.
- Roll each piece of dough into a rectangle about ¼-inch thick then spread the chicken filling over them.
- Fold up the ends and sides of each piece of dough around the fillings and press closed.
- Brush the calzones with egg white and sprinkle with parmesan then bake for 45 to 50 minutes until golden brown.

Nutrition Info

545 Calories

35g of Fat

40g of Protein

6.5g of Net Carbs

Day: 14

Breakfast

Cauliflower and bacon Hash Recipe

Prep time: 10 mins

Cooking time: 15 mins

Servings: 4 servings

Ingredients

- 3/4 lb. cauliflower, chopped into small pieces;
- 6 slices of bacon, diced;
- 1 medium onion, diced;
- 1/2 teaspoon smoked paprika;
- 3 tablespoons water;

- 1 clove garlic, minced;
- Juice from half a lemon;
- 2 teaspoon fresh parsley, minced;
- 2 tablespoons Paleo cooking fat;
- 4 eggs, fried; (optional)
- Sea salt and freshly ground black pepper to taste;

Instructions

- Cook the bacon in a skillet over a medium-high heat until crispy (about 10 minutes).
- Remove the bacon from the skillet and set aside, but leave the rendered fat in.
- In the same skillet, add the cauliflower, garlic, and onion. Cook 2 to 3 minutes or until it starts to golden.
- Add the smoked paprika and season to taste with salt and pepper.
- Add the water. Cover the skillet and cook until the cauliflower is tender, about 5 minutes.
- Return the bacon to the skillet.
- Add the lemon juice and cook for another 2 minutes; then remove from the heat and sprinkle fresh parsley on top.
- Serve with eggs, or as a side for any meal.

Nutrition Info

Protein: 14g 24%

Carbs: 15g 26%

Fat: 13g 50%

Lunch

Keto Brunch Spread

Prep Time: 10 minutes

Cook Time: 20 minutes

Total Time: 30 minutes

Servings: 4 servings

Ingredients

- 4 large eggs
- 24 asparagus spears
- 12 slices of pastured, sugar free bacon

Instructions

- Pre-heat your oven to 400F.
- Trim your asparagus about an inch from the bottoms. Then in pairs, wrap them with one slice of bacon. Hold your spears firmly and close together with one hand as you wind the slice of bacon starting from the bottom, to the top of the spear. Gently pull the bacon as you wind it, so it wraps tightly. Place it on a sheet pan.
- Repeat with the remaining asparagus, so you have 12 pairs wrapped in bacon.
- Place in the oven, set the timer for 20 minutes.
- In this time, bring a small pot of water to a rapid boil. Gently place 4 large eggs in the boiling water. Set another time for 6 minutes.
- Prepare a bowl with ice water. When the 6 minutes are up, use a slotted spoon or tongs to quickly transfer your

eggs to the ice bath. Let them sit for 2 minutes before peeling the tops off.

- Gently crack the top of the egg on a hard surface and peel away shell to reveal the tip of the egg.
- When the asparagus are ready, serve on a tray or cutting board. If you don't have an egg holder use espresso cups to hold your eggs up.
- With a small spoon scoop out the tops of the soft boiled eggs to reveal a perfectly runny yolk.
- Dip your asparagus spears into your eggs. Feast, enjoy!

Nutrition Info

Calories: 426 kcal
Fat: 38g
Saturated Fat: 13g
Carbohydrates: 3g
Protein: 17

Dinner

Instant Pot Beef Bourguignon

Instant Pot Beef Bourguignon is a pressure cooker recipe with beef, mushrooms, onions, and carrots cooked in red wine. Low carb, keto, and gluten free.

Prep Time: 30 minutes
Cook Time: 50 minutes

Servings: 6 servings

Ingredients

- 1.5 - 2 pounds beef chuck roast cut into 3/4-inch cubes
- 5 strips bacon diced
- 1 small onion chopped
- 10 ounces cremini mushrooms quartered
- 2 carrots chopped
- 5 cloves garlic minced
- 3 bay leaves
- 3/4 cup dry red wine
- 3/4 teaspoon xanthan gum (or corn starch)
- 1 tablespoon tomato paste
- 1 teaspoon dried thyme
- salt & pepper

Instructions

- Generously season beef chunks with salt and pepper, and set aside. Select the saute mode on the pressure cooker for medium heat. When the display reads HOT, add diced bacon and cook for about 5 minutes until crispy, stirring frequently. Transfer the bacon to a paper towel lined plate.

- Add the beef to the pot in a single layer and cook for a few minutes to brown, then flip and repeat for the other side. Transfer to a plate when done.
- Add onions and garlic. Cook for a few minutes to soften, stirring frequently. Add red wine and tomato paste, using a wooden spoon to briefly scrape up flavorful brown bits stuck to the bottom of the pot. Stir to check that the tomato paste is dissolved. Turn off the saute mode.
- Transfer the beef back to the pot. Add mushrooms, carrots, and thyme, stirring together. Top with bay leaves. Secure and seal the lid. Cook at high pressure for 40 minutes, followed by a manual pressure release.

- Uncover and select the saute mode. Remove bay leaves. Evenly sprinkle xanthan gum over the pot and stir together. Let the stew boil for a minute to thicken while stirring. Turn off the saute mode. Serve into bowls and top with crispy bacon.

Nutrition Info

Calories: 220 kcal
Total Fat: 5g

Sodium: 310mg

Potassium: 130mg

Total Carb: 6.5g

Dietary Fiber: 1g

Sugars 2g

Protein 27g

Day: 15

Breakfast

Ham & Cheese Breakfast Roll-Ups

Prep Time: 20 mins

Total Time: 20 mins

Servings: 2 servings

Ingredients

- 4 large eggs
- 1/4 cup milk
- 2 tablespoons Chopped chives
- kosher salt

- Freshly ground black pepper
- 1 tablespoon butter
- 1 cup shredded cheddar, divided
- 4 slices ham

Instructions

- In a medium bowl, whisk together eggs, milk, and chives. Season with salt and pepper.
- In a medium skillet over medium heat, melt butter. Pour half of the egg mixture into the skillet, moving to create a thin layer that covers the entire pan.
- Cook for 2 minutes. Add 1/2 cup cheddar and cover for 2 minutes more, until the cheese is melty. Remove onto plate, place 2 slices of ham, and roll tightly. Repeat with remaining ingredients and serve.

Lunch

Loaded Cauliflower Bake

Prep Time: 15 minutes

Cook Time: 45 minutes

Total Time: 1 hour

Servings: 4 servings

Ingredients

- 1 large head cauliflower, cut into florets
- 2 tablespoon butter
- 1 cup heavy cream
- 2 oz. cream cheese
- 1 1/4 cup shredded sharp cheddar cheese, separated
- Salt and pepper to taste
- 6 slices bacon, cooked and crumbled
- 1/4 cup chopped green onions

Instructions

- Preheat oven to 350 degrees.
- In a large pot of boiling water, blanch cauliflower florets for 2 minutes. Drain cauliflower.
- In a medium pot, melt together butter, heavy cream, cream cheese, 1 cup of shredded cheddar cheese, salt, and pepper until well-combined.
- In a baking dish, add cauliflower florets, cheese sauce, all but 1 tbsp. crumbled bacon, and all but 1 tbsp. green onions. Stir together.
- Top with remaining shredded cheddar cheese, crumbled bacon, and green onions.

- Bake until cheese is bubbly and golden and cauliflower is soft, about 30 minutes.
- Serve immediately and enjoy!

Nutrition Info

Calories: 498 kcal

Fat: 45g

Carbohydrates: 5.8g (Net: 4.1)

Protein: 13.9g

Dinner

One-Pan Chicken Stir-Fry Recipe

Prep Time: 10 minutes

Cook Time: 25 minutes

Servings: 4 servings

Ingredients

- 1/3 cup soy sauce
- 2 tablespoons rice vinegar

- 2 tablespoons of So-Nourished granulated erythritol
- 1 tablespoon sesame oil
- 1 teaspoon garlic powder
- 1 pound boneless chicken thighs
- 2 medium red peppers (cored and chopped)
- 2 cups green beans (sliced)
- 1 cup cauliflower florets
- 1 1/2 tablespoons olive oil
- 2 tablespoons sesame seeds

Instructions

- Whisk together the soy sauce, rice vinegar, granulated erythritol, sesame oil, and garlic powder in a small bowl.
- Chop the chicken into 1-inch pieces and place them in a zippered freezer bag.
- Pour in the sauce and shake to coat then chill for at least 4 hours.
- Preheat the oven to 425°F and line a large baking sheet with foil.
- Drain the chicken and spread it on the baking sheet and bake for 8 minutes.

- Toss the veggies with the olive oil and sprinkle onto the baking sheet with the chicken.
- Bake for another 12 to 15 minutes until the chicken is done then sprinkle with sesame seeds to serve.

Nutrition Info

400 Calories

28g of Fat

24g of Protein

8.5g of Net Carbs

Day: 16

Breakfast

Zucchini and Prosciutto Egg Muffins

Prep Time: 10 mins

Cook Time: 20 mins

Total Time: 30 mins

Servings: 12 muffins

Ingredients

- 1 tablespoon olive oil

- 1/2 onion, finely diced
- 3 garlic cloves, minced
- 1 bell pepper, finely diced
- 1 cup baby spinach, roughly chopped
- 1/4 cup fresh parsley, roughly chopped
- 8 large eggs
- 1/4 cup coconut milk, or nut milk
- salt and pepper, to taste
- 2 small zucchini, thinly sliced
- 12 slices prosciutto
- olive oil to coat the muffin tin

Instructions

- Preheat the oven to 350 degrees fahrenheit.
- Heat the olive oil in a pan on medium heat and sauté the onion and garlic for a minute. Add the sweet pepper, spinach and parsley and sauté for another 2 minutes or until the spinach has wilted.
- In a mixing bowl, whisk together the eggs, coconut milk and salt and pepper. When the veggies have finished cooking add them to the bowl along with the sliced zucchini and stir together.

- Grease a muffin tin with olive oil and line each muffin tin cup with one slice of prosciutto.
- Ladle the egg mixture into each muffin cup and bake for 20 minutes, or until cooked through.

Nutrition Info

Calories: 107kcal, Carbohydrates: 2g, Protein: 5g

Lunch

Loaded Chicken Salad

A delicious salad filled with plenty of vegetables and delicious grilled meat!

Prep Time: 10 minutes
Cook Time: 8 minutes
Total Time: 18 minutes
Servings: 4 servings

Ingredients

- 1 boneless chicken breast (about 300g, with or without skin)
- 1 tablespoon extra virgin olive oil
- 1/4 teaspoon Himalayan salt
- 1/4 teaspoon black pepper
- 1 avocado
- 100 g mozzarella balls
- 1 large tomato (any colour)
- 1 har artichoke hearts (my jar was 170g)
- 1/2 red onion
- 5 asparagus
- 20 leaves basil
- 4 cups baby spinach (I used about 200g)

Dressing

- 2 tablespoon extra virgin olive oil
- 1 1/2 tablespoon balsamic vinegar
- 1 teaspoon dijon mustard
- 1 clove garlic

- pinch Himalayan salt
- pinch black pepper

Instructions

- Peel and dice the avocado. Slice the red onion. Dice the tomato. Pile the basil leaves together, roll them up and slice. Cut the stems off the asparagus and slice in half. Mince the garlic.
- Slice the chicken breast in half lengthwise. Sprinkle the 1/4 teaspoon of salt and pepper on each sides. Heat the 1 tablespoon of olive oil in a cast iron skillet and place the chicken breasts in. Fry on each side, about 3 minutes each side, until they have a nice golden brown colour and cooked through. Add the asparagus beside the chicken breasts and cook a few minutes until soft and grilled. Take out the chicken and slice.
- In a small bowl, combine the minced garlic, olive oil, balsamic vinegar, dijon, and salt & peper.
- Add the baby spinach to a large bowl or plate. Cover with the grilled chicken, avocado, mozzarella, tomatoes, artichoke, red onions, asparagus and basil leaves. Pour the dressing over and enjoy!

Nutrition Info

Calories: 430 kcal

Calories from Fat: 264 kcal

Total Fat: 29.36g

Total Carbohydrates: 12.86g

Dietary Fiber: 6.12g

Sugars: 3.16g

Protein: 31.73g

Dinner

Chicken Bacon Ranch Casserole Recipe

Prep Time: 15 minutes

Cook Time: 35 minutes

Servings: 8 servings

Ingredients

- 1 pound broccoli (chopped well)
- 1 (8-ounce) package cream cheese (softened)
- 1 cup mayonnaise
- 1/2 cup sour cream
- 1 tablespoon fresh chopped parsley
- 2 teaspoons garlic powder
- salt and pepper
- 1 1/2 pounds cooked chicken thighs (chopped)
- 1/4 cup diced yellow onion
- 2 cups shredded cheddar cheese (divided)
- 4 slices cooked bacon (chopped)

Instructions

- Preheat the oven to 350°F and lightly grease a 9x13-inch glass baking dish with cooking spray.
- Fill a large saucepan with 1 inch of water then add a steamer insert.

- Add the broccoli then bring the water to boil and cook for 7 to 8 minutes until just tender.
- Drain the broccoli well and set it aside.
- Combine the cream cheese, mayonnaise, and sour cream in a large mixing bowl.
- Add the parsley, garlic powder, salt, and pepper then beat until smooth.
- Stir in the broccoli, chicken, onion, and 1 ½ cups shredded cheese.
- Fold in half the cooked bacon then spread it in the prepared baking dish.
- Top with the remaining cheese and bacon then bake for 35 minutes until hot and bubbling.

Nutrition Info

545 Calories

42g of Fat

38g of Protein

5g of Net Carbs

Day: 17

Breakfast

Shrimp and Cauliflower "Grits" Recipe

Total Time: 35 mins

Cook Time: 30 mins

Prep Time: 5 mins

Serves: 4 servings

Ingredients

For Shrimp

- 1 lb large shrimp, peeled/deveined (thawed if frozen)
- 1 tablespoon grass-fed butter (or ghee)
- 2 garlic cloves, minced
- 2 teaspoons paprika
- 1/2 teaspoon onion powder
- 1/2 teaspoon dried thyme
- 1/4 teaspoon cayenne pepper
- 1/4 teaspoon sea salt

For Cauliflower Grits

- 1 head of cauliflower, broken into florets
- 1/2 cup almond milk, unsweetened
- 1 tablespoon grass-fed butter (or ghee)
- 1 teaspoon nutritional yeast
- 1/4 teaspoon sea salt

Optional Toppings

- Green onion, finely chopped
- Lemon wedges
- Hot sauce

Instructions

- Start by placing cauliflower florets in a large pot with 1 cup water. Bring to a low boil and cover. Boil 20 minutes or until cauliflower is fork tender.
- Drain florets and place into a blender with 1/2 cup almond milk, 1 tablespoon butter, nutritional yeast and sea salt. Pulse until smooth.
- To cook shrimp, melt grass-fed butter in a large skillet over medium heat. Stir in shrimp and seasonings and cook 6 minutes, stirring occasionally.
- Pour grits onto serving plate and top with shrimp and sauce mixture. Finish with hot sauce, green onion and a squeeze of lemon.

Lunch

Caprese Tuna Salad Stuffed Tomatoes

Prep Time: 10 minutes

Servings: 1 serving

Ingredients

- 1 medium tomato
- 1 (5oz) can tuna, very well drained

- 2 teaspoon balsamic vinegar
- 1 tablespoon chopped mozzarella {1/4 oz.}
- 1 tablesoon chopped fresh basil
- 1 tablespoon chopped green onion

Instructions

- Cut the top 1/4-inch off the tomato. Use a spoon to scoop out the insides of the tomato. Set aside while you make the tuna salad.
- Stir together the drained tuna, balsamic vinegar, mozzarella, basil, and green onion. Put the tuna salad in the hollowed out tomato, and enjoy!
- Note: I prefer using fresh mozzarella but any mozzarella is good in here.

Nutrition Info

Calories per serving: 196 kcal

Fat per serving: 4.9g

Dinner

Easy Tomato Feta Soup Recipe

Prep Time: 5 mins

Cook Time: 25 mins

Total Time: 30 mins

Servings: 6 servings

Ingredients

- 2 tablespoon olive oil or butter

- 1/4 cup chopped onion
- 2 cloves garlic
- 1/2 teaspoon salt
- 1/8 teaspoon black pepper
- 1 teaspoon pesto sauce — optional
- 1/2 teaspoon dried oregano
- 1 teaspoon dried basil
- 1 tablespoon tomato paste — optional
- 10 tomatoes, skinned, seeded and chopped — or two 14.5 oz cans of peeled tomatoes
- 1 teaspoon honey, sugar or erythritol — optional
- 3 cups water
- 1/3 cup heavy cream
- 2/3 cup feta cheese — crumbled

Instructions

- Heat olive oil (butter) over medium heat in a large pot (Dutch Oven). Add the onion and cook for 2 minutes, stirring frequently. Add the garlic and cook for 1 minute. Add tomatoes, salt, pepper, pesto (optional), oregano, basil, tomato paste and water. Bring to a boil, then reduce to a simmer. Add sweetener.

- Cook on medium heat for 20 minutes, until the tomatoes are tender and cooker. Using an immersion blender, blend until smooth. Add the cream and feta cheese. Cook for 1 more minute.

- Add more salt if needed. Serve warm.

Nutrition Info

Calories: 170, Fat: 13g, Saturated Fat: 8g, Cholesterol: 43mg, Protein: 4g

Day: 18

Breakfast

Jalapeño Popper Egg Cups

Prep Time: 15 mins

Total Time: 35 mins

Servingss: 4 – 6 servings

Ingredients

- 12 slices bacon
- 10 large eggs
- 1/4 cup sour cream
- 1/2 cup shredded Cheddar

- 1/2 cup shredded mozzarella
- 2 jalapeños, 1 minced and 1 thinly sliced
- 1 teaspoon garlic powder
- kosher salt
- Freshly ground black pepper
- nonstick cooking spray

Instructions

- Preheat oven to 375°.

- In a large skillet over medium heat, cook bacon until slightly browned but still pliable. Set aside on a paper towel-lined plate to drain.

- In a large bowl, whisk together eggs, sour cream, cheeses, minced jalapeño and garlic powder. Season with salt and pepper.

- Using nonstick cooking spray, grease a muffin tin. Line each well with one slice of bacon, then pour egg mixture into each muffin cup until about two-thirds of the way to the top. Top each muffin with a jalapeño slice.

- Bake for 20 minutes, or until the eggs no longer look wet. Cool slightly before removing from the muffin tin. Serve.

Nutrition Info

Calories: 230kcal

Lunch

Keto Chicken Enchilada Bowl

This Keto Chicken Enchilada Bowl is a low carb twist on a Mexican favorite!

Prep Time: 20 minutes
Cook Time: 30 minutes
Total Time: 50 minutes

Serving: 4 servings

Ingredients

- 2 tablespoons coconut oil (for searing chicken)
- 1 pound of boneless, skinless chicken thighs
- 3/4 cup red enchilada sauce (recipe from Low Carb Maven)
- 1/4 cup water
- 1/4 cup chopped onion
- 4 oz can diced green chiles

Toppings (feel free to customize)

- 1 whole avocado, diced
- 1 cup shredded cheese (I used mild cheddar)
- 1/4 cup chopped pickled jalapenos
- 1/2 cup sour cream
- 1 roma tomato, chopped

Instructions

- In a pot or dutch oven over medium heat melt the coconut oil. Once hot, sear chicken thighs until lightly brown.

- Pour in enchilada sauce and water then add onion and green chiles. Reduce heat to a simmer and cover. Cook chicken for 17-25 minutes or until chicken is tender and fully cooked through to at least 165 degrees internal temperature.

- Careully remove the chicken and place onto a work surface. Chop or shred chicken (your preference) then add it back into the pot. Let the chicken simmer uncovered for an additional 10 minutes to absorb flavor and allow the sauce to reduce a little.

- To Serve, top with avocado, cheese, jalapeno, sour cream, tomato, and any other desired toppings. Feel free to customize these to your preference. Serve alone or over cauliflower rice if desired just be sure to update your personal nutrition info as needed.

Nutrition Info

Calories: 568 Calories
Total Carbs: 10.41g
Fiber: 4.27g
Net Carbs: 6.14g

Protein: 38.38g

Fat: 40.21g

Dinner

Chili Dog Casserole Recipe

Prep Time: 15 minutes

Cook Time: 45 - 50 minutes

Servings: 8 servings

Ingredients

- 8 all-beef hotdogs (sliced in half lengthwise)
- 1 pound ground beef (80% lean)

- 1 small red pepper (diced)
- 1 small yellow onion (diced)
- 2 cloves minced garlic
- 1 cup low carb tomato sauce
- 1 cup water
- 2 tablespoons tomato paste
- 1 teaspoon Worcestershire sauce
- 1 tablespoon chili powder
- 1 teaspoon ground cumin
- 1/2 teaspoon celery salt
- 1 cup shredded cheddar cheese
- salt and pepper

Instructions

- Preheat the oven to 400°F and lightly grease a 7x9-inch glass baking dish with cooking spray.
- Line the bottom of the baking dish with hotdogs then set aside.
- Combine the ground beef, peppers, onions, and garlic in a large skillet over medium-high heat.
- Cook until the beef is browned, breaking it up into chunks with a wooden spoon.

- Stir in the tomato sauce, water, tomato paste, Worcestershire sauce, and seasonings.
- Bring to a boil then reduce heat and simmer on medium-low for 30 minutes.
- Spoon the chili over the hotdogs and sprinkle with cheese.
- Bake for 15 to 20 minutes until the cheese is hot and bubbling.
- Rest for 10 minutes before serving.

Nutrition Info

365 Calories

27g of Fat

24.5g of Protein

4.5g of Net Carbs

Day: 19

Breakfast

Avocado Egg Boats

Prep Time: 10 mins
Total Time: 30 mins

Ingredients

- 2 ripe avocados, pitted and halved
- 4 large eggs
- kosher salt
- Freshly ground black pepper

- 3 slices bacon
- Freshly chopped chives, for garnish

Instructions

- Preheat oven to 350°. Place avocados in a baking dish, then crack eggs into a bowl. Using a spoon, transfer yolks to each avocado half, then spoon in as much egg white as you can fit without spilling over.
- Season with salt and pepper and bake until whites are set and yolks are no longer runny, about 20 minutes. (Cover with foil if avocados are beginning to brown.)
- Meanwhile, in a large skillet over medium heat, cook bacon until crisp, 8 minutes, then transfer to a paper towel-lined plate and chop.
- Top avocados with bacon and chives and serve with a spoon.

Lunch

Roasted Chicken Stacks

Prep Time: 10 minutes

Cook Time: 40 minutes

Total Time: 50 minutes

Servings: 5 servings

Ingredients

- 5 small chicken breasts or chicken breast cutlets
- 1 head of savoy cabbage
- 5 slices of prosciutto
- 3 tablespoon coconut flour
- 2 teaspoon salt, more to taste
- 1 teaspoon black pepper
- 2 teaspoon Italian herb blend
- 1/2 cup bone broth

- 1/4 cup avocado oil

Instructions

- Pre-heat oven to 400F.
- Combine the chicken breast, salt, pepper, herbs and coconut flour in a gallon sized plastic bag. Shake to evenly coat the chicken, yes, like shake and bake!
- Drizzle a tbsp. of the oil on the sheet pan.
- Shred the savoy cabbage and make 5 little piles of shredded cabbage on the sheet pan. Sprinkle with a little salt. Drizzle a little oil on them. Place a coated chicken breast over each one. Lastly, top each chicken piece with a slice of prosciutto. Drizzle with remaining oil.
- Roast at 400F for 30 minutes
- Pour the broth into the sheet pan. Roast for another 10 minutes.
- Remove from the oven and serve hot.
- Use a spatula to scoop up one stack at a time.

Nutrition Info

Calories: 369 kcal

Fat: 24.8g

Carbohydrates: 5.8g

Protein: 33.7g

Dinner

Easy Stir Fry Kimchi & Pork Belly

Stir fry kimchi and bork belly is so simple to make yet out of this world satisfying! Dinner under 30 minutes, and Keto friendly.

Prep Time: 5 mins

Cook Time: 15 mins

Marinating Time: 10 mins

Total Time: 25 mins

Servings: 3 servings

Ingredients

- 300 g naturally-raised pork belly
- 1 tablespoon naturally-brewed tamari or soy sauce (gluten-free option: use tamari or gluten-free soy sauce)
- 1 tablespoon naturally-brewed rice wine
- 1 lb kimchi (see notes below)
- 1 stalk green onion
- 1 tablespoon sesame seeds (optional)

Instructions

- Slice the pork belly as thin as possible. Marinate in tamari/soy sauce and rice wine for about 10 minutes. If your kimchi isn't pre-cut, then cut into 1 inch size.

- Heat a heavy bottom pan (I use cast iron). While the pan is very hot, add the marinated pork belly, stir fry until nicely browned, for approximately 5 to 10 minutes. You should see some fat being cooked out of the pork belly at this point.

- Add the kimchi into the pan, stir fry for another 2 minutes, for the flavour of kimchi and pork to completely mix.

- Turn off the heat. Thinly slice the green onion, and add to the stir fry.

- If available, sprinkle sesame seeds on top as garnish.

Nutrition Info

Calories: 804 kcal

Day: 20

Breakfast

Keto mushroom omelet

Looking for a quick and easy way to start your day? This hearty omelet is super healthy, and just takes a few minutes to make! Fresh mushrooms make a delicious filling. Enjoy this keto meal anytime

Prep Time: 5 mins
Total Tine: 10 mins

Ingredients

- 3 eggs
- 1 oz. butter, for frying
- 1 oz. shredded cheese
- 1/5 yellow onion
- 3 mushrooms
- salt and pepper

Instructions

- Crack the eggs into a mixing bowl with a pinch of salt and pepper. Whisk the eggs with a fork until smooth and frothy.
- Add salt and spices to taste.
- Melt butter in a frying pan. Once the butter has melted, pour in the egg mixture.
- When the omelet begins to cook and get firm, but still has a little raw egg on top, sprinkle cheese, mushrooms and onion on top (optional).
- Using a spatula, carefully ease around the edges of the omelet, and then fold it over in half. When it starts to turn golden brown underneath, remove the pan from the heat and slide the omelet on to a plate.

Tip!

Serve the omelet with a crispy, green salad with vinaigrette dressing on the side. Yum!

Nutrition Info

Calories: 510kcal

Lunch

Sesame Salmon With Baby Bok Choy & Mushrooms

Ingredients

Main Dish

- 4 each 4-6 oz. salmon fillet
- 2 each portobello mushroom caps (or 8 oz. baby bella mushrooms)
- 4 each baby bok choy
- 1 tablespoon toasted sesame seeds
- 1 each green onion

Marinade

- 1 tablespoon olive oil
- 1 teaspoon sesame oil
- 1 tablespoon Coconut Aminos
- 1/2 inch Ginger grated (approx. 1 tsp.)
- 1/2 lemon juice
- 1/2 teaspoon Salt
- 1/2 teaspoon black pepper

Instructions

- Whisk together all of your marinade ingredients

- Drizzle half of the marinade on the salmon and turn to coat. Cover and refrigerate the salmon while it marinates for one hour.
- Preheat oven to 400.
- Prepare vegetables: Trim the rough ends from the bok choy and cut into halves. Slice the mushrooms into ½ inch pieces.
- Drizzle the remaining marinade over the vegetables and lay on a lined baking sheet.
- Place salmon, skin side down, on a lined baking sheet as well. Bake until salmon is cooked through, about 20 minutes.
- Top with sliced green onions and sesame seeds.

Dinner

Keto Chicken Pot Pie

Cook Time 22 mins

Servings: 8 servings

Ingredients

For the Chicken Pot Pie Filling:

- 2 tablespoons of butter

- 1/2 cup mixed veggies could also substitute green beans or broccoli
- 1/4 small onion diced
- 1/4 teaspoon pink salt
- 1/4 teaspoon pepper
- 2 garlic cloves minced
- 3/4 cup heavy whipping cream
- 1 cup chicken broth
- 1 teaspoon poultry seasoning
- 1/4 teaspoon rosemary
- pinch thyme
- 2 1/2 cups cooked chicken diced
- 1/4 teaspoon Xanthan Gum

For the crust:

- 4 1/2 tablespoons of butter melted and cooled
- 1/3 cup coconut flour
- 2 tablespoons full fat sour cream
- 4 eggs
- 1/4 teaspoon salt
- 1/4 teaspoon baking powder
- 1 1/3 cup sharp shredded cheddar cheese or mozzarella shredded

Instructions

- Cook 1 to 1 1/2 lbs chicken in the slow cooker for 3 hours on high or 6 hours on low.
- Preheat oven to 400 degrees.
- Sautee onion, mixed veggies, garlic cloves, salt, and pepper in 2 tablespoons butter in an oven safe skillet for approx 5 min or until onions are translucent.
- Add heavy whipping cream, chicken broth, poultry seasoning, thyme, and rosemary.
- Sprinkle Xanthan Gum on top and simmer for 5 minutes so that the sauce thickens. Make sure to simmer covered as the liquid will evaporate otherwise. You need a lot of liquid for this recipe, otherwise, it will be dry.
- Add diced chicken.
- Make the breading by combining melted butter (I cool mine by popping the bowl in the fridge for 5 min), eggs, salt, and sour cream in a bowl then whisk together.
- Add coconut flour and baking powder to the mixture and stir until combined.
- Stir in cheese.

- Drop batter by dollops on top of the chicken pot pie. Do not spread it out, as the coconut flour will absorb too much of the liquid.
- Bake in a 400-degree oven for 15-20 min.
- Set oven to broil and move chicken pot pie to top shelf. Broil for 1-2 minutes until bread topping is nicely browned.

Nutrition Info

Calories: 297kcal

Carbohydrates: 5.3g

Protein: 11.6g

Fat: 17g

Fiber: 2g

Day: 21

Breakfast

Keto Fat Bombs

Prep Time: 5 mins

Total Time: 25 mins

Servingss: 8 servings

Ingredients

- 8 oz. cream cheese, softened to room temperature
- 1/2 cup keto-friendly peanut butter
- 1/4 cup coconut oil
- 1/2 teaspoon kosher salt
- 1 cup keto-friendly dark chocolate chips (such as Lily's)

Instructions

- Line a small baking sheet with parchment paper. In a medium bowl, combine cream cheese, peanut butter, ¼ cup coconut oil, and salt. Using a hand mixer, beat mixture until fully combined, about 2 minutes. Place bowl in freezer to firm up slightly, 10 to 15 minutes.
- When peanut butter mixture has hardened, use a small cookie scoop or spoon to create golf ball sized balls. Place in the refrigerator to harden, 5 minutes.
- Meanwhile, make chocolate drizzle: combine chocolate chips and remaining coconut oil in a microwave safe bowl and microwave in 30 second intervals until fully melted. Drizzle over peanut butter balls and place back in the refrigerator to harden, 5 minutes. Serve.
- To store, keep covered in refrigerator.

Lunch

Portobello Bun Cheeseburgers

Prep Time: 5 minutes

Cook Time: 15 minutes

Total Time: 20 minutes

Servings: 6 servings

Ingredients

- 1 lb. grassfed 80/20 ground beef
- 1 tablespoon Worcestershire sauce
- 1 teaspoon pink Himalayan salt

- 1 teaspoon black pepper
- 1 tablespoon avocado oil
- 6 portobello mushroom caps, destemmed, rinsed and dabbed dry
- 6 slices sharp cheddar cheese

Instructions

- In a bowl, combine ground beef, Worcestershire sauce, salt, and pepper.
- Form beef into burger patties.
- In a large pan, heat avocado oil over medium heat. Add portobello mushroom caps and cook for about 3-4 minutes on each side. Remove from heat.
- In the same pan, cook burger patties for 4 minutes on one side and 5 minutes on the other side, or until desired doneness is achieved. Add cheese to top of burgers and cover with a lid and allow cheese to melt, about 1 minute.
- Layer one portobello mushroom cap, then cheeseburger, desired garnishes, and top with remaining portobello mushroom cap.
- Enjoy!

Optional garnishes

- Sliced dill pickles
- Romaine
- Sugar-free barbecue sauce
- Spicy brown mustard

Nutrition Info

Calories: 336 kcal

Fat: 22.8g

Carbohydrates: 5.8g (Net Carbs: 4)

Dinner

Spinach Artichoke Stuffed Chicken Breast Recipe

Prep Time: 15 minutes

Cook Time: 15 minutes

Total Time: 30 minutes

Servings: 6 servings

Ingredients

- 1 ½ lbs. chicken breasts 6 4-oz. portions
- 2 tablespoons olive oil
- 4 ounces cream cheese softened

- ¼ cup Greek yogurt
- ½ cup Mozzarella cheese shredded
- ½ cup artichoke hearts thinly sliced
- ¼ cup frozen spinach drained, and tightly packed
- ½ teaspoon salt divided
- ¼ teaspoon pepper divided

Instructions

- Pound chicken breast to 1-inch thick. Using a sharp knife cut each chicken breast down the middle, being careful not to cut all of the way through, to make a pocket for the spinach artichoke filling. Sprinkle chicken breasts with ¼ teaspoon salt and 1/8 teaspoon pepper.
- In a medium-sized bowl combine the cream cheese, Greek yogurt, Mozzarella cheese, artichoke hearts, drained spinach, ¼ teaspoon salt and 1/8 teaspoon pepper. Mix until thoroughly combined.
- Carefully fill each chicken breast with equal amounts of the spinach artichoke filling. If you have extra filling, set it aside until the chicken is almost done cooking.
- In a large skillet over medium heat add olive oil and stuffed chicken breasts. Cover skillet and cook for 7-8

minutes on each side, or until chicken reaches 165 degrees with a meat thermometer.

- During the last few minutes of cooking, add additional filling to the skillet to heat it up. Serve chicken with cauliflower rice, regular rice, mashed cauliflower, or mashed potatoes and enjoy!

Nutrition Info

Calories: 288 kcal
Calories from Fat: 153 kcal

CONCLUSION

Losing weight can be a daunting challenge. With so many diet options it's hard to know which one will work best for you. However, there are certain fundamentals step anyone can take to start losing weight today.

The ketogenic diet was first introduced in the 1920's as a means to control epilepsy in children.

In more recent times, the principles of the ketogenic diet have been adapted for a highly effective weight loss plan.

The ketogenic diet is high in fat, low in carbohydrates, and is designed to provide adequate protein and calories for a healthy weight.

The essential aim of the diet is to prompt the body to burn fat instead of carbohydrate, which has the effect of fast weight loss.

The high fat content can cause surprise and concern in a health conscious society which associates 'fat' with 'bad.'

However, good fats are healthy and necessary as part of a controlled and balanced diet.

High levels of carbohydrates, on the other hand, can cause a spike in blood sugar levels, which can lead to obesity and low energy levels.

Part of the appeal of the ketogenic diet is its success in achieving fast weight loss, so it is ideal for those with many pounds to shed.

The diet excludes high carbohydrate foods such as starchy fruits and vegetables, bread, pasta and sugar, while increasing high fat foods such as cream and butter.

A typical meal might include fish or chicken with green vegetables, followed by fruit with lots of cream. Breakfast might be bacon and eggs, a snack cheese with cucumber.

There are many variants of the diet which including more relaxed versions of the regime.

The initial few days of a ketogenic diet involves the body adapting to a different way of eating, which can prompt a feeling of 'withdrawal'. This is no surprise as modern western diet and foods are heavy in starch and sugar.

Following this adaptation period, however, those eating a ketogenic diet begin to enjoy many benefits. In addition to fast weight loss, there are increased energy levels.

The ketogenic diet can also be very enjoyable, with delicious fish, steaks, bacon, eggs and fruit with cream on the menu. Enjoyment of food is important if the diet is to prove sustainable.

INTRODUCTION

If you're interested in going on a keto diet but can't even fathom giving up bread, the good news is cravings usually subside and relying on things like bread becomes a thing of the past.

But that doesn't mean you need to give bread up 100%. Foods like bread can help with your transition and fill a craving when the mood hits (which is better than falling off completely). These keto bread recipes give you many different ways to enjoy bread on your low-carb diet when needed.

In this book, there are recipes that are dairy-free so you can enjoy a good bun now and then too.

What exactly is a ketogenic diet?

The keto diet is an eating plan that consists of 80 percent fat and little to no carbohydrates. Staples of the keto diet are fish, meat, eggs, dairy, oils, and green vegetables. Pasta, rice and other grains, potatoes, and fruits are strictly prohibited.

Keto works by changing the way the body turns food into energy. Typically, during digestion, we break down carbohydrates — like those found in the verboten foods above — into molecules of fructose, galactose, and glucose, the last of which serves as the body's primary source of energy. When the body can't draw it from carbohydrates — either because they've been cut out of the diet or because a person hasn't eaten for a long time — it looks for other forms of energy. The keto diet deliberately places the body in a state of ketosis, where fat is released from cells and turned into ketones, the body's plan B for energy production.

What is ketosis?

Ketosis occurs when your body has run out of its glycogen (basically sugar) stores so it needs to find another fuel source. When this occurs your liver begins to process fat into ketones which become your body's main fuel source.

So to recap fat -> ketones = energy.

With that quick summary out of the way let's explore the benefits of the ketogenic diet.

Where did the keto diet start?

The keto diet is most assuredly not a fad, at least not in the usual sense of the word. It's been around for nearly a century, and has its roots in the medical world: In the 1920s, epilepsy researchers found that increased levels of ketones in their patients resulted in fewer seizures, and the diet is still a widely accepted treatment for epilepsy today. There's also some evidence that a ketogenic diet has therapeutic potential for a wide array of symptoms and diseases, including cancer, polycystic ovary syndrome, neurological conditions, diabetes, and even acne.

Benefits of the keto diet

Keto changes the way your body fuels itself. When you limit carbs, your body starts to burn fat, rather than glucose, for energy. You go into ketosis — when your liver converts fatty acids into molecules called ketones, an alternative source of fuel. Learn more about keto and how it works with this beginner's guide. Burning ketones carries all kind of benefits:

Better Mental Focus

The problem with carbs as an energy source is that they cause your blood sugar levels to rise and fall. Because the energy source isn't consistent it's harder for your brain to stay focused for long periods of time.

When you're in ketosis and your brain uses ketones as a fuel source, it has a consistent fuel source that it can rely on which means you can focus for longer periods of time.

You also don't have a cloudy mind.

It's really hard to explain the feeling because when you're eating carbs you don't realize that your mind isn't at 100%. Once you're in ketosis you will begin to see the difference, especially if you spend a day or two eating carbs again.

The Keto Diet Boosts Weight Loss

When you're on keto, your body uses stored body fat and fat from your diet as fuel. The result? Rapid weight loss. Ketones also influence the hormones that control appetite. Ketones suppress ghrelin (your hunger hormone) and increase cholecystokinin (CCK), which tells your brain when you've eaten enough.

Reduced Cravings

Many people don't realize how much their lives revolve around their next meal. Sudden intense hunger pangs and mood changes are seen as common and normal in our society. In reality, these things are caused by chronic blood sugar instability signaling the brain that you are starving. This is where the sudden urge to eat NOW comes from.

If you find yourself getting hangry a lot, you likely are dealing with blood sugar instability.

Getting into a state of ketosis balances blood sugar, provides the brain with stable energy, and completely eliminates cravings. In fact, I often have people tell me that they barely think about food between meals anymore.

Abundant Energy

You have increased amounts of energy for several reasons when following a ketogenic diet.

- Lowered Inflammation
- Upregulation of Mitochondrial Biogenesis
- More ATP per Molecule of ketone vs glucose
- Stable Blood Sugar

Combined, these benefits drastically increase energy output in the body. Mitochondria are basically your energy factories. So, taken together you get less inflammation, more efficient energy production, AND more energy production factories that result in an overall increase in energetic potential of your body.

Reduced inflammation

One of the most basic and most profound benefits of a ketogenic diet is that it drastically lowers inflammation. This is mainly due to the reduced amount of free radical production that occurs when burning ketones for energy instead of glucose. Less inflammation allows for more energy production and an overall more efficiently functioning body. This allows for a heightened ability of the body to heal in many different aspects.

Another reason that a ketogenic diet is so anti-inflammatory is that it allows blood sugar and insulin to stabilize. Blood sugar imbalance is one of the most pervasive inflammatory activities that goes on in the bodies of people who are heavily relying on sugar for energy.

Because of this anti-inflammatory benefit, a ketogenic diet may be well suited for improving cancer outcomes, autoimmunity, neurological disorders, and metabolic disorders alike.

Clearer Skin

Skin conditions like eczema, acne, and psoriasis are often rooted in chronic inflammation or autoimmunity. Often, inflammatory processes unnecessarily attack different structures of the skin which results in various conditions. For example, acne is associated with inflammation of the sebaceous glands in the skin whereas eczema is generalized inflammation of the skin cells.

Things like chemical exposure, environmental allergies, chronic stress, hormone imbalance, and imbalances in gut bacteria can all contribute to these skin conditions. While the factors should also be addressed, following a ketogenic diet can also help to quickly lower inflammation and accelerate healing.

Appettite Control

An amazing thing happens when your diet isn't carb heavy. You find that you're not as hungry as often and you don't end up with random cravings that cause you to eat bad things.

Many people that go on keto are able to do intermittent fasting where they only eat during a set period of the day. This is possible because your stomach isn't rumbling around telling you that you need to eat a donut.

What happens when you aren't consistently looking for things to eat?

Improved Fat Burning

By definition, being in a state of ketosis means you are burning fat for energy. If you have excess body fat, you will be able to burn it at a much more efficient rate.

In fact, there are several recent studies showing that a high-fat, low-carb diet is superior to a low-fat, high-carb diet for improving weight loss and improving lipid profiles.

Being overweight is considered a risk factor for several diseases. Additionally, having excess body fat (particularly in the gut) is associated with hormone imbalances and toxin accumulation in the body.

Keto Bread Recipes

1. Low Carb Carrot Cake Muffins

This low carb carrot cake muffins are great for snacking! Sugar free, gluten free, and keto recipe.

Prep Time: 10 minutes

Cook Time: 25 minutes

Cooling Time: 5 minutes

Total Time: 35 minutes

Servings: 6

Ingredients

- 1 carrot peeled and grated
- 1 cup almond flour
- 3 eggs
- ¼ cup melted butter
- 2 tbs low carb sweetener eg Swerve
- ½ tsp baking powder
- ½ tsp vanilla extract

Instructions

- Preheat the oven to 350F (175C).

- In a stand mixer bowl, add almond flour, eggs, melted butter, sweetener, baking powder and vanilla extract. Blend until fully combined.
- Stir in the grated carrot until mixed through the batter.
- Divide the mixture between a six-hole muffin pan that has been lined with paper or silicone liners.
- Bake in a preheated oven for 20-25 minutes or until cooked through. Let cool for 5 minutes before serving.

Nutrition Info

Calories 210 Calories from Fat 171

Total Fat 19g 29%

Saturated Fat 6g 30%

Cholesterol 102mg 34%

Sodium 105mg 4%

Potassium 102mg 3%

Total Carbohydrates 5g 2%

Dietary Fiber 2g 8%

Sugars 1g

Protein 6g 12%

2. Cheesy Skillet Bread

Easy low carb skillet bread with a wonderful crust of cheddar cheese. This keto bread recipe is perfect with soups and stews.

Prep Time 10 mins

Cook Time 16 mins

Total Time 26 mins

Servings: 10

Ingredients

- 1 tbsp butter for the skillet
- 2 cups almond flour
- 1/2 cup flax seed meal
- 2 tsp baking powder
- 1/2 tsp salt
- 1 & 1/2 cups shredded Cheddar cheese divided
- 3 large eggs lightly beaen
- 1/2 cup butter melted
- 3/4 cup almond milk

Instructions

- Preheat oven to 425F. Add 1 tbsp butter to a 10-inch oven-proof skillet and place in oven.
- In a large bowl, whisk together almond flour, flax seed meal, baking powder, salt and 1 cup of the shredded cheddar cheese.
- Stir in the eggs, melted butter and almond milk until thoroughly combined.
- Remove hot skillet from oven (remember to put on your oven mitts), and swirl butter to coat sides.
- Pour batter into pan and smooth the top. Sprinkle with remaining 1/2 cup cheddar.

- Bake 16 to 20 minutes, or until browned around the edges and set through the middle. Cheese on top should be nicely browned.
- Remove and let cool 15 minutes.

Nutrition Info

Calories 357 Calories from Fat 276

Total Fat 30.63g 47%

Total Carbohydrates 7.9g 3%

Dietary Fiber 4.77g 19%

Protein 12.48g 25%

3. 1-Minute Keto Muffins

The perfect quick keto bread is this 1-minute keto muffin. Grain free little snacks that can be made both sweet OR savoury depending on which flavours you decide to add.

Prep/Cook Time: 2 mins, Servings:4

Ingredients

- 1 egg
- 2 tsp coconut flour or more depending on brand used
- pinch baking soda
- pinch salt

Instructions

- Grease a ramekin dish (or very large coffee mug) with coconut oil or butter.
- Mix all the ingredients together with a fork to ensure it is lump free.
- Cook the 1-minute keto muffin in the microwave on HIGH for 45 seconds - 1 minute. Alternatively, they can be baked in an oven, at 200C/400F for 12 minutes.
- Cut in half and serve. (toasting or frying is optional)

Nutrition Info

Calories 113 Calories from Fat 54

Total Fat 6g 9%

Saturated Fat 2g 10%

Cholesterol 186mg 62%

Total Carbohydrates 5g 2%

Dietary Fiber 3g 12%

Protein 7g

4.   Low Carb Asparagus Egg Bites

These Asparagus Egg Bites make the perfect snack - especially on the go! Low carb, keto, and gluten free recipe.

Prep Time: 5 minutes

Cook Time: 15 minutes

Total Time: 20 minutes

Servings: 3

Ingredients

- non-stick cooking spray
- 3 medium asparagus stalks
- 6 eggs

- 1 tbs unsweetened almond milk

- salt and pepper

- 2 tbs grated Parmesan

Instructions

- Preheat the oven to 400F (200C).

- Prepare a six-hole muffin pan by spraying it liberally with some non-stick cooking spray. Chop up the asparagus (to make about half a cup) and divide between the muffin pan cups.

- Beat the eggs and unsweetened almond milk together in a jug. Season with salt and pepper then divide it between the muffin cups.

- Sprinkle some grated Parmesan over the top of each one, then bake in a preheated oven for 12-15 minutes, until golden brown on top and the egg is cooked through. They will puff up while cooking but deflate slightly as they cool.

- Remove the asparagus egg bites from the pan and enjoy warm - or let cool fully and store in the fridge.

Nutrition Info

Calories 143 Calories from Fat 81

Total Fat 9g 14%

Saturated Fat 3g 15%

Trans Fat 0g

Sodium 178mg 7%

Potassium 153mg 4%

Total Carbohydrates 1g 0%

Dietary Fiber 0g 0%

Sugars 0g

Protein 12g 24%

5. Low Carb Hot Cross Buns

Low-carb hot cross buns are perfect any time of the year. To ensure they bake evenly, ensure they are not too big and not too thick.

Prep Time15 mins

Cook Time20 mins

Total Time35 mins

Servings:4

Ingredients

Low Carb Hot Cross Buns

- 60 g coconut flour
- 30 g psyllium husks

- 1 tsp baking powder
- 2 tbsp granulated sweetener of choice or more, to your taste
- 1/2 tsp salt
- 1/2 tsp mixed spice
- 1/2 tsp cinnamon
- 1/2 tsp ground cloves
- 4 eggs - medium
- 250 ml boiling water
- raisins/chocolate chips/ cacao nibs optional

Icing

- powdered sweetener icing mix

Instructions

Low Carb Hot Cross Buns

- Mix all the dry ingredients in a mixing bowl.
- Add the eggs and mix.
- Add the boiling water and mix until evenly combined.
- Roll into 8 equal balls and place on a baking tray.

- Bake in a fan assisted oven at 180C/350F for 20-30 minutes until golden on the outside and cooked in the centre.

Icing

- Mark each hot cross bun with a cross using the powdered sweetener confectioners/icing mix and water paste.

Nutrition Info

Calories 84 Calories from Fat 28

Total Fat 3.1g 5%

Total Carbohydrates 8.9g 3%

Dietary Fiber 6.8g 27%

Sugars 0.7g

Protein 5.6g 11%

6. Fat Head Pizza Crust

Prep/Cook Time: 30 mins, Servings: 8

Ingredients

- 1 1/2 cups shredded mozzarella
- 3/4 cup almond flour
- 2 tablespoons of cream cheese, cubed
- 1 egg
- garlic powder, onion powder, and mixed herbs for seasoning *see notes

Instructions

- Put Mozzarella and cream cheese in a medium bowl
- Microwave for 1 min, stir and then another 30 sec, stir
- Stir in egg and almond flour
- Wet hands and spread "dough" thin on parchment paper. It should spread evenly with dough-like consistency.
- Poke rows of holes with a fork to avoid bubbles.
- Put in 425-degree oven
- After 8 minutes check the crust and poke holes if there are bubbles.
- Add desired pizza toppings.
- Continue cooking for a total of 12 to 14 minutes or until slightly brown and golden.

Nutrition Info

Serving Size: 1 slice

Calories: 143

Sugar: 1g

Sodium: 346mg

Fat: 12g

Carbohydrates: 2g

Fiber: 1g

Protein: 9g

7. AIP Bread Rolls Recipe

Prep/Cook Time: 60 minutes, Servings: 2 servings

Ingredients

- 2 Tablespoons coconut oil, melted
- 6 Tablespoons coconut flour
- 1/4 teaspoon baking soda
- 1 Tablespoon Italian seasoning
- 1/2 teaspoon salt
- 2 Tablespoons gelatin
- 6 Tablespoons hot water

Instructions

- Preheat the oven to 300 F (150 C).

- Mix together the coconut oil, coconut flour, and baking soda.
- In a separate bowl, whisk together the gelatin and hot water to create your gelatin egg.
- Pour the gelatin egg into the coconut flour mixture and combine well.
- Add in the Italian seasoning and salt to taste (you can taste the mixture to see if you want to add more) and mix well into a dough.
- Use your hands to form 2 small rolls from the dough, place the rolls on a baking tray lined with parchment paper, and bake in the oven for 40-50 minutes until the outside of each roll is slightly browned and crispy like you'd typically find in a regular bread roll.
- Let the rolls cool down before serving so that the gelatin sets a bit and can hold the roll together. Enjoy at room temperature with some ghee or coconut oil.
- This recipe can be doubled, tripled, etc. if you want to make more AIP bread rolls at the same time.

Nutrition Info

Calories: 200 Sugar: 2 g Fat: 16 g, Carbohydrates: 11 g, Fiber: 7 g, Protein: 3 g

8. Keto Chicken Sandwich Recipe with Toasted Italian Grain-Free Bread [Paleo, Keto]

Prep/Cook Time: 30 minutes, Servings: 2

Ingredients

For the chicken

- 1 chicken breast (200 g), sliced into thin pieces
- 1 egg, whisked
- 1 teaspoon (3 g) garlic powder
- 1/4 teaspoon (.5 g) paprika
- Dash of salt and pepper

- Avocado oil or olive oil to fry chicken in

For the Italian Grain-Free Bread

- 1/3 cup (35 g) almond flour
- 1/2 Tablespoon (1g) Italian seasoning
- 1/4 teaspoon (1 g) garlic powder
- 1/2 teaspoon (1 g) baking powder
- 1/8 teaspoon (1 g) salt
- 1 egg, whisked
- 2 and 1/2 tablespoons (37 ml) ghee (or butter if you tolerate it, coconut oil, or olive oil), melted

For serving with

- Mustard, Paleo mayo, and romaine lettuce

Instructions

- Preheat oven to 400 F (205 C).
- Place all the bread ingredients into a mug and mix well.
- Place the mug into the microwave and microwave on high for 90 seconds.

- Let the bread cool for a few minutes and then pop out of the mug and slice into 4 slices.
- Place the slices onto a baking tray and toast in the oven for 4 minutes.
- Meanwhile, slice the chicken breast into thin slices approximately the size of the mug (so that the chicken pieces won't hang out of the bread too much).
- Make the coating for the chicken pieces by mixing together the egg, garlic powder, paprika, salt and pepper.
- Place 2 tablespoons of olive oil into a frying pan. Dip each piece of chicken into the egg mixture and then place into the frying pan. Fry on medium heat until the outside of the chicken turns golden and then chicken is completely cooked. Place the chicken pieces on a plate.
- Put the sandwiches together by spreading some mustard and mayo onto 1 slice of bread, adding some lettuce leaves, and then putting a slice of chicken on top. Eat as an open-faced sandwich or place another slice of toasted Italian grain-free bread on top.

Nutrition Info

Calories: 714 Sugar: 1 g Fat: 65 g Carbohydrates: 4 g Fiber: 2 g Protein: 33 g

9. Monkey Bread

Prep/Cook Time: 1 hour, 30 mins

Ingredients

DOUGH:

- 3 cup blanched almond flour (10 oz) (or 1 cup coconut flour or 5 oz)
- 10 TBS psyllium husk powder (no substitutes) (90 grams)
- 4 tsp baking powder

- 2 tsp Celtic sea salt
- 1 cup Swerve (or erythritol and 1 tsp stevia glycerite)
- 8 egg whites (16 whites if using coconut flour)
- 5 TBS apple cider vinegar (2 oz)
- 2 cup BOILING water (14 oz)

FILLING:

- 8 oz cream cheese

TOPPING:

- 8 TBS butter (or coconut oil)
- 1 TBS cinnamon
- 1/2 cup Swerve (or erythritol)

Instructions

- Preheat the oven to 375 degrees F. In a large bowl, combine the flour, psyllium powder (no substitutes: flaxseed meal won't work), baking powder, salt and sweetener. Mix until combined. Add in the eggs and vinegar and combine until a thick dough. Add boiling water into the bowl. Mix until well combined. When you add the water the dough will be very sticky but after mixing for a couple minutes it will firm up.

- Separate dough into 20 equal sized disks. You can spray some more spray on top of the dough to help keep it from sticking to your fingers. Cut cream cheese into 20 squares. Place on square on top of each dough disk and form the disk around the sides of the cream cheese.
- monkey bread

- Place 10 of the squares in the bottom of a greased bundt pan with the cream cheese facing up. Sprinkle cinnamon and Swerve on top. Then put the remaining 10 squares inverted on top of the first 10 (making the cream cheese touch). Bake for 55 minutes.

Meanwhile, make the topping.

- Place all ingredients into a medium sized bowl and combine until smooth. After it has baked for 55 minutes, remove and quickly spread topping over the monkey bread. Return to oven and bake for 15 minute. Allow to cool for 20-30 minutes before turning over and removing from bundt pan. Makes 14 servings.

- monkey bread

Nutrition Info

308 calories, 21.1g fat, 2.9g protein, 28.9 carbs, trace fiber (28.9g effective carbs)

10. Easy Keto Almond Coconut Bread Recipe

Prep/Cook Time: 40 minutes, Servings: 12 servings

Ingredients

- 1/2 cup (120 ml) ghee, melted
- 6 eggs, whisked
- 3/4 cup (90 g) almond flour
- 1/4 cup (28 g) coconut flour
- 2 Tablespoons (14 g) flax meal
- 1 teaspoon (2 g) baking powder

- Dash of salt

Instructions

- Preheat oven to 350 F (175 C).
- Mix all the ingredients together well in a mixing bowl and pour into a greased 9-by-5 inch baking pan.
- Bake for 35-40 minutes until a cocktail stick comes out clean.

Nutrition Info

Calories: 159 Sugar: 0 g Fat: 15 g Carbohydrates: 3 g Fiber: 2 g Protein: 5 g

11. Keto Avocado Chocolate Bread Recipe

Prep/Cook Time: 50 minutes, Servings: 8 servings

Ingredients

- 2 ripe avocados, mashed
- 3 Tablespoons (45 ml) coconut oil
- 3 eggs, whisked
- 2 cups (240 g) almond flour
- 1/2 cup (48 g) cacao powder
- 1 teaspoon (4 g) baking soda
- 1/2 teaspoon (1 g) baking powder

- 1 teaspoon (5 ml) vanilla extract
- Stevia, to taste
- Dash of salt

Instructions

- Preheat oven to 350 F (175 C).
- Mix everything together.
- Place into a loaf pan.
- Bake for 40-45 minutes until a toothpick comes out clean.

Nutrition Info

Calories: 309 Sugar: 1 g Fat: 26 g Carbohydrates: 13 g Fiber: 8 g Protein: 10 g

12. Keto-Adapted Bread

Prep/Cook Time 40 mins, Serves: 18

Ingredients

- 12 eggs, separated
- ½cup Jay Robb unflavored egg white protein (or ¾ to 1 cup whey protein)
- ½ tsp onion powder (optional)

Instructions

- Preheat the oven to 325 degrees F.

- Separate the eggs (save the yolks), and whip the whites for a few minutes until VERY stiff (I use a stand mixer on high for a few minutes).
- Gently mix the protein powder into the whites.
- Slowly fold the reserved egg yolks into the whites (making sure the whites don't fall).
- Grease a bread pan with coconut oil spray and fill with "dough."
- Bake for 25-30 minutes or until golden brown.
- Let completely cool before cutting or the bread will fall. Cut into slices.
- I keep this bread in the freezer at all times to make sandwiches.
- OPTION: Make bread into 18 buns on a greased cookie sheet.
- NOTE: If having trouble with it falling after cooking, try 400 degrees for an hour. Some protein powders require longer.

Nutrition Info

80 calories, 2g fat, 2g protein, 24.5g carbs, 1g fiber

13. Lemon Poppy Seed Loaf Cake

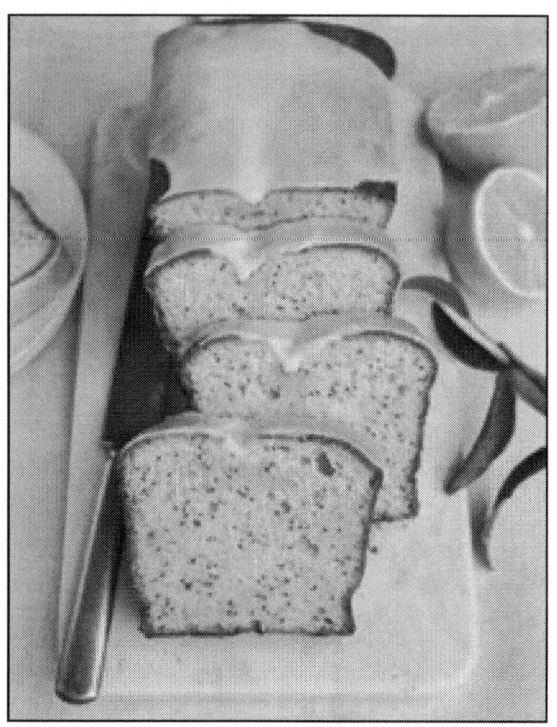

This Lemon Poppy Seed Loaf Cake is perfect for breakfast or dessert with some fresh berries or a smear of butter. It is low carb, keto, trim healthy mama friendly, gluten grain and sugar-free. It whips up in minutes and stores well for a week! All in all, it is a great healthy choice for your lemon poppy seed craving!

Prep Time 10 mins
Cook Time 1 hr

Total Time 1 hr 10 mins

Servings: 12

Ingredients

- 2/3 cup cottage cheese
- 4 tbsp butter softened
- 1/2 cup Trim Healthy Mama Gentle Sweet or my sweetener
- 4 eggs
- 3 tbsp lemon juice
- 1 1/2 cup almond flour
- 1/2 cup coconut flour
- 2 tsp baking powder
- 1 tsp lemon zest
- 2 tbsp poppy seeds

Instructions

- Preheat oven to 350. Grease a standard loaf pan well with cooking spray.

- Combine the cottage cheese, butter, and sweetener in the food processor. Pulse until smooth. Add the eggs, lemon juice, flours, baking powder, and zest. Pulse until well combined. Add the poppy seeds and pulse until they are evenly distributed in the batter. Transfer the batter to the prepared loaf pan.

- Bake for 55-65 min or until the center feels firm when lightly pressed and the edges are deep golden brown.
- Cool completely to make it easier to remove from the pan. Alternatively, you can line the loaf pan with parchment paper.

Recipe Notes

If you would like to make a glaze for your lemon poppy seed loaf simply mix together a powdered sweetener with lemon juice.

Nutrition Info

Calories 176 Calories from Fat 117

Total Fat 13g 20%

Saturated Fat 4g 20%

Cholesterol 66mg 22%

Sodium 108mg 5%

Potassium 130mg 4%

Total Carbohydrates 7g 2%

Dietary Fiber 3g 12%

Sugars 1g

Protein 7g 14%

14. Rosemary Keto Bagels

Prep/Cook Time: 55 minutes (10 minutes active)

Serves: 4

Ingredients:

- 1 1/2 cups almond flour
- 3/4 teaspoon baking soda
- 3/4 teaspoon xanthan gum
- 1/4 teaspoon salt
- 3 tablespoons psyllium husk powder
- 1 whole egg
- 3 egg whites
- 1/2 cup warm water

- 1 tablespoon rosemary, chopped
- Avocado oil

Instructions:

- Preheat oven to 250F.
- Mix almond flour, xanthan gum, baking soda and salt together in a bowl.
- In a separate bowl, whisk eggs and warm water together. Stir in psyllium husk until there are no clumps.
- Add liquid ingredients to dry ingredients.
- Coat bagel mold with avocado oil.
- Press dough into mold.
- Sprinkle rosemary on top.
- Place in oven and bake for 45 minutes.
- Remove and cool for 15 minutes before slicing.

Nutrition Info

Calories: 285

Protein: 13g

Carbs: 12g

Fiber: 7.5g

Net Carbs: 4.5g

Sugar: 1.75g

Fat: 22.5g

Saturated Fat: 2g

15. Keto Low Carb Mug Bread

A quick an easy bread to make that is keto and low carb friendly

Prep Time 2 mins

Cook Time 2 mins

Total Time 4 mins

Servings: 1mug

Ingredients

- Low carb flour alternative Carbalose- 2 tablespoons . OR 1 tablespoon of coconut flour plus 1 tablespoon of almond flour or other alternative flour is suggested.
- Baking powder- 1/2 teaspoon.
- Egg- 1.
- Oil- such as olive oil- 1 tablespoon.
- Seasonings- as desired.
- Optional- grated cheese- 1 tablespoon.

Instructions

- Using a microwave-safe mug and a fork, mix together your flours and baking powder. You can spray your mug for nonstick before adding the dry ingredients if desired.
- In a small bowl, whisk together the remaining ingredients (egg etc).
- Pour the wisked ingredients from the bowl into the mug and lightly blend together using your fork. Avoid lumps without over mixing. A good idea would be to tap the mug on the bottom to help the batter settle into the empty areas of the mug before baking. Mix enough so that you can get a 'bread in a cup' rather than an 'egg in a cup'.

- Microwave on high for 30 seconds. Rotate the mug and then microwave for another 45 seconds- 1 minute or until the bread seems baked to the eye.
- Carefully remove the mug from the microwave and turn it upside down on a plate or cutting board. The bread should slip out easily. However, you may need to give a quick tap to help it out.
- Slice the bread to your desired thickness.

16. Keto Fiber Bread Rolls Recipe

Perfectly made those Low Carb and Keto Fiber Bread Rolls Recipe are extremely delicious and irresistible to make. One look at them will convince you to try and make them right this moment.

Prep Time 10 minutes

Cook Time 40 minutes

Total Time 50 minutes

Serving: 11 Serving Size: 1

Ingredients

- 150g (1.5 Cups) Almond Flour
- 30g (1/4 Cup) Protein
- 1 Pkt (16g)(4tsp) Baking Powder
- 75g (3/4 Cup)Potato or Oat Fiber
- 15g (3Tbsp)Psyllium Husk
- 250g (1 Cup)Greek Yogurt
- 4 Eggs
- 4 Tbsp (25g) Oil
- 2 Tbsp Water
- 2 Tbsp Vinegar
- 1 tsp salt

Instructions

- Heat up the oven to 150C or 300F
- Mix all of the dry ingredience
- Separate eggs and mix all of the eggwhites first. Set aside
- Mix egg yolks fully.
- Add Yogurt and all of the wet ingredients
- Spoon by spoon keep adding all of the mixed dry ingredients
- At the end add egg whites and mix it gently and fully

- Cover the bowl and let it rest for half hour
- Prepare a baking sheet with Parchment paper
- Once rested, with wet hand make small balls, which you then flatten a bit at the end with hands to achieve rolls
- Once all is on the baking sheet, add a little bit of Potato or Oat Fiber to achieve the white look after baking
- With knife of your super Kaiser Roll Shaper Gadget press on each Roll to give it the perfect end touch
- Place it into the oven and bake for 40 Minutes
- Bon Appetit

Notes

- For this recipe you can use Potato Fiber or Oat Fiber to achieve the results, which are identical.

Nutrition Info

Calories: 177

Total Fat: 14g

Carbohydrates: 7g

Fiber: 7g

Protein: 11g

17. Cranberry Feta Dough Balls

Festive low carb dough balls with cranberry & feta

Prep Time: 15 minutes

Cook Time: 35 minutes

Total Time: 50 minutes

Servings: 4 People

Ingredients

- 1 cup mozzarella cheese grated
- 1/2 cup parmesan cheese grated
- 1/2 cup coconut flour
- 2 eggs beaten

- 1 cup Feta cheese crumbled
- 3 tablespoons cranberry chia jam
- 1/4 cup butter, melted unsalted
- 1/2 teaspoon baking powder
- 2 tablespoons chives, chopped optional garnish

Instructions

- Preheat the oven to 200C/400 degrees.
- In a bowl, mix the Mozzarella and Parmesan cheese together.
- Add the eggs and butter and mix thoroughly.
- Add the coconut flour and baking powder and mix until you almost have a dough like texture.
- Add the Feta cheese and cranberry chia jam, gently mixing this throughout the dough.
- Using your hands (clean!) make 15 even shaped balls for the tree shape. Anything left over can be used as the trunk if need be.
- Place the balls on a parchment covered baking tin in the shape of a Christmas Tree. You could try a festive wreath too!
- Bake for 30-35 until firm and golden.

Nutrition Info

Calories: 121kcal, Carbohydrates: 3.7g, Protein: 6g, Fat: 9g, Fiber: 1.9g

18. Paleo Chocolate Zucchini Bread

Paleo Chocolate Zucchini Bread. Easy, Healthy Gluten free loaf, super moist with almond meal and unsweetened cocoa powder. 100% KETO + Low carb + sugar free

Prep Time10 mins

Cook Time50 mins

Cool down4 hrs

Total Time1 hr

Servings: 12 slices

Calories: 185kcal

Ingredients

Dry ingredients

- 1 1/2 cup almond flour (170g)
- 1/4 cup unsweetened cocoa powder (25g)
- 1 1/2 teaspoon baking soda
- 2 teaspoons ground cinnamon
- 1/4 teaspoon sea salt
- 1/2 cup sugar free crystal sweetener (Monk fruit or erythritol) (100g) or coconut sugar if refined sugar free

Wet ingredients

- 1 cup zucchini, finely grated measure packed, discard juice/liquid if there is some - about 2 small zucchini
- 1 large egg
- 1/4 cup + 2 tablespoon canned coconut cream 100ml
- 1/4 cup extra virgin coconut oil , melted, 60ml
- 1 teaspoon vanilla extract
- 1 teaspoon apple cider vinegar

Filling - optional

- 1/2 cup sugar free chocolate chips

- 1/2 cup chopped walnuts or nuts you like

Instructions

- Preheat oven to 180C (375F). Line a baking loaf pan (9 inches x 5 inches) with parchment paper. Set aside.

- Remove both extremity of the zucchinis, keep skin on.

- Finely grate the zucchini using a vegetable grater. Measure the amount needed in a measurement cup. Make sure you press/pack them firmly for a precise measure and to squeeze out any liquid from the grated zucchini, I usually don't have any!. If you do, discard the liquid or keep for another recipe.

- In a large mixing bowl, stir all the dry ingredients together: almond flour, unsweetened cocoa powder, sugar free crystal sweetener, cinnamon, sea salt and baking soda. Set aside.

- Add all the wet ingredients into the dry ingredients : grated zucchini, coconut oil, coconut cream, vanilla, egg, apple cider vinegar.

- Stir to combine all the ingredients together.

- Stir in the chopped nuts and sugar free chocolate chips.

- Transfer the chocolate bread batter into the prepared loaf pan.
- Bake 50 - 55 minutes, you may want to cover the bread loaf with a piece of foil after 40 minute to avoid the top to darken too much, up to you.
- The bread will stay slightly moist in the middle and firm up after fully cool down.

Cool down

- Cool down 10 minutes in the loaf pan, then cool down on a cooling rack until it reach room temperature. It can take 4 hours as it is a thick bread. Don' slice the bread before it reach room temperature. If too hot in the center, it will be too oft and fall apart when you slice. For a faster result, cool down 40 minutes at room temperature then pop in the fridge for 1 hour. The fridge will create an extra fudgy texture and the bread will be even easier to slice as it firms up.
- Store in the fridge up to 4 days in a cake bow or airtight container.

Nutrition Info

Calories: 185kcal, Carbohydrates: 6.1g, Protein: 4.9g, Fat: 17.1g, Fiber: 2.7g, Sugar: 1.2g

19. Sweet Keto Challah Bread Recipe

Sweet Keto Challah Bread Recipe (Braided) is made into perfection without Flour, perfect for Low Carb option.

Prep Time 10 minutes

Cook Time 45 minutes

Total Time 55 minutes

20 Serving

Ingredients

- 4 Eggs
- 50g (1/3 Cup)Sukrin Plus
- 345g (1,5 Cup) Cream Cheese
- 60g (1/4 Cup)Butter
- 60g (1/4 Cup)Heavy Cream
- 50g (1/4 Cup)Oil
- 1 Cup (100g) Unflavored Protein
- 2/3 Cup (85g) Vanilla Protein
- 1/2 tsp salt
- 1/3 tsp (3g) Baking Soda
- 2 1/2 tsp (12g) Baking Powder
- 1 tsp (4g) Xanthan
- 1/2 of Lemon Zest
- 1/4 Cup (30g) Dried Berries (I have used cranberries)

Instructions

- Heat up the oven to 160C or 320F
- In a separate bowl, mix eggs into fluffiness, then add sugar substitute and mix again.
- Add Cream Cheese and all of the liquid ingredients and mix again
- Once that is properly mixed, add all of the dried ingredients and finish it with mixing it all together.

- Take it our of the mixer and add fresh lemon zest followed by dry cranberries
- Gently hand mix it into the dough, which is then poured into a silicone baking pan, depending on your desired shape.
- Bake for 45 Min
- Bon appetite

Nutrition Info

Calories: 158

Total Fat: 13g

Saturated Fat: 6g

Trans Fat: 0g

Unsaturated Fat: 6g

Cholesterol: 66mg

Sodium: 241mg

Carbohydrates: 2g

Protein: 9g

20. Low Carb Bagels-Gluten Free Onion Sesame

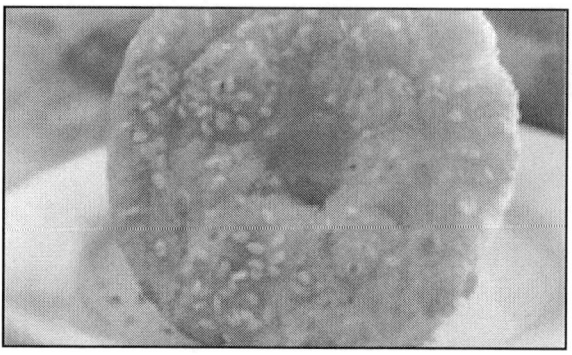

Prep/Cook Time:

Ingredients

- 2 1/2 cups mozzerella cheese
- 2 ounces cream cheese
- 3 eggs
- 1 1/2 cups almond flour
- 1 Tablespoon onion powder
- 1/2 teaspoon salt
- 1 Tablespoon sesame seeds

Instructions

- Preheat oven to 400 degrees F.

- Over a double boiler, melt mozzarella cheese and cream cheese together.

- When melted, stir together and beat in 2 eggs.

- In a separate bowl, add almond flour, onion powder, and salt. Stir to combine.

- Pour flour mixture into cheese/egg mixture and mix well.

- Using wet hands, take a small handful (about the size of an orange) and form into a ball. Flatten and make a hole in the center.

- Lay bagels on parchment lined baking sheet.

- Beat the remaining egg and brush over the bagels.

- Sprinkle sesame seeds over bagels and place in oven. Bake for 12 minutes, until golden brown. Remove and allow to cool on the baking sheet.

Nutrition Info

Calories: 287 Total Fat: 23g Saturated Fat: 7g Trans Fat: 0g Unsaturated Fat: 14g Cholesterol: 105mg Sodium: 401mg Carbohydrates: 7g Fiber: 3g Sugar: 2g Protein: 15g

21. Easy Low Carb Cheese Bombs

Make the perfect keto or low carb snack or appetizer with this recipe for Easy Low Carb Cheese Bombs that are so good to eat!

Prep Time 10 mins

Cook Time 12 mins

Total Time 22 mins

Servings: 4

Ingredients

- 12 Low Carb Biscuits

- 1 Egg
- 2 tbsp Milk
- 8 ounces Cheddar Cheese

Instructions

- Start by preheating your oven to 400 degrees. Also, prep one or two baking sheets for nonstick.
- In a small bowl, whip together your egg and milk. Set this bowl aside while you work.
- Prepare your biscuits as indicated in the recipe that you choose to use. Do not bake the biscuits. If you have not done as of yet, cut out each biscuit from the dough using a round cookie cutter. Place a cheese cube in the center of each cut out pieces of dough. The form the dough around the cheese to make a ball or bomb.
- Place the ball or bomb on to the prepared baking sheet. Then brush the egg and milk mixture on the surface of the ball.
- Lastly, bake for 10-12 minutes until they being to brown.
- You can brush with garlic butter if you desire. Allow to cool a bit before serving.

22. 1-2-3 Bread (Dairy-Free)

Prep/Cook Time: 50 minutes

Ingreients

- 1 teaspoon aluminium-free baking powder
- 2 cups = 480 ml = 8 oz = 230 g almond flour
- 3 extra large organic eggs

Intructions

- Preheat the oven to 300 °F (150 °C).
- Mix the baking powder with the almond flour in a medium bowl.

- In a large bowl, beat the eggs with an electric mixer until almost white and fluffy. The mixture will expand remarkably.
- Fold the almond flour mixture gently to the eggs preferably with a rubber spatula until there are no lumps.
- Put the dough into a generously greased small loaf pan or a silicone loaf pan and level the top with a rubber spatula.
- Bake for 30–40 minutes or until a stick inserted into the loaf comes out dry.
- Let cool and cut into slices.

Nutrition Info

1585 kcal

Protein 73.0 g

Fat 133.0 g

23. Simple and Fluffy Gluten-Free Low-Carb Bread

Prep/Cook Time: 50 minutes

Ingredients

- 1/2 cup = 120 ml = 45 g unflavored whey protein powder
- 2 teaspoons aluminium-free baking powder
- 1/2 cup = 120 ml = 125 g almond butter (natural, unsweetened)
- 4 extra large organic eggs

Intructions

- Preheat the oven to 300 °F (150 °C).
- Mix well the whey protein and baking powder in a small bowl.
- Beat the almond butter with an electric mixer in a large bowl until creamy.
- Add one egg at a time beating well after each addition until the batter is smooth, fluffy and bubbly.
- Combine the whey protein mixture with the almond butter mixture and beat well until creamy.
- Pour the batter in a 9 X 5 inch (23 X 13 cm) silicone loaf pan.
- Bake for 30–40 minutes.
- Let cool, remove from the pan and cut into slices.

24. Multi Seed Bagels Low-carb and Gluten Free

Prep/Cook Time: 1 hr 20 minutes, Servings: 8 servings

Ingredients

- 1 cup coconut flour
- ¼ cup Psyllium Fiber
- ½ cup sesame seeds
- ½ cup hemp hearts
- ½ cup pumpkin seeds
- 6 organic egg whites
- 1 tsp Celtic sea

- 1 Tbs Baking Powder (aluminum free)

Instructions

- Pre-heat the oven to 350 degrees.
- First combine all dry ingredients in a large bowl.
- Mix well.
- In a blender, blend the egg whites until very foamy.
- Add the foamy egg whites to the dry ingredients and mix well with a spoon, or in a food processor.
- The dough should still be crumbly.
- Now add 1 cup of boiling water to the mix and keep stirring until a smoother dough forms.
- The dough will still be a bit crumbly but will stick together when formed into a ball.
- Place a sheet of parchment paper on a cookie sheet.
- Form the dough into 6 balls.
- Now holding the ball in one hand stick your thumb though it, making a hole, then place the dough on the cookie sheet and form it into a bagel, pressing it together with your fingers.
- Sprinkle it with some sesame seeds or poppy seeds so it looks pretty!
- Bake at 350 for about 55 minutes.

- Let cool inside the oven for extra crunchy top.
- Makes 6 small bagels

Nutrition Info

Serves: 6 small bagels

Serving size: 1 bagel

Calories: 352

Fat: 19 gr

Carbohydrates: 8 gr Net

Fiber: 20 gr

Protein: 18 gr

25. Keto Dinner Rolls Recipe

Prep/Cook Time: 40 minutes, Servings: 9 rolls

Ingredients

- 1/3 cup (2.5 oz or 70 g) coconut flour
- 1/4 cup (1 oz or 30 g) almond flour
- 1/4 cup (0.9 oz or 25 g) psyllium husk powder
- 1 teaspoon (2 g) baking powder
- 1 teaspoon (4 g) baking soda
- Dash of garlic powder
- Dash of salt
- 4 large eggs

- 2 teaspoons (10 ml) olive oil
- 1/4 cup (60 ml) water
- 1/4 cup (60 ml) ghee

Instructions

- Preheat the oven to 350 F (175 C).
- Combine the coconut flour, almond flour, psyllium husk powder, baking powder, baking soda, garlic powder, and salt in a large bowl.
- In a separate bowl, whisk the eggs, olive oil and water together. Once the melted ghee has cooled a little, whisk this in too. Add the egg mixture to the flour mixture and combine well. Leave to settle for 5 minutes until the mixture firms up a little.
- Form 9 equal-sized balls with the mixture and place on a small tray lined with parchment paper.
- Bake in the oven for 25-30 minutes, reducing the temperature to 300 F (150 C) in the last 10 minutes. Leave to cool on a rack and store in a sealed container.

Nutrition Info

Calories: 149 Sugar: 1 g Fat: 12 g Carbohydrates: 5 g Fiber: 4 g Protein: 5 g

26. Keto Zucchini Bread Recipe

Prep/Cook Time: 50 minutes, Servings: 10 slices

Ingredients

- 4 medium eggs (176 g)
- 1 large zucchini, shredded (moisture squeezed out) (approx. 1–2 cups)
- 1/2 cup of almond flour (60 g)
- 1/4 cup of coconut flour (28 g)
- 8 Tablespoons of coconut oil (120 ml)

- 1 teaspoon of baking powder (2 g)
- 1 teaspoon of vanilla extract (5 ml)
- Dash of salt

Instructions

- Preheat oven to 350 F (175 C).
- Mix all the ingredients together in a large mixing bowl.
- Make sure to squeeze all the moisture out of the zucchini.
- Pour into a loaf pan and bake for 50 minutes.
- Let cool and slice.

Nutrition Info

Calories: 162 Sugar: 1 g Fat: 15 g Carbohydrates: 3 g Fiber: 2 g Protein: 4 g

27. Low Carb Paleo Tortillas Recipe - 3 Ingredient Coconut Flour Wraps

If you're looking for easy coconut flour recipes, try paleo low carb tortillas with coconut flour. Just 3 ingredients in these keto paleo coconut wraps!

Prep Time 5 minutes

Cook Time 10 minutes

Total Time 15 minutes

Servings 8" tortillas

Ingredients

- 1/2 cup Coconut flour

- 6 large Eggs (up to 7-8, see notes)

- 1 1/4 cup Unsweetened almond milk (up to 1 1/2 cup, see notes; can also use any milk of choice - use coconut milk beverage for nut-free)

- 3/4 tsp Sea salt (optional)

- 1 tbsp Gelatin powder (optional - for more pliable, sturdy tortillas)

- 1/2 tsp Cumin (optional)

- 1/2 tsp Paprika (optional)

Instructions

- In a large bowl, whisk all ingredients together until smooth. Let the batter sit for a minute or two to account for the natural thickening caused by coconut flour. The batter should be very runny right before cooking - it should pour easily (add more almond milk and eggs in *equal* proportions if needed to achieve this). If you are using the optional gelatin, add an extra 1/4 cup almond milk.

- Heat a small skillet (about 8 in (20 cm) diameter) over medium to medium-high heat and grease lightly (use oil of choice or an oil mister). Pour 1/4 cup (60 mL) of batter onto the skillet and immediately, rapidly tilt in different directions to evenly distribute, like making crepes. Cook, covered with a lid, until the edges are golden and you see bubbles forming in the middle. The edges will curl inward when you lift the lid (about 1-2 minutes). Flip over, cover again, and cook until browned on the other side (1-2 more minutes). Repeat until the batter is used up.

Recipe Notes

Exact amounts of eggs and milk needed can vary slightly based on your brand of coconut flour, how tightly it sits in the measuring cup, etc. The post above explains how to get the right consistency, and how to thin out the batter if it's too thick.

For the best low carb paleo tortillas, please see additional preparation and troubleshooting tips in the post above!

Nutrition Info

Calories 55
Fat 3g
Protein 5g

Total Carbs 4g

Net Carbs 1g

Fiber 3g

Sugar 1g

28. Low Carb Chelsea Buns

Low-carb Chelsea buns are so light and fluffy, who knew they could be this easy to make (and enjoy).

Prep Time15 mins

Cook Time20 mins

Total Time35 mins

Servings:4

Ingredients

- 200 g almond meal/flour
- 40 g psyllium husk
- 2 tsp baking powder

- 5 tbsp granulated sweetener of choice or more, to your taste
- 4 egg whites
- 1 tsp vanilla
- 250 ml boiling water

Cinnamon filling

- 2 tsp ground cinnamon
- 2 tsp granulated sweetener of choice
- lemon zest optional

Glaze

- 4 tbsp powdered sweetener
- 1 tsp vanilla optional
- water enough to make a liquid glaze

Instructions

Low Carb Chelsea Bun Dough

- Place all the dry ingredients together in a bowl and mix well.

- Make a hole in the middle of the dry ingredients and add the egg whites and vanilla. Mix just a little so you can't see the egg whites any more.
- Add 1/3 the boiling water gently and slowly, mix. Add another 1/3, mix. Add the final 1/3 and mix until it looks like a sticky dough.
- If the dough looks too wet, add an extra tablespoon of psyllium husk, if too dry, add a teaspoon of water at a time.
- Pour the dough onto a large sheet of baking parchment/paper. Place another piece of baking parchment/paper on top.
- Press out with your hands until it is a rectangle shape and 1cm / 1/2 inch thick.

Cinnamon filling

- Mix the cinnamon and sweetener together and sprinkle all over the rolled dough.
- Using the baking parchment/paper, start to roll the dough up along the longest side.
- Continue to roll it into one long roll, then cut into even slices.
- Place each slice in a ring tin that has been oiled and lined.

- Bake at 180C/350F for 20-30 minutes, or until golden, and baked in the centre of each Chelsea bun.

Glaze

- Mix the powdered sweetener, vanilla and water together to make a liquid glaze.
- Drizzle, pour or spoon all over.
- Enjoy warm or cold.

Nutrition Info

Calories 246 Calories from Fat 167

Total Fat 18.6g 29%

Total Carbohydrates 13.7g 5%

Dietary Fiber 8.2g 33%

Sugars 1.6g

Protein 10g

29. 15-Minute Gluten Free, Low Carb & Keto Tortillas

These 15-minute gluten free and keto tortillas are super pliable, easy and make the best low carb Mexican tacos!

Prep Time: 10 minutes

Cook Time: 5 minutes

Total Time: 15 minutes

Servings: 4

Ingredients

- 96 g almond flour
- 24 g coconut flour

- 2 teaspoons xanthan gum
- 1 teaspoon baking powder
- 1/8-1/4 teaspoon kosher salt depending on whether sweet or savory
- 2 teaspoons apple cider vinegar
- 1 egg lightly beaten
- 3 teaspoons water

Instructions

- Add almond flour, coconut flour, xanthan gum, baking powder and salt to food processor. Pulse until thoroughly combined.

- Pour in apple cider vinegar with the food processor running. Once it has distributed evenly, pour in the egg. Followed by the water. Stop the food processor once the dough forms into a ball. The dough will be sticky to touch.

- Wrap dough in cling film and knead it through the plastic for a minute or two. Think of it a bit like a stress ball. Allow dough to rest for 10 minutes (and up to two days in the fridge).

- Heat up a skillet (preferably) or pan over medium heat. You can test the heat by sprinkling a few water droplets, if the drops evaporate immediately your pan is too hot. The droplets should 'run' through the skillet.

- Break the dough into eight 1" balls (26g each). Roll out between two sheets of parchment or waxed paper with a rolling pin or using a tortilla press (easier!) until each round is 5-inches in diameter.

- Transfer to skillet and cook over medium heat for just 3-6 seconds (very important). Flip it over immediately (using a thin spatula or knife), and continue to cook until just lightly golden on each side (though with the traditional charred marks), 30 to 40 seconds. The key is not to overcook them, as they will no longer be pliable or puff up.

- Keep them warm wrapped in kitchen cloth until serving. To rewarm, heat briefly on both sides, until just warm (less than a minute).

- These tortillas are best eaten straight away. But feel free to keep some dough handy in your fridge for up to three days.

Notes

When cooking, coconut flour burns rather rapidly. So while this does help you to get the traditional charred marks of flour tortillas, you do need to keep an eye out for them to keep them from burning. Having said that, you do want your skillet to be very hot in order for the tortillas to cook quickly (in under a minute) and stay pliable. Like any tortilla, if the heat is not high enough it will harden and crack.

Nutrition Info

Calories 89 Calories from Fat 54

Total Fat 6g 9%

Saturated Fat 1g 5%

Cholesterol 20mg 7%

Sodium 51mg 2%

Potassium 58mg 2%

Total Carbohydrates 4g 1%

Dietary Fiber 2g 8%

Protein 3g 6%

30. The Best Keto Dinner Rolls

These are the best keto dinner rolls to help replace bread in your low carb lifestyle. This recipe is easy, filling, and delicious!

Prep Time: 5 minutes

Cook Time: 10 minutes

Total Time: 15 minutes

Serving: 6 rolls

Ingredients

- 1 Cup Mozzarella, shredded
- 1 oz Cream Cheese
- 1 Cup Almond Flour

- 1/4 Cup Ground Flax Seed
- 1 egg
- 1/2 Tsp Baking Soda

Instructions

- Preheat oven to 400
- Line baking sheet with parchment, set aside
- In a medium bowl, melt cream cheese and mozzarella together (microwave ~1 min)
- Stir cheeses together until smooth, add egg and stir until combined
- In separate bowl combine almond flour, ground flax seed and baking soda
- Mix cheese and egg mixture into dry ingredients and stir until dough forms soft ball (it will be sticky)
- Using wet hands, gently roll dough into 6 balls
- Roll tops in sesame seeds if desired and place onto lined baking sheet
- Bake for 10-12 minutes until golden brown
- Let cool for 15 minutes

Notes

Coconut flour is NOT a direct substitute for almond flour, you must adjust the amount

Dough will be sticky but should be able to form balls. Use wet hands to roll balls. If absolutely too wet to mold then add an additional tbsp of almond flour until pliable

4 large rolls work great for sandwiches and burgers, 6 smaller is good for dinner rolls

Nutrition Info

Serving Size: 1 roll

Calories: 219

Fat: 18g

Carbohydrates: 5.6g total (2.3g NET)

Fiber: 3.3g

Protein: 10.7g

31. Low Carb Keto Garlic Breadsticks

These soft, buttery garlic breadsticks taste like the ones served at restaurants, but they are also low carb, keto and gluten free.

Prep Time: 20 minutes

Cook Time: 18 minutes

Total Time: 38 minutes

Servings: 8 breadsticks (total Serving)

Ingredients:

Breadsticks dough

- 1 1/2 cups part skim low moisture shredded mozzarella cheese
- 2 oz full fat cream cheese
- 1 1/3 cups super-fine almond flour*
- 2 tbsp coconut flour
- 1 1/2 tbsp aluminum free baking powder
- 1 tsp garlic powder
- 1/4 tsp onion powder
- 3 large eggs one egg is reserved for egg wash

Garlic Butter Topping

- 2 cloves garlic minced
- 1 tbsp butter
- 1 tbsp olive oil
- 1 1/2 tbsp grated parmesan cheese
- 1 tsp parsley finely chopped

Instructions

- Preheat oven to 350°F. Line a baking sheet with parchment paper.

- In a small bowl, whisk together almond flour, coconut flour, baking powder, garlic powder and onion powder. Set aside.

- Add mozzarella and cream cheese to a large microwave-safe bowl. Cover the cream cheese with mozzarella (this will prevent the cream cheese from overheating and making a mess in your microwave). Melt in the microwave at 30 second intervals. After each 30 seconds, stir cheese until cheese is completely melted and uniform and resembles a dough in appearance (see photo for reference). This should only take around 1 minute total cooking time. Do not try to microwave the full time at once because some of the cheese will overcook. You can also melt the cheeses over the stove in a double boiler.

- Allow cheese dough to cool slightly (only a few minutes) so that it is still warm to the touch but not too hot. If the cheese is too hot it will cook the eggs. But don't let the cheese cool down completely because then it will turn hard and you will not be able to blend it with the other dough ingredients.

- Add cheese, 2 eggs (remember the third egg is for the egg wash finish at the end only), and almond flour mixture into a food processor with dough blade attachment. Pulse on high speed until the dough is uniform. The dough will be quite sticky, which is normal.

- Scoop out dough with a spatula and place onto a large sheet of plastic wrap. Cover the dough in plastic wrap and knead a few times with the dough inside the plastic wrap until you have a uniform dough ball.

- Wrap your pastry board with plastic wrap until the plastic wrap is taut. You should have the plastic wrap running across the bottom of the board so that the weight of the board will help keep the plastic wrap in place. The plastic wrap should keep your dough from sticking to the board. Lightly coat your hands with oil and divide dough into 8 equal parts. Roll each dough into smooth 1 inch thick sticks.

- Add the final egg to a small bowl and whisk. Generously brush the surface of rolls with egg wash.

- Bake rolls for about 15 minutes in the middle rack of your oven, or until breadsticks are just cooked and just starting to brown.

- While breadsticks are baking, make the garlic butter topping. Add garlic, butter and oil in a small saucepan. Bring to low-medium heat and stir until butter is melted and garlic is lightly browned.

- When breadsticks are just done baking but still pale, remove from oven. Quickly brush them generously with the garlic butter topping (You don't want to interrupt the cooking of the breadsticks for too long.) Sprinkle parmesan cheese and parsley over the breadsticks.

- Place breadsticks back into the oven and bake for an additional 3 minutes or until breadsticks turn a golden brown.

- If desired, sprinkle more parmesan cheese and parsley over breadsticks before serving. You can serve breadsticks plain or with low carb marinara sauce.

Nutrition Info

Calories 248 Calories from Fat 180
Total Fat 20g 31%
Saturated Fat 6g 30%

Cholesterol 78mg 26%

Sodium 194mg 8%

Potassium 279mg 8%

Total Carbohydrates 7g 2%

Dietary Fiber 2g 8%

Sugars 1g

Protein 12g 24%

32. Coconut Flour Pizza Crust

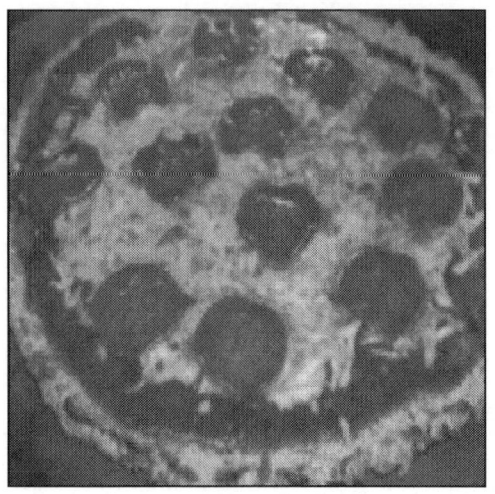

This coconut flour pizza crust is the best gluten-free pizza crust I've ever tried. It's soft and tasty, and sturdy enough to hold with your hands!

Prep Time10 mins

Cook Time20 mins

Total Time30 mins

Servings: 2 (8-inch) pizzas

Ingredients

- Olive oil spray for pans

- 4 large eggs
- 2 tablespoons water
- 1 teaspoon garlic powder
- 1 teaspoon onion powder
- 1 teaspoon dried oregano
- 1/4 cup coconut flour
- 6 tablespoons grated parmesan cheese (1 oz)

Topping:

- 1/2 cup marinara sauce
- 1 cup shredded part-skim mozzarella (4 oz)

Instructions

- Preheat oven to 400 degrees F.
- Line two pizza pans with parchment paper and spray the paper with olive oil. You can also make these pizzas side by side on a single, large baking sheet.
- In a large bowl, whisk the eggs with the water, garlic powder, onion powder and dried oregano.
- Measure out the coconut flour, breaking up any lumps with your hands. Stir the coconut flour into the egg mixture, mixing until smooth.

- Stir in the Parmesan cheese.

- Allow the mixture to rest and thicken for a couple of minutes. This will allow the coconut flour to soak up the liquid.

- Using a rubber spatula, transfer half of the mixture onto each of the prepared pans. Use a spatula to spread it out evenly into an 8-inch circle.

- Bake the pizzas until set and the edges are beginning to brown, about 15 minutes. The crust will still be light at this point, and that's OK.

- Remove the pizzas from the oven and switch the oven to broil. Position the top oven rack 6 inches below flame.

- Spread each pizza with half the pizza sauce, sprinkle with half the shredded mozzarella, and add any other toppings you like (I used Applegate's pepperoni).

- Broil each pizza until cheese is melted and crust is golden-brown, 2-3 minutes.

Nutrition Info

Calories 496 Calories from Fat 297

Total Fat 33g 51%

Saturated Fat 15g 75%

Sodium 885mg 37%

Total Carbohydrates 13g 4%

Dietary Fiber 5g 20%

Sugars 14g

Protein 35g 70%

33. Easy Paleo Keto Bread Recipe - 5 Ingredients

If you want to know how to make the BEST keto bread recipe, this is it! It makes fluffy white paleo bread that's quick & easy. Just 5 basic ingredients!

Course Breakfast, Main Course, Side Dish

Prep Time 10 minutes

Cook Time 1 hour 10 minutes

Total Time 1 hour 20 minutes

Ingredients

Basic Ingredients

- 1 cup Blanched almond flour
- 1/4 cup Coconut flour
- 2 tsp Gluten-free baking powder
- 1/4 tsp Sea salt
- 1/3 cup Butter (or 5 tbsp + 1 tsp; measured solid, then melted; can use coconut oil for dairy-free)
- 12 large Egg white (~1 1/2 cups, at room temperature)

Optional Ingredients (recommended)

- 1 1/2 tbsp Erythritol (can use any sweetener or omit)
- 1/4 tsp Xanthan gum (for texture - omit for paleo)
- 1/4 tsp Cream of tartar (to more easily whip egg whites)

Instructions

- Preheat the oven to 325 degrees F (163 degrees C). Line an 8 1/2 x 4 1/2 in (22x11 cm) loaf pan with parchment paper, with extra hanging over the sides for easy removal later.

- Combine the almond flour, coconut flour, baking powder, erythritol, xanthan gum, and sea salt in a large food processor. Pulse until combined.

- Add the melted butter. Pulse, scraping down the sides as needed, until crumbly.

- In a very large bowl, use a hand mixer to beat the egg whites and cream of tartar (if using), until stiff peaks form. Make sure the bowl is large enough because the whites will expand a lot.

- Add 1/2 of the stiff egg whites to the food processor. Pulse a few times until just combined. Do not over-mix!

- Carefully transfer the mixture from the food processor into the bowl with the egg whites, and gently fold until no streaks remain. Do not stir. Fold gently to keep the mixture as fluffy as possible.

- Transfer the batter to the lined loaf pan and smooth the top. Push the batter toward the center a bit to round the top.

- Bake for about 40 minutes, until the top is golden brown. Tent the top with aluminum foil and bake for another 30-45 minutes, until the top is firm and does not make a squishy sound when pressed. Internal temperature should be 200 degrees. Cool completely before removing from the pan and slicing.

Nutrition Info

Calories 82

Fat 7g

Protein 4g

Total Carbs 3g

Net Carbs 1g

Fiber 2g

Sugar 1g

34. Low Carb Focaccia Bread

Low carb focaccia bread can easily be made as a garlic bread too. Ensure before baking you have shaped the focaccia to be flat and cut little slices half way through the dough. This helps it cook evenly throughout.

Prep Time15 mins

Cook Time30 mins

Total Time45 mins

Servings: Loaf

Ingredients

- 50 g coconut flour
- 5 tbsp psyllium husk

- 2 tsp baking powder
- 1 tsp salt
- 4 eggs - medium
- 250 ml boiling water

Instructions

- Place the coconut flour, psyllium husks, baking powder and salt into a large mixing bowl and stir until combined.
- Add the eggs and mix. The mixture will be a very firm 'play-dough' like consistency so don't work it too hard at this point.
- Add the cup of boiling water and mix until thoroughly combined.
- Form into a focaccia shape and place on a baking tray lined with baking paper. Using a sharp knife, make diagonal cuts through the dough, sprinkle with plenty of salt, rosemary and place olives on top of the dough.
- Bake at 180C for 25-30 minutes. It is cooked when the centre is no longer 'spongy'.
- Serve hot with butter, cold with cheese, avocado slices, tomatoes, labna, etc.

Notes

To ensure you avoid any 'eggy' taste, add plenty of flavours such as rosemary, garlic, salt etc.* Psyllium husk 100% fibre and once added to water, swell and thicken. This property is used to thicken foods, added to gluten-free baking where it binds moisture and help make breads less crumbly, and as a laxative. Always drink plenty of fluids when taking psyllium, as the husks will swell and absorb liquids from your gut as it transits through.

Nutrition Info

Calories 528 Calories from Fat 234

Total Fat 26g 40%

Total Carbohydrates 58g 19%

Dietary Fiber 42g 168%

Sugars 5.9g

Protein 31g 62%

35. Healthy 3 Ingredient Mini Paleo Pizza Bases Crusts

These 3 Ingredient mini paleo pizza crusts or bases are an easy, delicious and low carb alternative to traditional pizzas! Made with just three ingredients and on the stovetop, these 3 Ingredient Pizza bases are naturally gluten free, grain free, high protein, low calorie and have a nut free option!

Servings: 4
Calories: 125kcal

Ingredients

For the coconut flour option

- 8 large egg whites for thicker bases, use 5 whole eggs and 3 egg whites
- 1/4 cup coconut flour sifted
- 1/2 tsp baking powder
- Spices of choice salt, pepper, Italian spices
- Extra coconut flour to dust very lightly

For the almond flour option

- 8 large egg whites
- 1/2 cup almond flour
- 1/2 tsp baking powder
- Spices of choice salt, pepper, Italian spices

For the pizza sauce

- 1/2 cup Mutti tomato sauce
- 2 cloves garlic crushed
- 1/4 tsp sea salt
- 1 tsp dried basil

Instructions

To make the pizza bases/crusts

- In a large mixing bowl, whisk the eggs/egg whites until opaque. Sift in the coconut flour or almond flour and whisk very well until clumps are removed. Add the baking powder, mixed spices and continue to whisk until completely combined.
- On low heat, heat up a small pan and grease lightly.
- Once frying pan is hot, pour the batter in the pan and ensure it is fully coated. Cover the pan with a lid/tray for 3-4 minutes or until bubbles start to appear on top. Flip, cook for an extra 2 minutes and remove from pan- Keep an eye on this, as it can burn out pretty quickly.
- Continue until all the batter is used up.
- Allow pizza bases to cool. Once cool, use a skewer and poke holes roughly over the top, for even cooking. Dust very lightly with a dash of coconut flour.

To make the sauce

- Combine all the ingredients together and let sit at room temperature for at least 30 minutes- This thickens up.

Notes

- For a crispy pizza base, bake in the oven for 3-4 minutes prior to adding your toppings.If you want to freeze them, allow pizza bases to cool completely before topping with a dash of coconut flour and a thin layer of pizza sauce. Ensure each pizza base is divided with parchment paper before placing in the freezer.

Nutrition Info

Calories: 125kcal, Carbohydrates: 6g, Protein: 8g, Fat: 1g, Fiber: 3g, Vitamin A: 1%, Vitamin C: 2%, Calcium: 1%, Iron: 2%

36. Gluten Free, Paleo & Keto Bread

Count on this paleo and keto bread to be soft, fluffy, absolutely delicious and with a killer crumb. Plus, with less than half the amount of eggs as your usual low carb bread recipe, this non-eggy sandwich bread will surely become a staple!

Prep Time: 15 minutes
Cook Time: 30 minutes
Resting Time: 40 minutes
Total Time: 45 minutes
Servings: 1

Calories: 174 kcal

Ingredients

For the paleo & keto bread

- 2 teaspoons active dry yeast
- 2 teaspoons maple syrup or honey, to feed the yeast (NO SUGAR WILL BE REMAIN POST BAKE)
- 120 ml water lukewarm between 105-110°F
- 168 g almond flour
- 83 g golden flaxseed meal finely ground
- 15 g whey protein isolate
- 18 g psyllium husk finely ground
- 2 teaspoons xanthan gum or 4 teaspoons ground flaxseed meal**
- 2 teaspoons baking powder
- 1 teaspoon kosher salt
- 1/4 teaspoon cream of tartar
- 1/4 teaspoon ground ginger
- 1 egg at room temperature
- 110 g egg whites about 3, at room temperature
- 56 g grass-fed butter or ghee, melted and cooled
- 1 tablespoon apple cider vinegar

- 58 g sour cream or coconut cream + 2 tsp apple cider vinegar

Instructions

For the paleo & keto bread

- See recipe video for guidance on keto yeast breads. And check out the post for deets, tips and possible subs!

- Line a 8.5 x 4.5 inch loaf pan with parchment paper (an absolute must!). Set aside.

- Add yeast and maple syrup (to feed the yeast, see notes) to a large bowl. Heat up water to 105-110°F, and if you don't have a thermometer it should only feel lightly warm to touch. Pour water over yeast mixture, cover bowl with a kitchen towel and allow to rest for 7 minutes. The mixture should be bubbly, if it isn't start again (too cold water won't activate the yeast and too hot will kill it).

- Mix your flours while the yeast is proofing. Add almond flour, flaxseed meal, whey protein powder, psyllium husk, xanthan gum, baking powder, salt, cream of tartar and ginger to a medium bowl and whisk until thoroughly mixed. Set aside.

- Once your yeast is proofed, add in the egg, egg whites, lightly cooled melted butter (you don't want to scramble the eggs or kill the yeast!) and vinegar. Mix with an electric mixer for a couple minutes until light and frothy. Add the flour mixture in two batches, alternating with the sour cream, and mixing until thoroughly incorporated. You want to mix thoroughly and quickly to activate the xanthan gum, though the dough will become thick as the flours absorb the moisture.

- Transfer bread dough to prepared loaf pan, using a wet spatula to even out the top. Cover with a kitchen towel and place in a warm draft-free space for 50-60 minutes until the dough has risen just past the top of the loaf pan. How long it takes depends on your altitude, temperature and humidity- so keep an eye out for it every 15 minutes or so. And keep in mind that if you use a larger loaf pan it won't rise past the top.

- Preheat oven to 350°F/180°C while the dough is proofing. And if you're baking at high altitude, you'll want to bake it at 375°F/190°C.

- Place the loaf pan over a baking tray and transfer gently into the oven. Bake for 45-55 minutes until deep golden, covering with a lose foil dome at minute 10-15 (just as it begins to brown). Just be sure that the foil isn't resting directly on the bread.

- Allow the bread to rest in the loaf pan for 5 minutes and transfer it to a cooling rack. Allow to cool completely for best texture- this is an absolute must, as your keto loaf will continue to cook while cooling! Also keep in mind that some slight deflating is normal, don't sweat it!

- Keep stored in an airtight container (or tightly wrapped in cling film) at room temperature for 4-5 days, giving it a light toast before serving. Though you'll find that this keto bread is surprisingly good even without toasting!

Recipe Notes

Before you scream sugar (got 5 emails about it right after posting!!) remember that the yeast will feed on such sugar to emit carbon dioxide, so it doesn't affect the carb count at all. And yes, this is a scientific fact.

If paleo (or in keto maintenance), feel free to sub 1/4 to 1/2 cup of almond flour with arrowroot flour for a lighter crumb.

Nutrition Info

Calories 174 Calories from Fat 126

Total Fat 14g 22%

Saturated Fat 3g 15%

Cholesterol 26mg 9%

Sodium 254mg 11%

Potassium 83mg 2%

Total Carbohydrates 6g 2%

Dietary Fiber 4g 16%

Protein 5g 10%

37. Cheesy Flax & Chia Seed Cracker Bread (Low Carb and Gluten Free)

Prep/Cook Time: 30 minutes, Servings: 28-30 crackers

Ingredients

- 1 1/2 c ground flax seeds (I used my Magic Bullet)
- 2 Tbsp chia seeds (highly recommend omitting)
- 2 eggs, beaten
- 1/2 c shredded cheddar (use extra sharp)
- 1/2 tsp garlic powder
- 1/2 tsp salt

- 1/2 tsp pepper

Instructions

- Combine all ingredients in a medium bowl and stir by hand until a thick dough forms.
- Spray a sheet of foil or plastic wrap with nonstick spray. Form the dough into a log shape with your hands and place on the wrap. Roll it until it is about a foot or so long and an inch and a half in diameter. You can keep round or press into a squared shape. Pop into the freezer for about 5 minutes until it firms up.
- Meanwhile, preheat the oven to 350 degrees. Remove the dough from the freezer and slice into about 1/4 to 1/2 inch thick slices.
- Lay flat on a greased cookie sheet and bake for 12 – 15 minutes until golden brown. Remove from the oven and cool. Taste.
- Don't throw them out yet. Put something yummy on top first and see if you can stand it. Report back asap.

38. Nearly No Carb Keto Bread

Prep/Cook Time 31 minutes, Servings 12 people

Ingredients

- 8 ounces cream cheese
- 2 cups mozzarella cheese grated (about 210 grams)
- 3 large eggs
- 1/4 cup parmesan cheese grated (about 27 grams)
- 1 cup crushed pork rinds about 46 grams
- 1 tablespoon baking powder

Optional:

- herbs and spices to taste

Instructions

- Preheat oven to 375°F. Line baking sheet (I used a 12 x 17 jelly roll pan) with parchment paper.
- Place cream cheese and mozzarella cheese in large microwaveable bowl.
- Microwave cheese on high power for one minute, stir, then microwave for another minute and stir again. The cheese should be fully melted.
- Add egg, parmesan, pork rinds, and baking powder. Stir until all ingredients have been incorporated.
- Spread mixture onto parchment paper lined pan. Bake at 375°F for 15-20 or until lightly brown on top.
- Allow pan to cool on rack for 15 minutes, then remove bread from pan and cool directly on rack.
- Slice into 12 equal sized pieces. Can be eaten plain or used to make sandwiches.

Nutrition Info

Calories 166 Calories from Fat 117

Total Fat 13g 20%

Saturated Fat 7g 35%

Cholesterol 86mg 29%

Sodium 294mg 12%

Potassium 158mg 5%

Total Carbohydrates 1g 0%

Dietary Fiber 0g 0%

Sugars 0g

39. Paleo and AIP Garlic Cauliflower Naan Bread [Nut-Free, Grain-Free]

Prep Time/Cook Time: 25 minutes, Servings: 1

Ingredients

- 1 cup (140 g) cauliflower florets
- 1/2 cup (64g) arrowroot flour
- 1 Tablespoon (7 g) garlic powder
- 2 Tablespoons (30 ml) avocado oil (or olive oil)
- Salt to taste

Instructions

- Preheat oven to 450 F (230 C).
- Place the cauliflower florets into a bowl with some water and microwave on high until tender (check every 2 minutes to make sure it doesn't burn). Alternatively, steam the florets until tender.
- Food process (or use a blender) to process the cauliflower florets into a mash.
- Mix the cauliflower mash with the arrowroot flour, garlic powder, avocado oil, and salt. Taste the mixture and add in more garlic powder and salt to taste. Mix into a springy dough.
- Use your hands to press the dough into a flat bread, place on some parchment paper, and bake in oven for 15 minutes.
- Let cool and serve.

Nutrition Info

Total Carbs: 4.3g

Fibre: 2.9g

40. Easy Keto Sandwich Bread Recipe

Prep/Cook Time: 30 min

Ingredients

- 2 1/2 cups almond flour
- 2 cups whey protein isolate
- 1 tbsp xantham gum
- 3 tsp baking powder
- 1/2 tsp salt

- 1 1/4 cups warm water

Instructions

- In a large mixing bowl, stir together the dry ingredients.
- Slowly add in the water and stir with a wooden spoon, stirring slowly as you add water, until your dough comes together.
- Pour bread dough into a loaf pan that has been lined with parchment paper or greased well (be sure to check your cooking spray to ensure it is in fact gluten free.)
- Bake at 375°F for 20 to 25 minutes - until puffy and golden brown. You will see air bubbles on the sides of the bread, similar to the way the bread looks inside.
- Remove from oven and let cool completely on a rack before slicing.
- Only slice off the bread you're going to eat - pre-slicing bread will cause it to dry out or mold faster.
- Enjoy!

Nutrition Info

Calories: 274 Total Fat: 12g Saturated Fat: 1g Trans Fat: 0g Unsaturated Fat: 10g Cholesterol: 5mg Sodium: 361mg Carbohydrates: 17g Fiber: 3g Sugar: 1g Protein: 27g

41. 90 Second Microwave Bread

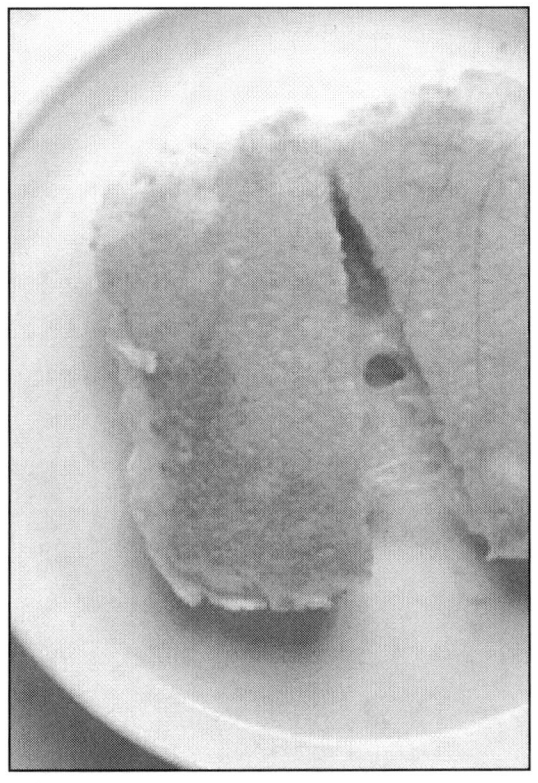

This 90 second bread is made in the microwave and you can use almond flour or coconut flour.

Prep Time: 3 minutes

Cook Time: 2 minutes

Total Time: 5 minutes

Servings: 1

Ingredients

- 3 tbsp almond flour or 1 1/3 tbsp coconut flour
- 1 tbsp oil (melted butter, melted coconut oil, avocado oil)
- 1/2 tsp baking powder
- 1 large egg
- tiny pinch of salt

Instructions

- Add all ingredients to a 4x4 microwave safe bowl, tap on the counter a few times to remove air bubbles, and microwave for 90 seconds. You can also bake in a oven safe container for 10 minutes at 375f

- Tap the container on the counter a few times to remove any air bubbles before you cook it
- You could really use any nut flour that you want if you are allergic to almonds or coconut. For alternative nut flours like pecan four, you would use 3 tbsp. You use half the amount for coconut flour because it's not really a nut and it is very absorbent!

- I found that a 4x4 microwave safe container made the perfect size piece of low carb bread that could be cut in half and stuffed with all the things
- You could also use a round container that is 4 inches in diameter for a keto mug bread
- If you would rather bake this in the oven, you can use an oven safe container and bake at 375 for 10 minutes
- Toasting this low carb bread makes it have a much better texture. You could also use a skillet to toast it in some butter. Yum!

Nutrition Info

Calories: 315kcal

42. Keto Pumpkin Bread

A delicious, moist, keto pumpkin bread full of warm spices and amazing pumpkin flavor. Made with almond and coconut flours to keep it healthy, gluten-free, and low-carb.

Prep Time: 10 minutes
Cook Time: 45 minutes
Total Time: 55 minutes
Serving: 10

Ingredients

- 1/2 cup butter, softened
- 2/3 cup erythritol sweetener, like Swerve
- 4 eggs large
- 3/4 cup pumpkin puree, canned (see notes for fresh)
- 1 tsp vanilla extract
- 1 1/2 cup almond flour
- 1/2 cup coconut flour
- 4 tsp baking powder
- 1 tsp cinnamon
- 1/2 tsp nutmeg
- 1/4 tsp ginger
- 1/8 tsp cloves
- 1/2 tsp salt

Instructions

- Preheat the oven to 350°F. Grease a 9"x5" loaf pan, and line with parchment paper.
- In a large mixing bowl, cream the butter and sweetener together until light and fluffy.
- Add the eggs, one at a time, and mix well to combine.

- Add the pumpkin puree and vanilla, and mix well to combine.
- In a separate bowl, stir together the almond flour, coconut flour, baking powder, cinnamon, nutmeg, ginger, cloves, salt. Break up any lumps of almond flour or coconut flour.
- Add the dry ingredients to the wet ingredients, and stir to combine. (Optionally, add up to 1/2 cup of mix-ins, like chopped nuts or chocolate chips.)
- Pour the batter into the prepared loaf pan. Bake for 45 - 55 minutes, or until a toothpick inserted into the center of the loaf comes out clean.
- If the bread is browning too quickly, you can cover the pan with a piece of aluminum foil.

Notes

- Want to use your own homemade puréed pumpkin? If it's thinner than canned pumpkin, try to remove some of the water to prevent soggy pumpkin bread.

- Want cream cheese frosting? Check the post above for an easy cream cheese frosting recipe.

- Want some nuts or chocolate chips? Feel free to add 1/2 cup of mix-ins to the batter before baking

- Want pumpkin muffins instead? Divide the batter into greased muffin tins. Be sure to reduce the baking time.

Nutrition Info

Calories: 165 Total Fat: 14g Saturated Fat: 7g Unsaturated Fat: 4g Cholesterol: 99mg Sodium: 76mg Carbohydrates: 6g Fiber: 3g Sugar: 1g Protein: 5g

43. Coconut Flour Flatbread

Coconut flour flatbread Ketogenic flatbread perfect as a side to curries or a low carb tortillas wraps. 100% Vegan + eggless + gluten free soft breads.

Prep Time10 mins

Cook Time5 mins

Total Time15 mins

Servings: 6 flatbreads

Ingredients

- 2 tablespoons psyllium husk (9g)

- 1/2 cup coconut flour fine, fresh, no lumps (60g)
- 1 cup lukewarm water (240ml)
- 1 tablespoon olive oil (15ml)
- 1/4 teaspoons baking soda
- 1/4 teaspoons salt - optional

Cooking

- 1 teaspoon olive oil to rub/oil the non stick pan

Instructions

Make the dough

- In a medium mixing bowl, combine the psyllium husk and coconut flour (if lumps are in your flour use a fork to smash them BEFORE measuring the flour, amount must be precise).
- Add in the lukewarm water (I used tap water about 40C/bath temperature), olive oil, and baking soda. Give a good stir with a spatula, then use your hands to knead the dough. Add salt now if you want. I never add the salt in contact with baking soda to avoid deactivating the leaving agent.

- Knead for 1 minute. The dough is moist and it gets softer and slightly dryer as you go. It should come together easily to form a dough as on my picture. If not, too sticky, add more husk, 1/2 teaspoon at a time, knead for 30 sec and see how it goes. The dough will always be a bit moist but it shouldn't stick to your hands at all. It must come together as a dough.
- Set aside 10 minute in the mixing bowl.
- Now the dough must be soft, elastic and hold well together, it is ready to roll.

Roll/ shape the flatbread

- Cut the dough into 4 even pieces, roll each pieces into a small ball.
- Place one of the dough ball between two pieces of parchment paper, press the ball with your hand palm to stick it well to the paper and start rolling with a rolling pin as thin as you like a bread. My breads are 20 cm diameter (8 inches) and I made 6 flatbread with this recipe.
- Un peel the first layer of parchment paper from your flatbread. Use a lid to cut out round flatbread. Keep the outside dough to reform a ball and roll more flatbread -

that is how I make 2 extra flatbread from the 4 balls above!

Cook in non stick pan

- Warm a non stick tefal crepe/ pancake pan under medium/high heat- or use any non stick pan of your choice, the one you would use for your pancakes.
- Add one teaspoon of olive oil or vegetable oil of your choice onto a piece of absorbent paper. Rub the surface of the pan to make sure it is slightly oiled. Don't leave any drops of oil or the bread will fry!
- Flip over the flatbread on the hot pan and peel off carefully the last piece of parchment paper.
- Cook for 2-3 minutes on the first side, flip over using a spatula and cook for 1-2 more minute on the other side.
- Cool down the flatbread on a plate and use as a sandwich wrap later or enjoy hot as a side dish. I recommend a drizzle of olive oil, crushed garlic and herbs before serving ! (optional but delish!)
- Repeat the rolling, cooking for the next 3 flatbread. Make sure you rub the oiled absorbent paper onto the saucepan each time to avoid the bread to stick to the pan.

- Store in the pantry in an airtight box or on a plate covered with plastic wrap to keep them soft, for up to 3 days.
- Rewarm in the same pan or if you want to give them a little crisp rewarm in the hot oven on a baking sheet for 1-2 minutes at 150C.

Nutrition Info

Serving: 1flatbread, Calories: 66kcal, Carbohydrates: 7.3g, Protein: 2g, Fat: 3.3g, Fiber: 4.7g, Sugar: 2g

44. Soul Bread Sesame Rolls

Have you tried Soul Bread yet? It just might be the most innovative and delicious low carb bread recipe around. These little keto rolls are perfect for making burgers, sliders and other sandwiches.

Prep Time 15 mins

Cook Time 35 mins

Total Time 50 mins

Servings: 12 small rolls

Ingredients

- 8 ounces cream cheese softened
- 3 tbsp butter melted
- 2 1/2 tbsp avocado oil
- 2 1/2 tbsp whipping cream
- 2 eggs
- 1 egg white
- 1 cup plus 3 tbsp unflavoured whey protein powder
- 1 1/2 tsp baking powder
- 1/2 tsp xanthan gum
- 1/2 tsp garlic powder
- 1/4 plus 1/8 tsp salt
- 1/4 tsp baking soda
- 1/4 tsp cream of tartar
- Toasted sesame seeds

Instructions

- Preheat oven to 325F and grease a muffin top pan or a square brownie pan very well. You can also use a muffin pan.

- In a large bowl, beat together cream cheese, butter, avocado oil, whipping cream, eggs, and egg white.
- In another bowl, whisk together the protein powder, baking powder, xanthan gum, garlic powder, salt, baking soda, and cream of tartar. Break up any clumps with a fork.
- Add dry ingredients to the cream cheese mixture and fold in by hand until just combined. Do not over mix.
- Fill the cavities of prepared pan to almost full (for the muffin top pan, you may need to work in batches). Sprinkle tops with toasted sesame seeds.
- Bake 25 to 35 minutes, until golden brown on top and firm to the touch. Remove and let cool in pan 15 minutes, then flip out onto a wire rack to cool completely. *If using a muffin top pan, they won't take as long to bake. Keep your eye on them!

Nutrition Info

Calories 175 Calories from Fat 130

Total Fat 14.42g 22%

Cholesterol 67mg 22%

Total Carbohydrates 2.5g 1%

Dietary Fiber 0.33g 1%

Protein 9.34g 19%

45. Brie, Ham and Green Apple Panini

Prep/Cook Time: 20 mins, Servings: 10 sandwiches

Ingredients

- 1 recipe Low Carb Flatbread
- 2 tbsp Dijon mustard
- 2 tbsp mayonnaise
- ½ lb black forest ham
- 6 oz brie thinly sliced
- 1 medium green apple very thinly sliced
- Oil or melted butter for brushing outside of sandwich

Instructions

- Preheat panini press.
- Cut bread into 10 sections, then cut through the bready center of each section to get two flat, thin slices.
- In a small bowl, mix mustard and mayonnaise.
- Take two matching sections of bread and spread one side with mustard/mayo combo. Layer with a few slices of cheese, meat and green apple. Repeat with remaining sections of bread.
- Brush outside of each sandwich with oil or melted butter.
- Place on panini press and grill until bread is toasted and cheese is melted.

Nutrition Info

Serves 10. Each serving has 15.5 g of carbs and 7.1 g of fiber. Total NET CARBS = 8.4 g.

46. Parmesan & Tomato Keto Bread Buns

Prep Time: 10-15 minutes

Total Time: 55-60 minutes

Ingredients (makes 5 buns)

Dry ingredients:

- 3/4 cup almond flour (75 g/ 2.7 oz)
- 2 1/2 tbsp psyllium husk powder (20 g/ 0.7 oz)
- 1/4 cup coconut flour (30 g/ 1.1 oz)
- 1/4 cup packed cup flax meal (38 g/ 1.3 oz)
- 1 tsp cream of tartar or apple cider vinegar
- 1/2 tsp baking soda

- 2/3 cup grated Parmesan cheese (60 g/ 2.1 oz)
- 1/3 cup chopped sun-dried tomatoes (37 g/ 1.3 oz)
- 1/4 - 1/2 tsp pink sea salt
- 2 tbsp sesame seeds (18 g/ 0.6 oz) - or use 2 tbsp sunflower, flax, poppy seeds, or 1 tbsp caraway seeds

Wet ingredients:

- 3 large egg whites
- 1 large egg
- 1 cups boiling water (240 ml/ 8 fl oz)

Instructions

- Preheat the oven to 175 °C/ 350 °F (fan assisted). Use a kitchen scale to measure all the ingredients and add them to a mixing bowl (apart from the sesame seeds which are used for topping): almond flour, coconut flour, flax meal, psyllium husk powder, cream of tartar, baking soda, salt, parmesan cheese and sun dried tomatoes. Mix all the dry ingredients together. Parmesan & Tomato Keto Bread Buns
- Add the egg whites and eggs and process well using a mixer until the dough is thick.

- The reason you shouldn't use only whole eggs is that the buns wouldn't rise with so many egg yolks in. Don't waste them - use them for making Home-made Mayo, Easy Hollandaise Sauce or Lemon Curd. Parmesan & Tomato Keto Bread Buns

- Add boiling water and process until well combined. Parmesan & Tomato Keto Bread Buns

- Using a spoon, divide the keto buns mix into 5 and roll into buns using your hands. Place them on a non-stick baking tray or on parchment paper. They will grow in size, so make sure to leave some space between them. You can even use small tart trays.

- Top each of the buns with sesame seeds (or any other seeds) and gently press them into the dough, so they don't fall out. Place in the oven and cook for about 45 - 50 minutes until golden on top. Parmesan & Tomato Keto Bread Buns

- Remove from the oven, let the tray cool down and place the buns on a rack to cool to room temperature. Parmesan & Tomato Keto Bread Buns

- Enjoy just like you would regular bread — with butter, ham or cheese! Parmesan & Tomato Keto Bread Buns Store in a tupperware for 2-3 days or freeze for up to 3 months.

Note:

You Can make 5 regular/large buns as per recipe, or up to 10 small buns.

Nutrition Info

Calories261 kcal

Net carbs4.9 grams

Protein14.5 grams

Fat18.9 grams

47. Coconut Flour Psyllium Husk Bread - Paleo

Want an easy low carb keto Paleo bread? Try this gluten free coconut flour psyllium bread recipe. It's a tasty bread to serve with breakfast or dinner.

Prep Time 5 minutes

Cook Time 55 minutes

Total Time 1 hour

Servings 15 slices

Calories 127kcal

Ingredients

- 6 tablespoons whole psyllium husks 27g, may want to finely grind
- 3/4 cup warm water
- 1 cup coconut flour 125g
- 1 1/2 teaspoons baking soda
- 3/4 teaspoon sea salt
- 1 pint egg whites 2 cups (or use 8 whole eggs)
- 2 large eggs see note
- 1/2 cup olive oil
- 1/4 cup coconut oil melted

Instructions

- Preheat oven to 350°F.
- If not using silicone pan, grease or line pan with parchment paper. I used an 8x4-in pan.
- Dump all ingredients into a food processor and pulse until well combined. If you don't have a food processor, you can use a mixing bowl with electric mixer.
- Spread batter into 8x4 loaf pan. Smooth top.
- Bake for 45-55 minutes or until edges are brown and toothpick inserted comes out clean.

- Let bread sit in pan for 15 minutes. Remove bread from pan and allow to cool completely on rack.

Notes

Original recipe used a carton of eggs which can result in an ammonia smell. Therefore, the recipe has changed to use 1 pint egg whites and 2 whole eggs.

Nutrition Info

Calories 127 Calories from Fat 120

Total Fat 13.3g 20%

Sodium 243mg 10%

Total Carbohydrates 6g 2%

Dietary Fiber 4.1g 16%

Protein 3g 6%

48. Paleo Gluten-Free Low Carb English Muffin Recipe in a Minute

A paleo low carb English muffin recipe that's soft and buttery inside, crusty on the outside. These gluten-free English muffins are easy to make in 2 minutes, with 5 ingredients!

Prep Time 2 minutes

Cook Time 3 minutes

Total Time 5 minutes

Ingredients

- 3 tbsp Blanched almond flour

- 1/2 tbsp Coconut flour
- 1 tbsp Butter (or ghee, or coconut oil)
- 1 large Egg (or equivalent egg whites)
- 1 pinch Sea salt
- 1/2 tsp Gluten-free baking powder

Instructions

- Melt ghee (or butter) in a microwave or oven safe ramekin or other container, about 4 in (10 cm) diameter with a flat bottom. This takes about 30 seconds. (If using the oven only, you can melt it in the oven while it preheats. Remove once melted.)
- Add the remaining ingredients and stir until well combined. Let sit for a minute to allow the mixture to thicken.

Microwave method:

- Microwave for about 90 seconds, until firm.

Oven method:
- Bake for about 15 minutes at 350 degrees F (177 degrees C), until the top is firm and spring-y to the touch.

- Run a knife along the edge and flip over a plate to release. Slice in half, then toast in the toaster.

Recipe Notes

- If you prefer more/smaller slices, you can also make it in a mug instead of a ramekin, then just pop those in the toaster in batches.

Serving size: 2 large slices (entire recipe)

Nutrition Info

Calories 307

Fat 27g

Protein 12g

Total Carbs 8g

Net Carbs 4g

Fiber 4g

Sugar 2g

49. Keto Cranberry Orange Bread

This recipe makes a keto cranberry orange bread. It's a low carb quick bread that features the flavors of fresh cranberries and orange zest and extract.

Prep Time: 10 minutes

Cook Time: 1 hour

Additional Time: 10 minutes

Total Time: 1 hour 20 minutes

Serving: 12

Ingredients

Keto Cranberry Orange Bread Batter

- 2 1/2 cups of finely milled almond flour
- 1 cup of sugar substitute
- 2 teaspoons of baking powder
- 1/2 teaspoon of sea salt
- 8 whole eggs
- 8 ounces of room temperature full-fat cream cheese
- 2 teaspoons of orange extract
- 1/2 cup of room temperature unsalted butter
- 2 cups of fresh or frozen whole cranberries
- 1 tablespoon of orange zest

Keto Orange Glaze

- 3/4 cup of confectioners sugar substitute
- 3 tablespoons of freshly squeezed lemon juice
- 2 tablespoons of heavy whipping cream
- 1 teaspoon of orange extract
- 2 teaspoons of orange zest

Instructions

Keto Cranberry Orange Bread

- Preheat oven to 350 degrees.

- Grease and line with parchment paper a 10 inch loaf pan or two 6 inch loaf pans. (note if using two smaller pans check for doneness at 35 minute mark)
- In a medium-sized bowl measure then sift the almond flour. To the sifted flour add the baking powder, sea salt and stir. Set this aside.
- In a large bowl using an electric hand-held mixer or stand-up mixer blend the butter, cream cheese, and sugar-substitute until mixture is light fluffy.
- Next add the eggs one at a time, making sure to scrape the bowl several times.
- To the wet batter add the dry ingredients and combine until well-incorporated.
- Fold in the cranberries in the bread batter.
- Spread the batter into the greased loaf pan.
- Bake for 60-70 minutes or until an inserted toothpick comes out clean.
- Allow the loaf to cool in the pan for about 30 minutes before taking it out of the pan. Then let the pan cool on a baking rack for another 30 minutes before adding the icing or freezing.

Keto Orange Icing

- In a small mixing bowl whisk the confectioners sugar substitute, lemon juice, orange zest, orange extract and heavy cream. Stir until fully combined.
- Spread/drizzle the icing over the cooled keto cranberry bread.

Nutrition Info

Calories: 337 Total Fat: 30.6g Saturated Fat: 11.4g Cholesterol: 154mg Sodium: 157mg Carbohydrates: 6.9g Fiber: 3.2g Sugar: 1.9g Protein: 10.3g

50. Turmeric Cauliflower Buns

These 4-Ingredient Turmeric Cauliflower Buns are an easy grain-free, low-carb, and super healthy side dish.

Prep Time: 30 mins

Cook Time: 30 mins

Serving: 6 1

Ingredients

- 1 medium head of cauliflower or about 2 cups of firmly packed cauliflower rice (see directions for making the cauliflower rice)
- 2 eggs

- 2 tablespoons coconut flour
- ¼ teaspoon ground turmeric
- pinch each of salt and pepper

Instructions

- Preheat oven to 400°F.
- Line a baking sheet with parchment paper and set aside.
- Take your cauliflower and use a sharp knife to cut off the base. Pull off any green parts and use your hands to break the cauliflower into florets. Give the florets a quick rinse and pat dry.
- Next, make cauliflower rice by placing the florets into the bowl of a food processor with the "S" blade. Pulse for about 30 seconds until the cauliflower is about the size of rice. You should have about two cups of firmly packed cauliflower rice.
- Place the cauliflower rice into a microwavable-safe bowl with about a teaspoon of water. Cover with plastic wrap and poke a few holes to let the steam escape. Microwave the cauliflower rice for about 3 minutes. Alternatively, you can steam the cauliflower rice on the stovetop in a steamer basket.

- Uncover the bowl and let the cauliflower rice cool for about 5 minutes. Then, use a large spoon to put the cauliflower rice into a nut milk bag or a clean dish towel. Squeeze the excess moisture out, being careful not to burn your hands.
- Pour the cauliflower rice into a medium mixing bowl and stir in the eggs, turmeric, and a pinch of salt and black pepper.
- Use your hands to form the mixture into 6 buns, placing them on the baking sheet.
- Bake for 25-30 minutes or until the top becomes slightly browned.
- The cauliflower buns are best served hot right out of the oven. They do not refrigerate or re-heat well (they will get mushy), but they are so delicious that you'll no doubt eat them right away!

Nutrition info

Calories Per Serving: 59

% Daily Value

3% Total Fat 2.1g

21% Cholesterol 62mg

6% Sodium 151.7mg

2% Total Carbohydrate 6.6g

51. Ultimate Dairy-Free Keto Bread

Prep Time 5 minutes

Cook Time 30 minutes

Servings 4

Ingredients

- 2 oz. macadamia butter OR 3.5 T almond butter + 0.5 T oil (2 oz. total)
- 2 large eggs
- 1 large egg white
- 1 oz. coconut flour

- 1/2 tsp. baking powder
- 1/4 tsp. salt
- 1/2 tsp. erythritol
- 1/2 tbsp. psyllium husks powder

Instructions

- Preheat the oven to 350°F (180°C). Line a baking pan with a sheet of parchment paper.
- In a small bowl, combine all the dry ingredients, leaving out only the psyllium husks powder. The coconut flour is best sifted.
- Ultimate Keto Bread
- Make macadamia butter if you don't have any. Just pulse the nuts in a bowl of an S-blade food processor (scraping the sides of the bowl once or twice) until you get runny butter.
- Ultimate Keto Bread
- Mix the eggs and the egg white in a medium bowl using an electric mixer. Add the macadamia butter and mix again until well incorporated.
- Ultimate Keto Bread
- Combine the egg mixture and the dry mixture, and mix well. At the very end, add the psyllium husks powder and

mix some more. If you find the mixture to be runny, add in another T of coconut flour and mix well.

- Ultimate Keto Bread
- Use your hands or a spoon to form four disks on the baking pan. Wet your hands to make this step less sticky.
- Bake for 30 minutes.

Nutrition Info

170 Calories,

Fat: 13.4 g (of which Saturated: 3.4 g, MUFA's: 9.3 g),

Total Carbs: 7.5 g,

Fiber: 4.9 g,

Net Carbs: 2.6 g,

Protein: 6.5 g

52. Low Carb Blueberry English Muffin Bread Loaf

Prep Time 15 minutes

Cook Time 45 minutes

Total Time 1 hour

Servings 12

Ingredients

- 1/2 cup almond butter or cashew or peanut butter
- 1/4 cup butter ghee or coconut oil
- 1/2 cup almond flour
- 1/2 tsp salt

- 2 tsp baking powder
- 1/2 cup almond milk unsweetened
- 5 eggs beaten
- 1/2 cup blueberries

Instructions

- Preheat oven to 350 degrees F.

- In a microwavable bowl melt nut butter and butter together for 30 seconds, stir until combined well.

- In a large bowl, whisk almond flour, salt and baking powder together. Pour the nut butter mixture into the large bowl and stir to combine.
- Whisk the almond milk and eggs together then pour into the bowl and stir well.

- Drop in fresh blueberries or break apart frozen blueberries and gently stir into the batter.
- Line a loaf pan with parchment paper and lightly grease the parchment paper as well.
- Pour the batter into the loaf pan and bake 45 minutes or until a toothpick in center comes out clean.

- Cool for about 30 minutes then remove from pan.

- Slice and toast each slice before serving.

Nutrition Info

Net Carbs: 3g

53. Low Carb Flatbread

Prep/Cook Time 35 mins, Servings: 10 servings

Ingredients

- 3 1/4 cups almond flour
- 6 tbsp coconut flour
- 1/3 cup unflavoured whey protein powder
- 2 tsp baking powder
- 1/2 tsp garlic powder
- 1/2 tsp salt
- 4 large eggs
- 1/4 cup oil (avocado or olive)
- 1/4 cup water

Instructions

- Preheat oven to 325F.
- In a large bowl, whisk together almond flour, coconut flour, whey protein, baking powder, garlic and salt. Whisk in eggs, oil and water until well combined. Dough should be quite sticky.
- Turn out onto a large piece of parchment paper and pat into a rough rectangle. Top with another piece of parchment.
- Roll into a large, rough rectngle about ½ inch to ¾ inch thick. Place on a large baking sheet and remove top layer of parchment.
- Bake 20 minutes or until firm to the touch.
- Remove from oven and let cool completely before cutting.
- Using a bread knife, cut into 10 sections. Cut each section carefully through the bready center into two halves. Fill with your favourite sandwich fillings.

Nutrition Info

Calories 316 Calories from Fat 233

Total Fat 25.9g 40%

Total Carbohydrates 11g 4%

Dietary Fiber 5.4g 22%

Protein 13.2g 26%

54. Zucchini Coconut Bread

Prep/Cook Time 60 minutes, Servings: 6

Ingredients

- 3/4 cup coconut flour
- 1/2 cup zucchini (grated and drained)
- 1/4 cup Pecan (chopped)
- 3/4 tbsp baking powder
- 1 tsp vanilla extract
- 1 scoop unflavored protein powder (around 28 - 30g)
- 6 large eggs
- 1/2 cup butter salted
- 1/2 cup So Nourished Erythritol (or less, up to your liking)

- 1/2 teaspoon salt

Instructions

-
- Preheat your oven to 350°F.
- Rinse the zucchini well with water and use a hand grater to shred it. Salt the grated zucchini in a bowl. Move to a colander to drain any unnecessary liquids. You should obtain about 1/2 cup of drained and shredded zucchini.
- Start making the dry mixture in a bowl. Fold the coconut flour, baking powder, and protein powder with the sweetener. Mix until blended entirely.
- Beat the eggs in a mixer together with vanilla extract and melted butter. Transfer the grated zucchini in and carefully add the dry mixture too. Whisk together until incorporated. Drop the chopped pecan.
- Coat a loaf pan with melted butter. Evenly spread the bread batter into the pan. Place in the oven for 40-45 minutes or until the bread is browned and cooked. Once the surface turns golden, take out from the oven and let sit for 10 minutes before removing from the pan.
- Slice and enjoy!

Nutrition info

Calories: 160, Fat: 14.3g, Net carbs: 0.9g (total carbs: 1.7g, dietary fiber: 0.8g), Protein: 6.9g

55. Low Carb and Keto Fluffy Waffles Recipe

Prep/Cook Time: 10 minutes, Servings: 4 full waffles

Ingredients

- 4 oz Cream Cheese
- 4 eggs
- 1 tablespoon melted butter
- 1 teaspoon vanilla extract
- 1 tablespoon powdered stevia
- 4 tablespoons coconut flour
- 1 1/2 teaspoons baking powder

Instructions

- Add all the ingredients to a blender and blend it on high for about 1 minute until all the ingredients come out nice and smooth. If you don't have a blender, you can mix it in a small bowl on medium speed for a minute or two. You will want to make sure you cream together all of the cream cheese so you don't have any lumps.
- Optional: Add cinnamon for extra flavor.
- Preheat the waffles iron.
- Spray the waffle iron with non-stick cooking spray.
- Pour about 1/8 to a 1/4 cup batter for each waffle. Note: the batter only spreads a bit more than the amount you put on the waffle iron. It's not like the regular carb filled waffle recipe where you put a small amount on the iron and it's dripping over the edges after a few minutes.
- These are very filling so don't be surprised if you only end up eating 2 out of the 4 waffle squares.
- Optional: Top with butter and sugar-free syrup.

Nutrition Info

Calories: 231kcal, Carbohydrates: 7.7g, Protein: 9.6g, Fat: 18.2g

56. Cranberry Jalapeño "Cornbread" Muffins

Low carb, grain-free muffins that taste like cornbread! Made with coconut flour and bursting with cranberries and jalapeño, these delicious muffins would make a great addition to any Thanksgiving table.

Prep Time 10 mins
Cook Time 30 mins
Total Time 40 mins
Servings: 12 muffins
Calories: 157 kcal

Ingredients

- 1 cup coconut flour (I used Bob's Red Mill)
- 1/3 cup Swerve Sweetener or other erythritol

- 1 tbsp baking powder
- 1/2 tsp salt
- 7 large eggs, lightly beaten
- 1 cup unsweetened almond milk
- 1/2 cup butter, melted OR avocado oil
- 1/2 tsp vanilla
- 1 cup fresh cranberries, cut in half
- 3 tbsp minced jalapeño peppers
- 1 jalapeño, seeds removed, sliced into 12 slices, for garnish

Instructions

- Preheat oven to 325F and grease a muffin tin well or line with paper liners.
- In a medium bowl, whisk together coconut flour, sweetener, baking powder and salt. Break up any clumps with the back of a fork.
- Stir in eggs, melted butter and almond milk and stir vigorously. Stir in vanilla extract and continue to stir until mixture is smooth and well combined. Stir in chopped cranberries and jalapeños.
- Divide batter evenly among prepared muffin cups and place one slice of jalapeño on top of each.

- Bake 25 to 30 minutes or until tops are set and a tester inserted in the center comes out clean. Let cool 10 minutes in pan, then transfer to a wire rack to cool completely.

Nutrition Info

Calories 157 Calories from Fat 101

Total Fat 11.22g 17%

Saturated Fat 7.11g 36%

Cholesterol 128mg 43%

Sodium 362mg 15%

Total Carbohydrates 7.08g 2%

Dietary Fiber 3.84g 15%

Protein 5.21g 10%

57. Collagen Keto Bread

Prep/Cook Time: 1 hour and 50 minutes (10 minutes active)

Ingredients:

- 1/2 cup Unflavored Grass-Fed Collagen Protein
- 6 tablespoons almond flour (see recipe notes below for nut-free substitute)
- 5 pastured eggs, separated
- 1 tablespoon unflavored liquid coconut oil
- 1 teaspoon aluminum-free baking powder
- 1 teaspoon xanthan gum (see recipe notes for substitute)
- Pinch Himalayan pink salt
- Optional: pinch of stevia

Instructions:

- Preheat oven to 325 degrees F.

- Generously oil only the bottom part of a standard size (1.5 quart) glass or ceramic loaf dish with coconut oil (or butter or ghee). Or you may use a piece of parchment paper trimmed to fit the bottom of your dish. Not oiling or lining the sides of your dish will allow the bread to attach to the sides and stay lifted while it cools.

- In a large bowl, beat the egg whites until stiff peaks form. Set aside.

- In a small bowl, whisk the dry ingredients together and set aside. Add the optional pinch of stevia if you're not a fan of eggs. It'll help offset the flavor without adding sweetness to your loaf.

- In a small bowl, whisk together the wet ingredients — egg yolks and liquid coconut oil — and set aside.

- Add the dry and the wet ingredients to the egg whites and mix until well incorporated. Your batter will be thick and a little gooey.

- Pour the batter into the oiled or lined dish and place in the oven.

- Bake for 40 minutes. The bread will rise significantly in the oven.

- Remove from oven and let it cool completely — about 1 to 2 hours. The bread will sink some and that's OK.
- Once the bread is cooled, run the sharp edge of a knife around the edges of the dish to release the loaf.
- Slice into 12 even slices.

Nutrition Info

Calories: 77

Protein: 7g

Carbs: 1g

Fiber: 1g

Sugar: 0g

58. Cheesy Low Carb Biscuits

Easy and delicious low carb biscuits recipe made with Cheddar cheese and sour cream. Perfect with soup, or as a breakfast biscuit. They even make great sandwiches.

Prep Time 10 mins

Cook Time 25 mins

Total Time 35 mins

Servings: 10 biscuits

Ingredients

- 1/2 cup coconut flour
- 1/2 cup almond flour
- 2 tsp baking powder
- 1 tsp garlic powder
- 1/2 tsp salt
- 3/4 cup shredded Cheddar cheese divided (I recommend Cabot Private Stock)
- 4 large eggs OR 3 large egg whites and 2 large eggs
- 3/4 cup sour cream or Greek yogurt I recommend Cabot full fat sour cream
- 1/4 cup butter melted

Instructions

- Preheat oven to 350F and line a large baking sheet with parchment or a silicone mat.
- In a large bowl, whisk together the coconut flour, almond flour, baking powder, garlic powder and salt. Whisk in 1/2 cup of the shredded Cheddar.
- Stir in eggs, sour cream and melted butter until well combined.

- Drop by rounded spoonfuls onto prepared baking sheet. These are very filling and they spread and rise so make the mounds smallish. You should get 10 to 12 biscuits.
- Sprinkle with remaining 1/4 cup Cheddar.
- Bake 20 to 23 minutes, until firm to the touch and cheese is just starting to brown.
- Remove and let cool 5 minutes.

Nutrition Info

Calories 185 Calories from Fat 128

Total Fat 14.2g 22%

Total Carbohydrates 5.6g 2%

Dietary Fiber 2.6g 10%

Protein 6.8g 14%

59. Keto + Low Carb Cornbread Muffins

These muffins are completely corn-free, but they are reminiscent of real cornbread muffins without the high carb count. They're perfect as a side, breakfast, or snack!

Prep Time: 15 minutes
Cook Time: 25 minutes
Total Time: 40 minutes
Servings: 12

Ingredients

- 3 eggs, slightly beaten
- 1/2 cup heavy whipping cream
- 1/2 cup unsweetened coconut milk (from a carton, not a jar)
- 5 tbsp salted butter, melted
- 3 oz cream cheese, softened
- 1 cup (128g) coconut flour
- 1/4 cup (30g) almond meal
- 3 tbsp (27g) Swerve Confectioners
- 1 1/2 tsp baking powder
- 1/8 tsp salt

Instructions

- Pre-heat oven to 350 F.
- If you're using a silicone muffin pan like I did, you don't need to grease the pan. However, if you're not using silicone, I recommend lightly greasing it or using liners for easy removal.
- In a large bowl, combine eggs, heavy whipping cream, coconut milk, melted butter (cooled slightly), and cream cheese. Using a hand mixer, mix everything until the cream cheese is well-incorporated. (It's okay if you have a few small flecks remaining.) Set aside.

- In a medium-sized bowl, combine coconut flour, almond meal, Swerve Confectioners, baking powder, and salt. Mix thoroughly.

- Add dry ingredients to wet and mix thoroughly using your hand mixer.

- Evenly distribute the batter across the holes, pressing the batter down a bit with the back of a spoon. (The batter is thick and easily forms pockets.) They will be about 80% full.

- Place in the oven and bake for 20-25 minutes until the edges start to brown and an inserted toothpick comes out mostly clean. Do not overbake. The center should still be slightly soft (but not uncooked) when you pull the pan out of the oven.

- Cool and enjoy!

Nutrition Info

Calories 169 Calories from Fat 126

Total Fat 14g 22%

Saturated Fat 8g 40%

Cholesterol 64mg 21%

Sodium 105mg 4%

Potassium 105mg 3%

Total Carbohydrates 7.8g 3%

Dietary Fiber 3.7g 15%

Sugars 0g

Protein 4g 8%

60. Keto Croissants

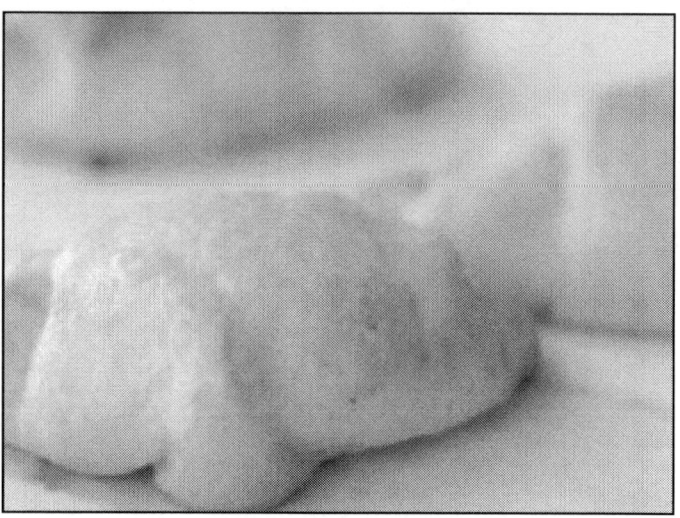

Fluffy with a crispy crust, these keto-style croissants will hit the spot when you are looking for something doughy on the side!

8 Servings

Prep Time 10 mins

Cook Time 13 mins

Total Time 23 mins

Ingredients

- 3 cups mozzarella cheese, shredded
- 2 oz cream cheese

- 3 egg whites
- ½ cup coconut flour
- 2 tbsp butter, melted
- 1 tbsp psyllium husk
- 2 tbsp sparkling water (room temperature)
- salt to taste

Instructions

- Preheat oven to 385°F and line baking sheet with parchment paper.
- Beat the egg whites until soft peaks form.
- Add cheese and cream cheese to a large microwavable bowl, stir and microwave until melted.
- Stir in the beaten egg whites, coconut flour, psyllium husk, and pinch of salt.
- Knead with hands until a dough-like consistency is reached, add sparkling water, and continue kneading.
- Note: If the dough becomes hard, microwave it for 10-15 seconds.
- Place dough between two sheets of parchment paper and spread with rolling pin to about ½ inches thickness.
- Brush half of the melted butter onto the dough.

- With a pizza cutter, start dividing the dough into 4 equal squares and further cut each square into two triangles that have a bottom approximately 4 inches wide.
- Roll the triangles upward, starting at the widest part, and gradually curve into a crescent shape.
- Place croissants onto baking sheet at least 2 inches apart.
- Brush remaining butter on top and bake for 12 minutes or until golden brown.

Nutrition Info

Servings 8

Calories 248

Total Fat 17.2g 27%

Net Carbohydrate 7.2g 3%

Dietary Fiber 3.8g 16%

Protein 16g 32%

61. Low Sugar Gluten Free Pumpkin Bread

A moist low sugar, low carb, and gluten free coconut flour pumpkin bread with no added sugars, and a delicious blend of spices to bring out the pumpkin flavor.

Prep time: 10 mins

Cook time: 60 mins

Total time: 1 hour 10 mins

Ingredients

- 1 cup coconut flour
- ½ cup Swerve Sweetener, granulated
- 8 eggs (I used large)
- 1 tsp baking soda
- ½ tsp baking powder
- ½ tsp salt
- 1 tsp Sweetleaf Stevia
- 2 tsp cinnamon
- ½ tsp ginger
- 1 tsp ground cloves
- 2 tbsp vanilla extract
- 1 stick butter
- 1, 15-oz can of pureed Pumpkin

Instructions

- Preheat oven to 350 degrees F, and grease a 9x5 bread pan with butter. (Using oil or butter vs spray helps the bread not to stick to the pan.)
- In a large bowl, mix together the dry ingredients of coconut flour, Swerve Sweetener, baking soda, baking powder, salt, Sweetleaf Stevia, cinnamon, ginger and ground cloves.

- In another bowl, mix together the wet ingredients. When well mixed, add the wet ingredients into the large ingredients and whisk well. (If using a blender, a low-medium blend is fine.)
- Fill the 9x5 bread pan with the pumpkin bread, and bake in the oven until a tooth pick comes out clear. For me, the 50-1 hr mark was perfect.

62. 3-Ingredient Grain-Free Bagels

Prep/Cook Time: 30 mins

Ingredients

- 3 eggs (organic and fresh!)
- 1/4 c. yogurt or sour cream (use dairy-free yogurt, if necessary)
- 1 1/2 c. almond flour

Instructions

- Preheat oven to 350 and grease 5 wells in a donut pan. (I use this donut pan.)

- Using a hand mixer, beat the eggs until they're light and creamy. Stir in the yogurt or sour cream until smooth.

- Slowly fold in the almond flour, 1/2 cup at a time.

- Spoon batter evenly into prepared donut molds and bake for 20 minutes.

- Slice, toast, and serve with butter, more sour cream, crème fraîche, coconut butter, whatever floats your boat!

63. Turmeric Cauliflower Buns

These 4-Ingredient Turmeric Cauliflower Buns are an easy grain-free, low-carb, and super healthy side dish.

Prep Time: 30 mins
Cook Time: 30 mins
Serving: 6

Ingredients

- 1 medium head of cauliflower or about 2 cups of firmly packed cauliflower rice (see directions for making the cauliflower rice)

- 2 eggs
- 2 tablespoons coconut flour
- ¼ teaspoon ground turmeric
- pinch each of salt and pepper

Instructions

- Preheat oven to 400°F.
- Line a baking sheet with parchment paper and set aside.
- Take your cauliflower and use a sharp knife to cut off the base. Pull off any green parts and use your hands to break the cauliflower into florets. Give the florets a quick rinse and pat dry.
- Next, make cauliflower rice by placing the florets into the bowl of a food processor with the "S" blade. Pulse for about 30 seconds until the cauliflower is about the size of rice. You should have about two cups of firmly packed cauliflower rice.
- Place the cauliflower rice into a microwavable-safe bowl with about a teaspoon of water. Cover with plastic wrap and poke a few holes to let the steam escape. Microwave the cauliflower rice for about 3 minutes. Alternatively, you can steam the cauliflower rice on the stovetop in a steamer basket.

- Uncover the bowl and let the cauliflower rice cool for about 5 minutes. Then, use a large spoon to put the cauliflower rice into a nut milk bag or a clean dish towel. Squeeze the excess moisture out, being careful not to burn your hands.
- Pour the cauliflower rice into a medium mixing bowl and stir in the eggs, turmeric, and a pinch of salt and black pepper.
- Use your hands to form the mixture into 6 buns, placing them on the baking sheet.
- Bake for 25-30 minutes or until the top becomes slightly browned.
- The cauliflower buns are best served hot right out of the oven. They do not refrigerate or re-heat well (they will get mushy), but they are so delicious that you'll no doubt eat them right away!

Nutrition Info

Calories Per Serving: 59
% Daily Value
3% Total Fat 2.1g
21% Cholesterol 62mg
6% Sodium 151.7mg

2% Total Carbohydrate 6.6g

Sugars 2.4g

9% Protein 4.5g

2% Vitamin A 26.7μg

79% Vitamin C 47.2mg

3% Calcium 31.2mg

4% Magnesium 17mg

64. Nut-Free Keto Buns

Hands-on 10-15 minutes

Overall 1 hour 15 minutes

Serving: 10 buns

Ingredients

Dry ingredients

- 1 1/4 cup fine defatted sesame seed flour (100 g / 3.5 oz)
- 2/3 cup flaxmeal (100 g / 3.5 oz)
- 2/3 cup coconut flour (80 g / 2.8 oz)

- 1/3 packed cup psyllium husk powder (40 g / 1.4 oz)
- 2 tsp garlic powder
- 2 tsp onion powder
- 2 tsp cream of tartar or apple cider vinegar
- 1 tsp baking soda
- 1 tsp salt (pink Himalayan or sea salt)
- 5 tbsp sesame seeds (or sunflower, flax, poppy seeds) or 1-2 tbsp caraway seeds for topping

Wet ingredients

- 6 large egg whites
- 2 large eggs
- 2 1/4 - 2 1/2 cups water depending on the consistency, boiling or lukewarm depending on the method - see intro (540 ml / 18 fl oz) - Use only 2 cups if using ground sesame seeds / sesame seed meal instead of defatted sesame seed flour.

Instructions

- Preheat the oven to 175 °C/ 350 °F. Use a kitchen scale to measure all the ingredients carefully. I used defatted sesame seed flour but you can try sesame seed meal instead and use less water. To make sesame seed meal, I just blend the seeds until powdered (just like I do with flax seeds to make flax meal).

- I used Sukrin sesame flour (UK) but you can use this brand too (US) - both should be defatted. Nut-Free Keto Buns

- Mix all the dry ingredients apart from the seeds for the topping in a bowl: sesame flour, coconut flour, flaxmeal, psyllium powder, ...

- Do not use whole psyllium husks - if you cannot find psyllium husk powder, use a blender or coffee grinder and process until fine. If you get already prepared psyllium husk powder, remember to weigh it before adding to the recipe. I used whole psyllium husks which I grinded myself. Do not use just measure cups - different products have different weights per cup! Nut-Free

- ..., baking soda, cream of tartar, garlic powder, ...

- Cream of tartar and baking soda act as leavening agents. This is how it works: To get 2 teaspoons of gluten-free baking powder, you need 1/2 a teaspoon of baking soda and 1 teaspoon of cream of tartar (double in this recipe of 10 buns). If you don't have cream of tartar, instead you can use apple cider vinegar and add it to the wet ingredients. Nut-Free Keto Buns

- ... onion powder and salt

- Add the egg whites and eggs and process well using a mixer until the dough is thick.

- Nut-Free Keto Buns The reason you shouldn't use only whole eggs is that the buns wouldn't rise with so many egg yolks in. Don't waste them - use them for making Home-made Mayo, Easy Hollandaise Sauce or Lemon Curd.

- Add boiling water and mix until well combined. Nut-Free Keto Buns

- Using a spoon or hands, form the buns and place them on a non-stick baking tray or a parchment paper. They will grow in size as they bake, so make sure to leave some space between them. Top each of the buns with sesame seeds (or any other seeds) and press them into the dough, so they don't fall out.

- Place in the oven and cook for 55-60 minutes. Remove from the oven, let the tray cool down and place the buns on a rack to cool down to room temperature. Store them at room temperature if you plan to use them in the next couple of days or in the freezer for future use.

- Top with butter or cream cheese, burger meat and meat-free toppings. Enjoy!

Nutrition Info

Net carbs3.5 grams

Protein12.3 grams

Fat10.6 grams

Calories180 kcal

65. Keto Breakfast Pizza

Prep/Cook Time: 25 minutes

Ingredients:

- 2 cups grated cauliflower
- 2 tablespoons coconut flour
- 1/2 teaspoon salt
- 4 eggs
- 1 tablespoon psyllium husk powder (Use a mold-free brand like this one)
- Toppings: smoked Salmon, avocado, herbs, spinach, olive oil (see post for more suggestions)

Instructions:

- Preheat the oven to 350 degrees. Line a pizza tray or sheet pan with parchment.
- In a mixing bowl, add all ingredients except toppings and mix until combined. Set aside for 5 minutes to allow coconut flour and psyllium husk to absorb liquid and thicken up.
- Carefully pour the breakfast pizza base onto the pan. Use your hands to mold it into a round, even pizza crust.
- Bake for 15 minutes, or until golden brown and fully cooked.
- Remove from the oven and top breakfast pizza with your chosen toppings. Serve warm.

Nutrition Info

Calories: 454

Total Fat: 31g

Saturated Fat: 75g

Cholesterol: 348mg

Total Carbs: 26g

Fiber: 17.2g

Sugars: 4.4g

Net Carbs: 8.8g

Protein: 22g

66. Keto Flax Seed Bread

Prep Time 5 minutes

Cook Time 2 minutes

Total Time 7 minutes

Servings 2 Slices

Ingredients

- 1 tablespoon Softened Butter
- 4 tablespoons Organic Ground Flaxseed Meal
- 1 Large Egg
- ½ teaspoon Baking Powder

- ½ teaspoon Salt

Instructions

- Grab your Pyrex glass square dish and add the butter. Melt it in the microwave for a few seconds.
- Crack your egg into the dish and give it a good mix with a fork.
- Mix the ground flax seed, salt and baking powder in a separate bowl and combine.
- Add all the mixed dry ingredients, ground flax, salt, and baking powder directly into the baking dish and combine all ingredients thoroughly.
- It will turn into a thick texture. Flatten out the surface of the mixture to ensure even cooking.
- Cook in the microwave for two minutes.
- Leave to cool for a few minutes before taking out.
- Use a spatula and gently pull the bread away from the side of the dish. After you turn it upside down, it should come out without difficulty.
- Grab your bread knife and cut it in half to make two slices

67. Keto Paleo Low-Carb Stuffing

A paleo-friendly, low-carb, keto stuffing made with homemade coconut flour bread. Savory and delicious for everyone at the holiday dinner table.

Prep time: 20 mins

Cook time: 30 mins

Total time: 50 mins

Serves: 12

Ingredients

- 1 loaf low-carb coconut flour bread
- ¼ cup fresh parsley
- 2 tablespoons tallow, coconut oil or red palm oil
- ½ red onion (200 grams), diced
- 4 celery sticks (200 grams), diced
- 2 teaspoons dried thyme leaves
- 1 teaspoon dried rosemary
- ½ teaspoon dried ground sage
- ¼ teaspoon black pepper
- ¼ teaspoon Himalayan rock salt
- ¼ teaspoon ground ginger
- ¼ teaspoon ground cinnamon
- ¾ cup homemade beef broth
- ¼ cup stevia-sweetened ginger ale (soda), or additional beef broth

Instructions

- Roughly chop fresh-baked bread into 1 inch chunks (it doesn't have to be perfect). Place the pieces on a large baking sheet and place in the oven (do not turn it on!).

Keep it there for 24-48 hours. If it's still moist, let it sit in a 170F oven for about 1 hour or so. The bread should be a bit more moist than croutons, but not soft. This step will help the bread retain its shape in the stuffing, so don't skip it! Alternatively, you can dehydrate in your dehydrator, 130F for 24 hours.

- Place the bread chunks in a large bowl, toss with fresh parsley and set aside.
- Preheat oven to 350F and lightly grease a 2.3 L/2.5 qt. casserole dish with a dab of tallow, coconut oil or red palm oil.
- Heat tallow in a large pan on medium-high heat. Add onion and cook until soft, about 5 minutes. Add celery, thyme, rosemary, sage, pepper, salt, ginger and cinnamon. Cook for another 3 minutes.
- Remove from heat and add vegetable mixture to bread and toss to combine being sure not to over mix.
- Now, combine the beef broth and stevia-sweetened soda in a small dish. Pour the mixture over top of the bread. Again, be sure not to over mix, just toss, then add to the prepared casserole dish.
- Cover and bake in preheated oven for 30 minutes.
- Remove from the oven and let sit with the cover on for 5 minutes.

Nutrition Info

Calories: 234

Calories from Fat: 158.4

Total Fat: 17.6 g

Saturated Fat: 12.2 g

Cholesterol: 55 mg

Sodium: 169 mg

Carbs: 11.1 g

Dietary Fiber: 5.7 g

Net Carbs: 5.4 g

Sugars: 3.1 g

Protein: 7.7 g

68. Low Carb Pumpkin Bread

Prep Time: 15 minutes

Cook Time: 45 minutes

Total Time: 1 hour

Serving: 20

Ingredients

- 15 oz. can of pumpkin puree
- 2 cups granulated of sugar substitute
- 3 teaspoons of baking powder

- 2 teaspoon vanilla extract
- 3 tablespoons of pumpkin pie spice
- 3 tablespoons of cinnamon powder
- 1/4 teaspoon sea salt
- 10 large eggs
- 3 cups of almond flour
- 1 cup of golden flax meal
- Optional
- Cream Cheese Frosting
- 8 oz package of softened cream cheese
- 4 tablespoons of heavy whipping cream
- 1 cup of sugar-free confectioners sugar

Instructions

- Preheat oven to 350 degrees.
- Grease two 8x4 inch loaf pans well.
- Using an electric mixer, beat the pumpkin puree, sugar substitute, and vanilla extract until well blended.
- Next add in the eggs one at time making sure to beat until fully combined.
- To the wet batter add the almond flour, flax meal, baking powder, spices and salt.

- Note that batter will be thick. Pour the batter into the two prepared pans and bake at 350 degrees for 45 minutes, or until an inserted toothpick comes out clean.

Nutrition Info

Calories: 200 Total Fat: 15.8g Saturated Fat: 5.5g Cholesterol: 59mg Sodium: 60mg Carbohydrates: 4.8g Fiber: 2.9g Sugar: 0.8g Protein: 6.4g

69. Low Carb Keto Banana Walnut Bread

This recipe for low carb keto banana walnut bread uses a mixture of yellow squash and banana extract to mimic the taste of bananas.

Prep Time: 20
Cook Time: 1:00
Total Time: 1 hour 20 minutes
Serving: 12 slices

Ingredients

- cooking spray
- 1 cup super fine almond flour
- 1 cup flaxseed meal
- 3/4 cup Swerve or equivalent granulated sweetener
- 1/4 cup Isopure Whey Protein Powder or equivalent zero carb protein powder
- 1/4 cup oat fiber
- 1 tablespoon baking powder
- 1 teaspoon ground cinnamon
- 1/4 teaspoon salt
- 3 oz yellow squash (1/2 a squash), grated
- 5 large eggs
- 1 cup whole milk ricotta cheese
- 2 teaspoons vanilla extract
- 4 teaspoons banana extract
- 1/4 cup walnuts, chopped

Instructions

- Preheat oven to 350 degrees F. Cut a piece of parchment paper to fit in and over the side of a loaf pan. You'll use it to remove the bread to cool. Spray with non-stick cooking spray.

- In medium sized mixing bowl, add almond flour, flaxseed meal, sweetener, whey protein, oat fiber, baking powder, cinnamon and salt. Whisk together.

- Grate the yellow squash and blot the liquid from it with paper towels. Add to a large bowl along with eggs, ricotta cheese, vanilla and banana extract. Mix well to combine.

- Add the dry ingredients to the wet ingredients and mix well.

- Add batter to prepared loaf pan and use a spatula to smooth the top. Sprinkle walnuts over the top of the batter.

- Bake for 55-65 minutes until browned on top and a toothpick in the middle comes out clean. Check in at minute 40 and place a sheet of aluminum foil over the top to prevent further browning.

- Cool for 10 minutes in the pan. Cut around the edges of the pan and remove the loaf using the sides of parchment paper. Place loaf on cooling rack and cool for at least 10 more minutes before cutting.

Nutrition Info

Calories: 193

Fat: 14

Carbohydrates: 9

Fiber: 5

Protein: 10

70. Gluten Free, Paleo & Keto Drop Biscuits

Ultra tasty, easy, tender and moist. These gluten free, paleo and keto drop biscuits check all the right boxes! Whip them up in 30, for an awesome low carb bread that goes great with sweet and savory alike.

Prep Time: 10 minutes
Cook Time: 20 minutes
Total Time: 30 minutes
Servings: biscuits

Ingredients

- 1 egg
- 77 g sour cream or coconut cream + 2 tsp. apple cider vinegar, at room temp
- 2 tablespoons water
- 1 tablespoon apple cider vinegar
- 96 g almond flour
- 63 g golden flaxseed meal or psyllium husk, finely ground
- 21 g coconut flour
- 20 g whey protein isolate or more almond flour
- 3 1/2 teaspoons baking powder
- 1 teaspoon xanthan gum or 1 TBS. flaxseed meal
- 1/2 teaspoon kosher salt
- 112 g organic grass-fed butter or 7 TBS. ghee/coconut oil

Instructions

- Prehcat oven to 450°F/230°C. Linc a baking tray with parchment paper or a baking mat.

- Add eggs, sour (or coconut) cream, water and apple cider vinegar to a medium bowl and whisk for a minute or two until fully mixed. Set aside.

- Add almond flour, flaxseed meal, coconut flour, whey protein, baking powder, xanthan gum (or more flax) and kosher salt to a food processor and pulse until very thoroughly combined.

- Add in the butter and pulse a few times until pea-sized. Pour in the egg and cream mixture, pulsing until combined. The dough will be very shaggy.

- Drop 6 rounds of dough onto the prepared baking tray. Brush with melted butter and bake for 15-20 minutes until deep golden. Allow to cool for 10 minutes before serving. These guys keep well, stored in an airtight container at room temperature, for 3-4 days.

- You can freeze the shaped biscuit dough for 1-2 months, and bake straight from the freezer as needed.

Nutrition Info

Calories 290 Calories from Fat 270

Total Fat 30g 46%

Saturated Fat 11g 55%

Cholesterol 74mg 25%

Sodium 455mg 19%

Potassium 113mg 3%

Total Carbohydrates 8g 3%

Dietary Fiber 5g 20%

Sugars 1g

Protein 7g 14%

71. Low Carb Keto Bagels Recipe (Fathead Dough)

Prep/Cook Time: 22 minutes, Servings: 6

Ingredients

- 1 1/2 cup part-skim shredded mozzarella cheese (about 6 ounces)
- 2 ounces full-fat cream cheese, cut into pieces
- 1 large egg
- 1 1/4 cup almond flour (nut-free options in post) (see conversion chart in site menu)
- 1 tbsp baking powder

- 1 tbsp oat fiber (or 2 tbsp whey protein powder or 1/4 cup more almond flour)*

Instructions

- Place the mozzarella cheese and cream cheese in a microwave safe bowl and microwave for 1 minute. Stir and microwave for 30 seconds to 1 minute more. Scrape the cheese into a food processor with the egg and process until smooth.
- Add the dry ingredients and process until a dough forms. It is very sticky! Scrape onto a piece of cling film and place into the freezer.
- Preheat oven to 400 F and place rack into the middle of the oven. Line a baking sheet with parchment.
- When oven is ready, remove the bagel dough from the freezer and divide into 6 equal pieces. Lightly oil hands and roll each portion into a snake and seal the ends together forming a ring. Place on the parchment paper and top with your favorite topping, pressing gently to adhere.
- Bake for 12 minutes or until the outside has browned. They will still be soft, so let them cool before removing

from the baking sheet. Once cool, store in a bag in the refrigerator. Warm slightly to enjoy or toast.

- Makes 6 average sized bagels. Dividing the dough into 8 portions results in mini bagels and dividing into 4 results in gourmet sized bagels. (Don't have a food processor? Read the post for other methods.)
- Keep bagels in the refrigerator in an airtight container. They keep for 7-10 days and also freeze well.

Nutrition Info

Calories 245 Calories from Fat 189

Total Fat 21g 32%

Sodium 316mg 13%

Total Carbohydrates 6g 2%

Dietary Fiber 3g 12%

Protein 12g

72. The Best Cloud Bread Recipe

Prep/Cook Time 25 mins

Ingredients

- 4 large eggs, separated
- 1/2 teaspoon cream of tartar
- 2 ounces low-fat cream cheese
- 1 teaspoon Italian herb seasoning
- 1/2 teaspoon sea salt
- 1/4 - 1/2 teaspoon garlic powder

Instructions

- Preheat the oven to 300 degrees F. If you have a convection oven, set on convect. Line two large baking sheets with parchment paper.

- Separate the egg whites and egg yolks. Place the whites in a stand mixer with a whip attachment. Add the cream of tartar and beat on high until the froth turns into firm meringue peaks. Move to a separate bowl.

- Place the cream cheese in the empty stand mixing bowl. Beat on high to soften. Then add the egg yolks one at a time to incorporate. Scrape the bowl and beat until the mixture is completely smooth. Then beat in the Italian seasoning, salt, and garlic powder.

- Gently fold the firm meringue into the yolk mixture. Try to deflate the meringue as little as possible, so the mixture is still firm and foamy. Spoon 1/4 cup portions of the foam onto the baking sheets and spread into even 4-inch circles, 3/4 inch high. Make sure to leave space around each circle.

- Bake on convect for 15-18 minutes, or in a conventional oven for up to 30 minutes. The bread should be golden on the outside and firm. The center should not jiggle when shaken. Cool for several minutes on the baking sheets, then move and serve!

Nutrition Info

Calories 36 Calories from Fat 18

Total Fat 2g 3%

Saturated Fat 1g 5%

Cholesterol 68mg 23%

Sugars 0g

Protein 2g 4%

73. Keto Focaccia Bread Recipe

Prep/Time: 25 minutes, Servings: 1 serving

Ingredients

- 2 Tablespoons (12 g) gelatin powder
- 2 Tablespoons (30 ml) water
- 2 Tablespoons (30 ml) hot water
- 1 Tablespoon (8 g) nutritional yeast flakes
- 1 cup (240 ml) hot water
- 2 cups (8 oz or 225 g) coconut flour

- 1/4 cup (0.9 oz or 25 g) psyllium husk powder
- 1 teaspoon (2 g) baking powder
- 1 teaspoon (4 g) baking soda
- Dash of garlic powder
- Dash of salt
- 3 large eggs
- 2 teaspoons (10 ml) olive oil
- Handful of fresh rosemary tips
- Sea salt flakes

Instructions

Preheat the oven to 350 F (175 C).

- Make a gelatine egg by sprinkling the gelatine powder over two tablespoons water. Once dissolved, stir in two tablespoons boiling hot water and set aside while you prepare the remaining ingredients.
- Dissolve the nutritional yeast flakes in a cup of hot water and set aside.
- Combine the coconut flour, psyllium husk powder, baking powder, baking soda, garlic powder and salt in a bowl.
- In a separate bowl, whisk the eggs with the olive oil and add in the gelatine mixture once it has cooled slightly (else it will scramble the eggs). Check the temperature of

the nutritional yeast water, once that has sufficiently cooled to add to the egg mixture, whisk this in too.

- Add the egg mixture to the flour mixture and combine well. Tip the mixture into a greased baking dish (approx. 6-in x 6-in) so the mixture comes up at least an inch high. Make small indentations using the back of a chopstick and pierce with little washed rosemary tips.
- Bake in the oven for 25 minutes, or until a cake tester inserted comes out clean. Scatter over sea salt flakes and trim into pieces once cooled.

Nutrition Info

Calories: 212 Sugar: 3 g Fat: 9 g Carbohydrates: 17 g Fiber: 14 g Protein: 13 g

74. 3 Ingredient Paleo Naan (Indian bread)

Prep Time: 5 minutes Serving: 6 small naans Method: Stovetop Cuisine: Indian

Ingredients

- ½ cup almond flour
- ½ cup tapioca flour or arrowroot flour
- 1 cup coconut milk, canned and full fat
- Salt, adjust to taste, optional
- Ghee (slather that bread!), optional

Instructions

- Preheat a crepe pan OR nonstick pan over medium heat.
- Mix all the ingredients together in a bowl, and pour ¼ cup of the batter onto the pan.
- After the batter fluffs up and looks firm/mostly cooked, flip it over to cook the other side (be patient, this takes a little time!).
- Serve immediately or cool on a wire rack.

Nutrition Info

Calories Per Serving: 129

15% Total Fat 9.6g

0% Cholesterol 0mg

0% Sodium 6mg

4% Total Carbohydrate 11g

Sugars 1.4g

2% Protein 1g

75. Rosemary and Garlic Coconut Flour Bread

Prep Time: 10 minutes

Cook Time: 45 minutes

Total Time: 55 minutes

Servings: 10 Slices

Ingredients

- 1/2 cup Coconut flour
- 1 stick butter (8 tbsp)
- 6 large eggs
- 1 tsp Baking powder

- 2 tsp Dried Rosemary
- 1/2-1 tsp garlic powder
- 1/2 tsp Onion powder
- 1/4 tsp Pink Himalayan Salt

Instructions

- Combine dry ingredients (coconut flour, baking powder, onion, garlic, rosemary and salt) in a bowl and set aside.
- Add 6 eggs to a separate bowl and beat with a hand mixer until you get see bubbles at the top.
- Melt the stick of butter in the microwave and slowly add it to the eggs as you beat with the hand mixer.
- Once wet and dry ingredients are fully combined in separate bowls, slowly add the dry ingredients to the wet ingredients as you mix with the hand mixture.
- Grease an 8x4 loaf pan and pour the mixture into it evenly.
- Bake at 350 for 40-50 minutes (time will vary depending on your oven).
- Let it rest for 10 minutes before removing from the pan. Slice up and enjoy with butter or toasted!

Nutrition Info

Calories: 147kcal, Carbohydrates: 3.5g, Protein: 4.6g, Fat: 12.5g, Fiber: 2g

76. Keto Cream Cheese Bread

Keto cream cheese bread is a low carb bread recipe that is made with coconut flour making it keto-friendly as well as nut-free.

Prep Time: 5 minutes

Cook Time: 25 minutes

Additional Time: 5 minutes

Total Time: 35 minutes

Serving: 12

Ingredients

- 8 large eggs

- 8 ounces of full-fat cream cheese (room temperature)
- ½ cup of unsalted butter (room temperature)
- 1 ½ cups coconut flour
- ½ cup of full-fat sour cream
- 4 teaspoons of baking powder
- 1 teaspoon of sea salt
- 1 tablespoon of sugar substitute
- 2 tablespoons of sesame seeds (optional)

Instructions

- Allow your eggs, cream cheese, butter to come to room temperature.
- Pre-heat your oven to 350 degrees.
- Grease a 12 cavity muffin pan generously with butter or a 10 inch loaf pan.
- In a medium-sized bowl combine your coconut flour, baking powder, sea salt, sugar substitute and set aside.
- In a large bowl using a handheld electric mixer or a standup mixer beat together the room temperature butter, cream cheese until light and fluffy. Be sure to scrape the sides of bowl several times to make sure the mixture is well blended.

- To this butter and cream cheese mixture add the 8 eggs one at a time. Making sure to scrape the sides of the bowl several times. Note that due to the large number of eggs the mixture will not fully combine, this is normal. Once you add the dry ingredients to this wet mixture, the ingredients will come together perfectly.

- To the wet ingredients slowly add all the dry ingredients on a low mixing setting. Making sure to scrape the bowl a couple of times.

- Once the two mixtures are fully combined stop using the electric mixture and fold in the 1/2 cup of sour cream gently. Making sure the sour cream gets fully incorporated into the batter but being careful to not over mix.Note that the batter will be very thick and fluffy. This is the normal texture when using coconut flour exclusively in a recipe.

- Overfill the muffin pan just slightly. The thick batter will not cause the muffins to spread. Slightly overfilling your muffin tins will create a nice muffin top.

- With one additional whole egg and a tablespoon of water create an egg wash. Baste the top of each muffin with the egg wash and then sprinkle the sesame seeds on top of each muffin. This step is optional.

- Bake the muffins for 25-30 minutes until lightly brown on the top and when an inserted toothpick comes out clean.
- Report this ad
- If you are baking your keto cream cheese bread in a 10 inch loaf, bake the bread for up to 90 minutes. Check your bread at 60 minutes for doneness and allow to cook longer if necessary.

Nutrition Info

Calories: 204 Total Fat: 19.4g Saturated Fat: 11.4g Cholesterol: 154mg Sodium: 160mg Carbohydrates: 2.2g Fiber: 0.6g Sugar: 0.4g Protein: 5.8g

77. Sunflower Pumpkin Seed Psyllium Bread

A low carb gluten free pumpkin sunflower seed psyllium bread. It's packed with hearty seeds and fiber. Enjoy it as a snack or along with a meal.

Prep Time 5 minutes

Cook Time 1 hour 10 minutes

Total Time 1 hour 15 minutes

Servings 10 people

Ingredients

- 1/2 cup whole psyllium husks finely ground, 60g
- 1/4 cup chia seeds 40g
- 1/4 cup pumpkin seeds 40g
- 1/4 cup sunflower seeds 40g
- 2 tablespoons flaxseed meal (15g) or sesame seed flour
- 1 teaspoon baking powder
- 1/4 teaspoon salt
- 3 tablespoons coconut oil melted
- 1 1/4 cup egg whites (300g) I used pasteurized in a carton
- 1/2 cup almond milk

Instructions

- In large mixing bowl, stir together psyllium, chia, pumpkin seeds, sunflower seeds, flax, baking powder, and salt.
- Stir in coconut oil.
- Blend in egg whites and almond milk being careful not to over mix.
- When thickened, spread out into a greased or lined 8x4-inch loaf pan.
- Bake for about 70 minutes at 325°F or until internal temperature reaches about 215°F.

Nutrition Info

Calories 155 Calories from Fat 72

Total Fat 8g 12%

Saturated Fat 4g 20%

Cholesterol 0mg 0%

Sodium 126mg 5%

Potassium 153mg 4%

Total Carbohydrates 14g 5%

Dietary Fiber 11g 44%

Sugars 0g

Protein 5g 10%

78. Buttery Low Carb Flatbread

Prep time 5 mins

Cook time 2 mins

Total time 7 mins

Serves: 4

Ingredients

- 1 cup Almond Flour
- 2 tbsp Coconut Flour
- 2 tsp Xanthan Gum
- ½ tsp Baking Powder
- ½ tsp Falk Salt + more to garnish

- 1 Whole Egg + 1 Egg White
- 1 tbsp Water
- 1 tbsp Oil for frying
- 1 tbsp melted Butter-for slathering

Instructions

- Whisk together the dry ingredients (flours, xanthan gum, baking powder, salt) until well combined.
- Add the egg and egg white and beat gently into the flour to incorporate. The dough will begin to form.
- Add the tablespoon of water and begin to work the dough to allow the flour and xanthan gum to absorb the moisture.
- Cut the dough in 4 equal parts and press each section out with cling wrap. Watch the video for instructions!
- Heat a large skillet over medium heat and add oil.
- Fry each flatbread for about 1 min on each side.
- Brush with butter (while hot) and garnish with salt and chopped parsley.

79. Keto Fathead Bagels

Truly chewy keto bagels - you want them and I've got them! These bagels are low carb, nut-free, and take only 5 ingredients to make. Easy and delicious, they will take your healthy breakfast to a whole new level.

Prep Time 20 mins
Cook Time 20 mins
Total Time 40 mins
Servings: 8 servings

Ingredients

- 1/2 cup coconut flour (56g)
- 2 tsp baking powder
- 3/4 tsp xanthan gum
- 12 oz pre-shredded part skim mozzarella
- 2 large eggs

Optional Topping for Everything Bagels

- 1 tsp sesame seeds
- 1 tsp poppyseed
- 1 tsp dried minced onion
- 1/2 tsp coarse salt
- 1 tbsp butter melted

Instructions

- Preheat the oven to 350F and line a large baking sheet with a silicone liner. In a medium bowl, whisk together the coconut flour, baking powder, and xanthan gum. Set aside.

- In a large microwave safe bowl, melt the cheese on high in 30 second increments until well melted and almost liquid. Stir in the flour mixture and the eggs and knead in the bowl using a rubber spatula.

- Turn out onto the prepared baking sheet and continue to knead together until cohesive. Cut the dough in half and cut each half into 4 equal portions so that you have 8 equal pieces of dough.

- Roll each portion out into a log about 8 inches long. Pinch the ends of the log together.

- In a shallow dish, stir together the sesame seeds, poppyseed, dried onion, and salt. Brush the top of each bagel with melted butter and dip firmly into the everything seasoning. Set back on the silicone mat.

- Bake 15 to 20 minutes, until the bagels have risen and are golden brown.

Nutrition Info

Calories 190 Calories from Fat 111
Total Fat 12.3g 19%
Total Carbohydrates 5.5g 2%

Dietary Fiber 2.6g 10%

Protein 12.1g 24%

80. Keto Banana Bread

A delicious version of Keto Banana Bread. I may be a little controversial with this recipe but I am providing options to satisfy all keto needs.

Prep Time: 10 minutes

Cook Time: 1 hour

Total Time: 1 hour 5 minutes

Servings: 16 serves

Ingredients

- 80 g butter melted
- 25 g sugar free maple syrup
- 1 cup (150g) Sukrin Gold sweetener or Lakanto Gold sweetener
- 2 teaspoons ground cinnamon
- 1/2 teaspoon nutmeg fresh grated
- 1 teaspoon vanilla
- 100 g banana
- 60 g golden flax meal or golden flax seeds milled extra fine
- 20 g coconut flour
- 150 g almond meal
- 1 tablespoon baking powder I totally recommend Bobs Red Mill Baking Powder for best rise
- 10 g psyllium husk powder or chia flour
- 1 teaspoon xanthan gum
- 4 eggs
- 80 g Greek natural yogurt

OPTIONAL

- 2 teaspoons banana extract INSTEAD of banana
- 1 cup walnuts or brazil nuts chopped

Instructions

- Preheat oven 170°. Line a 22cm x 11cm loaf tine with baking paper.

Conventional Method

- Over medium heat cook butter, maple syrup, sweetener, cinnamon and nutmeg until butter has melted.
- In a large mixing bowl mash bananas. Pour in melted butter mixture and combine well.
- Add remaining ingredients including nuts (if using) and fold until combined.
- Scoop batter into prepared loaf tin. Smooth over top of loaf with wet spatula.
- Bake 60 minutes or until a skewer comes out clean. Cool 5 minutes in pan before transferring to wire rack to cool completely.

Thermomix Method

- Add butter, maple syrup, sweetener, cinnamon and nutmeg and cook 5 minutes/100°/stir.
- Add banana and mix 10 seconds speed 4. Scrape sides of bowl
- Add remaining ingredients. Mix 30 seconds/speed 3. Fold though nuts (if using) Follow instructions from Step 4 above.

Nutrition Info

Calories: 141kcal, Carbohydrates: 6g, Protein: 4g, Fat: 11g, Saturated Fat: 3g, Cholesterol: 51mg, Sodium: 63mg, Potassium: 150mg, Fiber: 2g, Sugar: 1g, Vitamin A: 3.8%, Vitamin C: 0.7%, Calcium: 7.7%, Iron: 5%

81. 3 Minute Low Carb Biscuits

Prep Time: 2 minutes

Cook Time: 3 minutes

Total Time: 5 minutes

Servings: 1 Servings

Calories: 392kcal

Ingredients

- 1 tbsp Butter
- 2 tbsp Coconut flour

- 1 large Egg
- 1 tbsp Heavy Whipping Cream
- 2 tbsp Water
- 1/4 cup Cheddar Cheese
- 1/8 tsp garlic powder
- 1/8 tsp Onion powder
- 1/8 tsp Dried Parsley
- 1/8 tsp Pink Himalayan Salt
- 1/8 tsp black pepper
- 1/4 tsp Baking powder

Instructions

- Melt butter in a coffee mug by microwaving for 20 seconds.
- Add coconut flour, baking powder, and seasonings. Mix to incorporate with a fork.
- Add egg, water, cheese and heavy whipping cream. Mix until combined.
- Microwave for 3 minutes. Immediately remove from mug and allow to cool for 2 minutes.
- Slice and enjoy.

Nutrition Info

Calories: 392kcal, Carbohydrates: 9g, Protein: 15g, Fat: 32g, Fiber: 5g

82. Keto Mini Bread Loaves

Prep/Cook Time: 1 hour 10 mins

Serving:32

Ingredients

- 2 cups almond flour
- 1/2 cup psyllium husk powder
- 1/2 cup ground flax
- 4 teaspoons baking powder
- 2 tablespoons coconut flour
- 2 teaspoons Pink Himalayan sea salt
- 5 teaspoons Apple Cider Vinegar
- 1 3/4 cups boiling water

- 4 egg whites
- 2 eggs

Instructions

- Preheat oven to 350 degrees.
- Mix the almond flour, coconut flour, psyllium husk, flax, sea salt, and baking powder in a medium bowl.
- Meanwhile, boil the water.
- In a small bowl beat the eggs whites, eggs and vinegar lightly (just quick enough to combine it all).
- Add the eggs and vinegar mixture into the bowl with the dry ingredients. Mix with a hand whisk for about 20-30 seconds.
- Add the hot water and whisk for another 30 seconds. Then use your hand (be careful, it will still be hot) and mix for another 10 seconds using a folding motion. The dough will get more "doughy" as you do this.
- Since your hands will already be goopy, just scoop it equally into the 4 mini loaf molds.
- Smooth out the top a bit, but it doesn't need to be perfect.
- Bake for 50-55 minutes and remove from oven.

- While they are still hot, remove from loaf pan. You can use a knife or thin spatula to separate the sides and then pop it out.
- Let cool on a wire rack.

Nutrition Info

Calories 73.28 Total Fat 4.38g Saturated Fat 0.45g Sodium 78.76mg Carbohydrates 6.78g Fiber 4.77g Sugar 0.31g Protein 2.71g

83. Cinnamon Almond Flour Bread {Paleo}

This delicious cinnamon almond flour bread is a versatile low carb, gluten free and paleo bread recipe the whole family loves! Simple ingredients, nourishing, soft and delicious.

Prep Time: 10

Cook Time: 30 minutes

Total Time: 40 minutes

Serving: 8

Ingredients

- 2 cups fine blanched almond flour (I use Bob's Red Mill)

- 2 tbsp coconut flour
- 1/2 tsp sea salt
- 1 tsp baking soda
- 1/4 cup Flax seed meal or chia meal (ground chia or flaxseed, see notes for how to make your own)
- 5 Eggs and 1 egg white whisked together
- 1.5 tsp Apple cider vinegar or lemon juice
- 2 tbsp maple syrup or honey
- 2–3 tbsp of clarified butter (melted) or Coconut oil; divided. Vegan butter also works
- 1 tbsp cinnamon plus extra for topping
- Optional chia seed to sprinkle of top before baking

Instructions

- Preheat oven to 350F. Line an 8×4 bread pan with parchment paper at the bottom and grease the sides.
- In a large bowl, mix together your almond flour, coconut flour, salt, baking soda, flaxseed meal or chia meal, and 1/2 tablespoon of cinnamon.
- In another small bowl, whisk together your eggs and egg white. Then add in your maple syrup (or honey), apple cider vinegar, and melted butter (1.5 to 2 tbsp).

- Mix wet ingredients into dry. Be sure to remove any clumps that might have occurred from the almond flour or coconut flour.
- Pour batter into a your greased loaf pan.
- Bake at 350º for 30-35 minutes, until a toothpick inserted into center of loaf comes out clean. Mine too around 35 minutes but I am at altitude.
- Remove from and oven.
- Next, whisk together the other 1 to 2 tbsp of melted butter (or oil) and mix it with 1/2 tbsp of cinnamon. Brush this on top of your cinnamon almond flour bread.
- Cool and serve or store for later.

Nutrition Info

Serving Size: 1

Calories Per Serving: 221

24% Total Fat 15.4g

13% Dietary Fiber 3.1g

Sugars 3.7g

19% Protein 9.3g

0% Vitamin C 0mg

9% Iron 1.5mg

84. Hot Ham and Cheese Roll-Ups with Dijon Butter Glaze

Prep/Cook Time: 40 minutes

Ingredients

For the Hot Ham and Cheese Roll-Ups

- 1/4 cup almond flour (get it here)
- 3 tablespoons coconut flour (get it here)
- 1 teaspoon onion powder
- 1 teaspoon garlic powder
- 1 1/2 cup low-moisture, part skim mozzarella cheese, shredded

- 4 tablespoons salted butter
- 2 tablespoons cream cheese
- 1 large pastured egg
- 10 ounces sliced ham
- 1 1/2 cups sharp white cheddar cheese, shredded

For the Dijon Butter Glaze

- 2 tablespoons salted butter
- 1 tablespoon Dijon mustard
- 1 teaspoon Worcestershire sauce
- 1 teaspoon garlic powder
- 1/2 teaspoon dried Italian seasoning

Instructions

- Preheat oven to 375°F.
- In a small mixing bowl, combine almond flour, coconut flour, onion powder and garlic powder.
- In a separate mixing bowl, combine mozzarella cheese, butter, and cream cheese. Microwave for 1 minute and 30 seconds to soften. Mix together until everything is well combined. If if gets stringy or is not quite melted enough, put it back in for another 30 seconds.

- To the cheese mixture, add the dry ingredients and the egg. Mix until all ingredients are well incorporated. If you are having a hard time mixing it, put it back in the microwave for another 20-30 seconds.

- Once the ingredients are combined, spread the dough out on parchment paper or a silpat in a thin and even layer – about 9 1/2 by 13 1/2. If it starts to get sticky, wet your hands a little bit to prevent it from sticking to you.

- Once you have the dough in a nice, even rectangle, sprinkle the cheddar over top, covering all of the dough.

- Next, layer on the ham.

- Roll the dough up tightly lengthwise. This will produce smaller rolls, but you will get almost twice as many. Turn so that the seam is facing down

- Cut the ends off each side of the roll-up to even it out. Then cut it into 1 1/2 slices.

- Place your individual roll-ups in a baking dish.

- Bake for 20-25 minutes or until they are fluffy and golden brown.

- While they are baking, melt the butter and mix it with the Dijon, Worcestershire, garlic powder and Italian seasoning. Fork whisk until all ingredients are well incorporated.

- Take your rolls out of the oven, brush the glaze over top of them. Return them to the oven and bake for an additional 5 minutes.

Nutrition Info

Calories – 482 ,Fat – 41g , Protein – 25g. , Carbs – 6.8g ,Fiber – 2.8g, Net Carbs – 4g

85. Rosemary Olive Bread

This rosemary olive bread is baked with coconut flour in the shape of a circular loaf. Although the shape is not mandatory, it looks pretty.

Prep Time: 10 minutes

Cook Time: 35 minutes

Total Time: 45 minutes

Servings: 10 Slices

Ingredients

- 1/2 cup Coconut flour

- 4 medium Eggs
- 4 tablespoons Olive oil
- 2 tablespoons Pysllium husk powder
- 1 tablespoon Apple cider vinegar
- 1 tablespoon Baking powder
- 1/2 teaspoon Salt
- 1 1/2 tablespoons Rosemary dried or fresh
- 75 grams Black or green olives chopped
- 1/2 cups Boiling water

Instructions

- Preheat the oven to 180C/350F degrees
- Place the coconut flour, baking powder, rosemary, psyllium husk powder and salt in a bowl and mix thoroughly.
- Add the oil and eggs and blend well until the mixture looks like breadcrumbs.
- Add the apple cider vinegar and mix well.
- Add the chopped olives to the bread and mix.
- Gently add the water, a bit at time and stir into the mixture (you may not need it all).
- Line a baking tray with parchment paper.

- Using your hands, make a large ball of the dough (I find keeping my hands wet helps with the sticky dough).
- Place the dough on the parchment paper lined baking tray.
- Score the top to make a pattern is optional!
- Bake for 35 minutes until golden and firm.
- Eat and enjoy!

Nutrition Info

Serving: 1 Slice, Calories: 123kcal, Carbohydrates: 6g, Protein: 3g, Fat: 9g

86. Almond Flour Bread

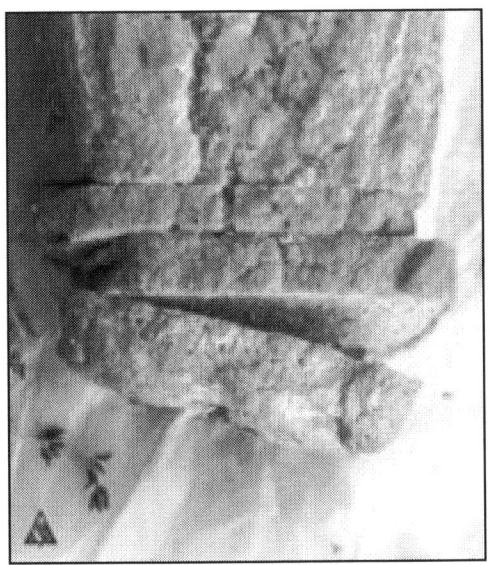

An easy recipe for a quick, filling and tasty almond flour bread. This almond flour bread is keto and paleo, and works great with both savory and sweet toppings.

Prep Time10 mins

Cook Time45 mins

Rest time30 mins

Total Time1 hr 25 mins

Servings: 16 slices

Ingredients

- 1 teaspoon coconut oil for pan
- 5 large eggs
- 5 tablespoons refined coconut oil, gently melted in microwave (2.5 oz)
- 1 teaspoon apple cider vinegar (don't skip – helps the bread rise)
- 1/4 teaspoon kosher salt
- 1 3/4 cup almond flour (7 oz)
- 1/2 teaspoon baking soda

Instructions

- Preheat oven to 350 degrees F. Grease an 8-inch loaf pan (a 9-inch pan will be too big).
- In a medium bowl, whisk the eggs. Whisk in the coconut oil, vinegar, salt, almond flour and finally the baking soda.
- Pour the batter into the prepared loaf pan.
- Bake until bread is golden-brown and set, and a toothpick inserted in center comes out clean, about 45 minutes.
- Cool 10 minutes in pan on a wire rack before gently releasing the bread from the pan (carefully run a knife along edges if needed). Cool to room temperature, about 20 minutes more, before slicing and serving.

- Keep leftovers in a ziploc bag in the fridge for a few days, or freeze.

Nutrition Info

Calories 131 Calories from Fat 108

Total Fat 12g 18%

Sodium 83mg 3%

Total Carbohydrates 3g 1%

Dietary Fiber 1g 4%

Protein 5g

87. Cauliflower Tortillas

Great low carb alternative to traditional corn or flour tortillas.

Prep Time 30 minutes

Cook Time 20 minutes

Total Time 50 minutes

Servings 6 tortillas

Calories 37

Ingredients

- 3/4 large head cauliflower (or two cups riced)
- 2 large eggs (Vegans, sub flax eggs)
- 1/4 cup chopped fresh cilantro
- 1/2 medium lime, juiced and zested
- salt & pepper, to taste

Instructions

- Preheat the oven to 375 degrees F., and line a baking sheet with parchment paper.
- Trim the cauliflower, cut it into small, uniform pieces, and pulse in a food processor in batches until you get a couscous-like consistency. The finely riced cauliflower should make about 2 cups packed.

- Place the cauliflower in a microwave-safe bowl and microwave for 2 minutes, then stir and microwave again for another 2 minutes. If you don't use a microwave, a steamer works just as well. Place the cauliflower in a fine cheesecloth or thin dishtowel and squeeze out as much liquid as possible, being careful not to burn yourself. Dishwashing gloves are suggested as it is very hot.
- In a medium bowl, whisk the eggs. Add in cauliflower, cilantro, lime, salt and pepper. Mix until well combined.

Use your hands to shape 6 small "tortillas" on the parchment paper.

- Bake for 10 minutes, carefully flip each tortilla, and return to the oven for an additional 5 to 7 minutes, or until completely set. Place tortillas on a wire rack to cool slightly.

- Heat a medium-sized skillet on medium. Place a baked tortilla in the pan, pressing down slightly, and brown for 1 to 2 minutes on each side. Repeat with remaining tortillas.

88. Jalapeno Low Carb Bagel

Prep Time: 10 minutes

Cook Time: 30 minutes

Total Time: 40 minutes

Servings: 6 Bagels

Calories: 273kcal

Ingredients

- 2 cups Mozzarella cheese grated

- 2 oz Cream cheese

- 1 cup Almond flour

- 1 teaspoon baking powder

- 3 Jalapeno peppers
- 2 Eggs
- 1 oz Cheddar cheese grated

Instructions

- Preheat the oven to 200C/400F
- Chop and deseed the jalapeno peppers. Slice a few thin circles and set them aside for the decoration.
- In a bowl, mix the almond flour and baking powder.
- Add the chopped jalapeno peppers and eggs. Mix well.
- In another bowl add the mozzarella and cream cheese.
- Cook in the microwave for 2 minutes, stopping after 1 minute to give it a gentle stir (you'll end up with crispy bits around the bowl otherwise).
- Remove and stir, then add in the almond flour mixture.
- Stir well and combine until you have a blended dough.
- Break the dough up into 6 pieces and roll out the pieces to make into a bagel shape OR use a donut tray to place the dough in. (I find this easier to keep them neater).
- Decorate the bagels with sliced jalapenos and sprinkle with some grated Cheddar cheese.
- Bake for 20-30 minutes, keeping an eye on them that they bake until golden.

- Eat and enjoy!

Nutrition Info

273 Calories, 22g Fat, 16g Protein, 6g Total Carb, 2g Fibre, 4g Net Carbs

89. Keto Low Carb Buns with Psyllium Husk

Delicious low carb buns that taste just like multigrain bread!

Prep Time 10 minutes

Cook Time 30 minutes

Total Time 40 minutes

Servings buns

Ingredients

- 4 tbsp boiling water

Dry Ingredients

- 100 g blanched almond flour (about 3/4 cup tightly packed)
- 2 tbsp psyllium husk powder
- 1 tsp baking powder
- 1 tsp black sesame seeds
- 1 tsp white sesame seeds
- 2 tsp sunflower seeds
- 1 tsp black chia seeds
- 1/2 tsp Himalayan salt
- 1/2 tsp garlic powder

Wet Ingredients

- 1 egg
- 2 egg whites
- 1 tbsp apple cider vinegar (or lemon juice, white vinegar)
- 3 tbsp melted refined coconut oil (or butter, lard, shortening, ghee)

Instructions

- Preheat the oven to 180C/350F.
- In a bowl, mix the dry ingredients with a whisk. In a separate bowl, mix the wet ingredients. Pour the wet

ingredients into the dry ingredients and mix with a silicone spatula.

- Slowly pour in the boiling water and continue mixing. The dough will be quite thick and expand as it absorbs the water.
- Separate the dough into 5 and form 5 balls with your hands (the batter is pretty sticky). You can spray some olive oil on your hands to make the dough not stick to you.
- Place the balls over parchment paper on a baking tray and bake for 30 minutes. Take out and let cool before serving or you'll burn your fingers! These come out piping hot!

Notes

- You cannot substitute the psyllium husk powder.
- Please don't leave out the boiling water. You need it to activate the psyllium.
- Make sure to use REFINED coconut oil and not the normal extra-virgin kind as you'll get a huge coconut taste.
- If you double the recipe, you may need to add 1-2 tbsp of hot water to the batter.

- All of our ovens are different, so if you find yours to be too moist, just add 5 more minutes in the oven, or cook them at 190C/375F instead for 30 minutes.

Nutrition Info

Calories 236 Calories from Fat 187

Total Fat 20.81g 32%

Saturated Fat 8.37g 42%

Cholesterol 42mg 14%

Sodium 41mg 2%

Total Carbohydrates 8.34g 3%

Dietary Fiber 5.34g 21%

Sugars 0.96g

Protein 7.53g 15%

90. Low-Carb Focaccia Bread with Thyme and Onion

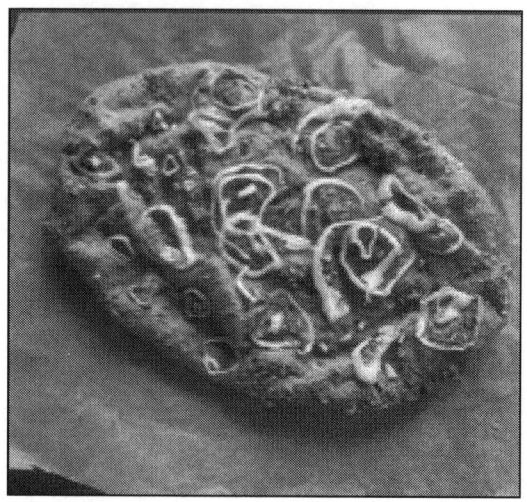

This delicious Low-Carb Focaccia Bread recipe is easy to make, and tastes so rich and wonderful with the addition of thyme and onion.

Prep Time 15minutes

Cook Time 30minutes

Servings 1loaf

Ingredients

- 1/2 cup coconut flour
- 5 tablespoons psyllium husk powder

- 2 teaspoons baking powder
- 1 teapsoon salt
- 4 whole egg
- 1 cup boiling water
- 1 teaspoon dried thyme
- 1 small onions

Instructions

- Add coconut flour, psyllium husk, baking powder and salt in a mixing bowl and combine.
- Mix in the eggs. Work quickly, stirring until the powders firm up into a thick dough.
- Add a cup of boiling water and mix thoroughly.
- Line a baking sheet with parchment paper. Form dough into a flat oval on top of the paper. Use a sharp knife to score diagonal cut through the dough. Sprinkle the top with thyme and additional salt. Thinly slice the onion into rings and arrange evenly over the thyme and salt. Press gently into the dough to stick.
- Bake at 350 degrees F for 25-30 minutes. The dough rises about twice as high, with a firm crust once done. If the bread feels spongy to the touch, continue cooking.`

- Remove from the oven and cool slightly before cutting; serve warm or cold. Store in the fridge.

Recipe Notes

Marcos per serving: 3.0 g fat, 9.0 g carb, 2.6 g net carb, 3.7 g protein

Nutrition Info

Calories per slice: 79.5 total calories

CONCLUSION

If you still want to try the keto diet, it's important to talk to your doctor first about your body's nutrient needs, your cholesterol levels, and your risk of heart disease. For a diet that has this dramatic an effect on the inner workings of your body, best to equip yourself with advice of a medical professional. When it comes to your health, you don't always have to keep up with the Kardashians — but if you do, don't do it on your own.

Made in the USA
Monee, IL
22 December 2019